CAMRA'S
London
Pub Walks

CAMRA'S
London

Pub Walks
BOB STEEL

Published by the Campaign for Real Ale Ltd.
230 Hatfield Road
St Albans
Hertfordshire AL1 4LW
www.camra.org.uk/books

Design and layout © Campaign for Real Ale Ltd. 2013
Text © Bob Steel

All rights reserved.
No part of this publication may be reproduced, stored in a retrieval
system or transmitted in any form or by any means – electronic,
mechanical, photocopying, recording or otherwise – without the
prior permission of the Campaign for Real Ale

ISBN 978-1-85249-310-3

A CIP catalogue record for this book is available
from the British Library

Printed and bound in China by 1010 Printing Intl Ltd

Head of Publishing: Simon Hall
Project Editor: Katie Hunt
Editorial Assistance: Emma Haines
Design/Typography: Stephen Bere
Cover Design: Dale Tomlinson
Cartography: Stephen Bere
Marketing Manager: Chris Lewis

Photographs: Bob Steel
Additional photography: Cath Harries p2-3, p4 (top right), p5 (top
centre), p29, p35, p53, p58 (top), p59, p60, p61, p64, p66 (top),
p67, p74 (left), p112 (bottom), p121 (top), p122; David Kirkby p135;
Ewan Munro p5 (top left) p31, p56 (left), p77 (top), p83 (right), p85,
p89, p134, p167 (top), p172 (left), p182; Exmouth Arms p82, p84
(bottom); Fuller's p14, p33; garryknight (flickr) p72; John Butler
p134 (bottom); Rob Gale p79, p81; Shaun O'Connor p137; Shepherd
Neame p15 (top), p16 (top), p181; Stephen May p27 (bottom right);
Stephen Bere p17, p19 (top right), p20, p21 (bottom left), p22
(bottom), p47, p51 (top), p57, p69 (top), p75 (right), p83 (left), p84
(top), p96, p97 (top right); stevecadman (flickr) p151

Cover photography: Top: Michael K Berman-Wald / Alamy;
Left: Renato Granieri / Alamy; Centre: Justin Kase zsixz / Alamy;
Right: Alex Segre / Alamy

Acknowledgements
I'd like to thank all those who have helped in the preparation of
this guide: to those members of London branches of the Campaign for
Real Ale who have contributed suggestions, but in particular Martin
Butler, Paul Charlton, Stephen Harris, Roy Hurry, John Norman, John
Pardoe, Geoff Strawbridge and Ian White; to those publicans, pho-
tographers and others who have given permission to use images, and
made suggestions. I'd also like to thank Jane Jephcote for permission to use material from her London pub heritage itineraries.

Finally, I would like to pay tribute to the small but steadfast band
of licensees who propagate in their pubs ideals of good service; and
take pride in their craft in an age of globalisation, homogeneity and
mediocrity. Let us resist together those who see this great institution
simply as an entry on an accountant's balance sheet!
Bob Steel

Contents

Walk location map

Numbers represent the approximate centre of each walk.

KEY FOR WALK MAPS

- 🚶 Walk start point
- ▬ ▬ Walk route
- ⋮⋮⋮⋮ Detour/Alternative route
- ▭▭▭ Bus route
- 🔲 Featured pub
- 🔲 'Try also' pub
- ➤ Direction of walk

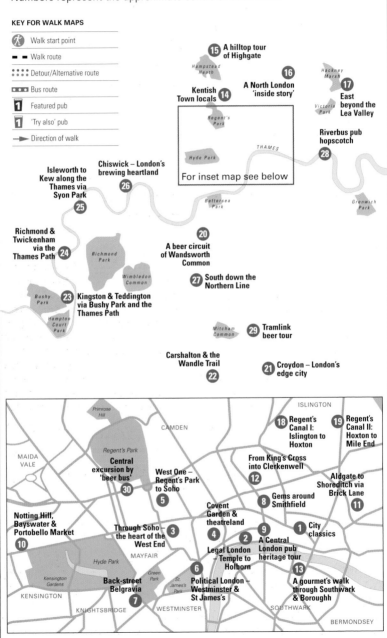

15 A hilltop tour of Highgate

Hampstead Heath

16 A North London 'inside story'

Hackney Marsh

17 East beyond the Lea Valley

14 Kentish Town locals

Victoria Park

Regent's Park

THAMES

Hyde Park

Riverbus pub hopscotch

28

For inset map see below

26 Chiswick – London's brewing heartland

25 Isleworth to Kew along the Thames via Syon Park

Battersea Park

Greenwich Park

24 Richmond & Twickenham via the Thames Path

Richmond Park

Wimbledon Common

20 A beer circuit of Wandsworth Common

27 South down the Northern Line

Bushy Park

23 Kingston & Teddington via Bushy Park and the Thames Path

Hampton Court Park

Mitcham Common

29 Tramlink beer tour

22 Carshalton & the Wandle Trail

21 Croydon – London's edge city

ISLINGTON

Primrose Hill

CAMDEN

18 Regent's Canal I: Islington to Hoxton

19 Regent's Canal II: Hoxton to Mile End

Regent's Park

30 Central excursion by 'beer bus'

MAIDA VALE

5 West One – Regent's Park to Soho

12 From King's Cross into Clerkenwell

11 Aldgate to Shoreditch via Brick Lane

10 Notting Hill, Bayswater & Portobello Market

3 Through Soho – the heart of the West End

4 Covent Garden & theatreland

8 Gems around Smithfield

1 City classics

2 A Central London pub heritage tour

Hyde Park

MAYFAIR

Kensington Gardens

Green Park

St. James's Park

9

6 Political London – Westminster & St James's

13 A gourmet's walk through Southwark & Boroughh

7 Back-street Belgravia

6 Legal London – Temple to Holborn

KENSINGTON

KNIGHTSBRIDGE

WESTMINSTER

SOUTHWARK

BERMONDSEY

Introduction

It's seven years since the first edition of CAMRA's London Pub Walks was prepared. A great deal has happened in the beer and pub scene in that time, so a complete re-write of this popular best-seller for the Campaign is now due. Interest in beer has reached new heights, many new pubs and bars have appeared, and new breweries have blossomed in London, which had almost no microbreweries when I embarked on the first edition. On the other hand, a number of the pubs which appeared in that guide have become casualties of change, and a few have closed altogether. For these reasons you'll find that there are a large number of completely new routes for the discerning drinker, taking you to places you may not have ventured before. These include suburban areas such as the depths of East London, once a beer desert but now with some worthwhile beer destinations; and, at the other side of the city, the bustling town of Croydon.

The changing London pub and beer scene

In 2006, I remarked that very few London pubs indeed acted as true free houses offering a wide range of beers; and in that respect London lagged behind other parts of the country. I'm happy to say that that situation no longer exists, and finding a wide range of ales from Britain's excellent brewers is now much easier in the capital. And as for the variety of tastes, there has been a real explosion in the few years since the first edition of London Pub Walks. The new microbreweries are undoubtedly leading the way in this, with younger brewers experimenting with all sorts of interesting recipes and providing a feast for the palate, alongside the more traditional British milds, bitters and stouts. There has also been a bit of a revolution in the way we're drinking our beer, towards smaller measures of stronger beers in the continental tradition. In this sense, the term 'craft beer' which is being used to encapsulate this trend is appropriate, although the term has also now, confusingly, become synonymous with those new beers served in keg form, often

FROM LEFT: **Jerusalem Tavern, Walk** 8 **Cittie of Yorke, Walk** 9 **Churchill Arms, Walk** 10 **Palm Tree, Walk** 19

filtered and/or pasteurised, chilled, and under some gas pressure. I am not going to venture too far in the controversy this has created both within and outside of CAMRA save to say that these new kegged beers are a galaxy apart from the appalling, gassy and tasteless liquids that caused CAMRA's birth in the early 1970s. What is undeniable is that interest in beer is at record levels in modern times and there has been renaissance in beer and pub culture as a result. And what better which to enjoy all this than London?

That's the good news; now the bad. Pubs are still closing at a rate of around a dozen a week across the country, ostensibly because people are turning away from the pub in favour of drinking cheap supermarket booze at home – or are they? My traditional local in South London is current CAMRA London Pub of the Year. Turnover has grown by several hundred percent since the free-of-tie lease was acquired by a consortium of shareholders. It focuses upon good beer in a quiet, conversation-friendly environment. Looking at the list of recent past winners of the Pub of the Year award, most share these characteristics: free houses offering a traditional welcome, a convivial atmosphere and a choice of well-kept beers. In contrast, when one looks at the sort of pub that is struggling, many of them are characterless, poorly run, expensive and bland. So who's to blame? In my view the biggest villains are often the owners of the pubs themselves – too often the giant pub companies view their estates not as community assets but

only as a property portfolio from which to extract the maximum profit, and to sell off if it doesn't yield the expected corporate return. It's well documented how tenants are being squeezed by these 'pubcos', forced to endure frequent rent hikes and compelled to buy their beers in from them at greatly inflated prices. This on top of the destructive duty escalator imposed by the government until recently, and it's no wonder that pump prices continue to rise steeply. Sadly the family brewers who in the past were held up by CAMRA and others as a shining examples of champions of British pubs and beer have become among the greediest and most ruthless of them all and that, in my opinion, certainly includes what were the last two large London brewers. Young's (now no more than a property company) and Fuller's, who although at least are still brewing very good beer, are in the forefront of aggressive price hikes in their increasingly extensive tied estate.

CAMRA's main aim has always been to safeguard traditional British beer, but we also need convivial pubs in which to drink. The first edition of *London Pub Walks* was, in part, a celebration of the work done by CAMRA to publicise the Real Heritage pubs of the capital, and to increase awareness of the fine range of architectural features – some grand, some more humble but increasingly rare – which survived as evidence of the pub as part of our social history. No other body apart from CAMRA, working in conjunction with English Heritage, has

FROM LEFT: **Tipperary, Walk ⑨ White Cross, Walk ㉔ Harp, Walk ④ Market Porter, Walk ⑬**

anything approaching a definite guide to our best remaining pub interiors. Sadly these are still under threat and being whittled away, not least by some of the more irresponsible 'pubcos' and again I will single out Young's, who have sold off a significant number of their pubs to developers and undertaken wholly insensitive alterations in many others, particularly in the last few years. They are not alone, but there is no excuse for refurbishments which trash our pub heritage and turn our pubs into, at best, upmarket restaurants and brasseries.

Joining CAMRA, and enjoying beer in the pub, rather than at home, will ensure you're playing your part in ensuring the survival of one of our most enduring institutions.

The geography of London's pub heritage

Another objective of this guide is to put the pubs in a spatial context: plenty of books have been published about London pubs, but few London pub guides take you from one to the next. Most of these trails take you to five or six pubs, and many link to adjacent trails if you have the stamina! Wherever possible, trails start and end at an Underground station, or failing that a National Rail station. Visitors to London will find the public transport system pretty good, despite what its detractors say. It's probably worth buying a Travelcard at the start of the day – if you are making more than a couple of journeys by public transport it will be cost effective.

There are several routes at the end of the book designed around public transport – enabling you to navigate your way to the best London pubs by Tube, tram, bus and Riverbus.

Food

Food of course is now widely available in pubs; and the great majority of pubs in this book offer at least snacks and sandwiches. I have not religiously included food information for each pub. If you want to eat whilst on one of these trails, you should have no trouble, unless you decide to go at a very busy time or late in the evening.

Opening times, and when to go

It's important to bear in mind that there are some weekend closures and restricted opening hours in parts of the capital. Broadly speaking, pubs in the City, towards the east of the central area, are more likely not to be open at weekends – most of those in the West End will be. Check the times on each entry, which were correct when going to press, but are subject to alteration.

Another thing to remember is that London pubs can get very busy – in the City at lunchtimes and after work; in the West End of an evening. Not everyone is able to go at quieter times, but I think a great time to enjoy pubs is in the morning, soon after they open – particularly if you want to appreciate the architecture!

RWS
Carshalton 2013

FROM LEFT: **Coal Hole, Walk ❹** **Ship, Walk ❶** **Hand & Shears, Walk ❽** **Ship Tavern, Walk ❷**

The London brewing scene

London is an exciting place to be a brewer at the moment. The interest in hand-crafted beers has never been greater and it seems that barely a week goes by without another brewery launch. I would hesitate to commit to say how many breweries there are in London at the time of writing but the London Brewers' Alliance website counts 32, whilst beer writer Des de Moor puts the number in development at 15. Might we soon see in excess of 45 breweries in London? That would be a far cry from the handful which were in operation when the first edition of CAMRA's *London Pub Walks* appeared in 2006. They come in all shapes and sizes too: we have breweries with as little as an 18 gallon brewlength, all the way up to London's biggest player, Fuller's.

One of the biggest strengths in the London scene at the moment is the diversity of beers being brewed. If I've been hesitant to say how many breweries currently operate in London, I'm even more reluctant to guess at how many beers are being brewed. It must number close to 200. From American, European, and myriad British styles to experimentation with new hops, ingredients 'out of leftfield' whether they be fruit or spices, or multiple hop additions, there's diversity such that you can drink tasty micro-brewed keg beers (to some, an unthinkable development only few years ago), drink from breweries focusing almost exclusively on bottled beer, opt for high strength keykeg dispense ales, or find yourself some of the very best cask beer available in the UK brewed just minutes from the pub where you're drinking it.

This variety is driven by the consumer looking for something brewed locally, something which is high-quality, and something which is interesting and different to drink. Today the consumer is prepared to seek out alternatives to global brands. Local does not, however, mean the consumer has lower expectations. We've only been brewing for three months, but the common refrain from potential publicans and licensees who've not sampled the quality of our beers is 'people will support and drink local beer as long as it tastes good'. Something, to use a CAMRA phrase, which is LocAle (see p188) might guarantee the first pint sold; but only quality will guarantee pints number two, three, and four sold quickly afterwards.

To sustain such growth both in numbers of breweries and in their production figures, London brewers have to carve out a niche which works for them, and do everything possible to combat the biggest challenge facing them: pub closures.

As breweries in London have opened, pubs have closed. Many of them permanently; many of them in spite of being perfectly viable as pubs. Close to Clarence & Fredericks we've seen rapacious property development companies and predatory supermarkets combining, in the face of protest and offers from community and cooperative pub-ownership groups, to close pub after pub in favour of conversion to shops and apartments. Over the past four years we've seen large numbers of pubs shutting their doors for the last time: the most recent figures, released by CAMRA in November 2012, speak of 18 pubs closing each week. London may fare better than other parts of the country but this is no time to be complacent. The majority of London breweries are small and, for the most part, draught products, whether cask or keg, are the lifeblood they need to produce (and sell) to survive. Lose the pubs into which small breweries can sell, and the breweries will begin to fold.

But it is not only the fault of property developers and supermarkets. It's the failure of regulation of the large pub-owning companies especially around fair rents and the 'tie' system; it's down to the lack of strong planning laws and the presence of frameworks to guide rather than compel local authorities in their planning decisions; and it's due to the duty escalator, a treasury policy which saw beer duty rise 42% between 2008 and 2013 when it was scrapped in response to consumer pressure.

We're fans of pubs. It's where we sell 99% of the beer we brew. And, with the help of people like you who use pubs and appreciate quality we will, we hope, be part of a movement that will keep the great British pub and fine British beer at the heart of our nation and our way of life. Cheers!

Duncan Woodhead, Head Brewer, Clarence & Fredericks Brewery, Croydon

City classics

WALK INFORMATION

Start: ⊖ ⊖ Bank

Finish: ⊖ Aldgate or ⇌ Fenchurch Street

Distance: 1.3 miles (2km)

Key attractions: The Royal Exchange; Bank of England; Leadenhall Market; Museum of London

The pubs: Counting House; Crosse Keys; Lamb Tavern; Ship (Talbot Court); Ship (Hart Street); East India Arms. Try also: Cock & Woolpack; Peacock

This compact walk traces a route right across the heart of London's financial district, close to many famous financial institutions like the Stock Market in Threadneedle Street, and the futuristic Lloyd's building. The Royal Exchange, which greets you at the start of the walk, is these days a swanky shopping centre but still well worth seeing. Another highlight is Leadenhall Market, which is relatively unspoilt in comparison to other London markets. The pubs themselves are a mixed bunch from the grand conversions to little tucked away side-street taverns; but expect them all to get very busy when the city workers spill out for lunch or at the end of the day.

The splendid Lamb Tavern occupies a key site in Leadenhall Market

Emerging from your train at Bank, you're greeted immediately by the grand Royal Exchange building, rebuilt in the 1840s, and which as noted above, is now used as an up-market indoor shopping mall; but a flying visit is recommended if only for the architecture. Either way, proceed east along Cornhill. Depending upon the time (as it only opens at noon) and if you're keen to try an extra pub, you could look into the hidden little **Cock & Woolpack 7**

on narrow Finch Lane, a turning on the left (north side) of Cornhill. It's a Shepherd Neame house so expect a range from their portfolio. Otherwise continue a little further to reach the **Counting House 1**. This sumptuous late Victorian building was built as a bank, and has only been a pub since 1997.

TIMING TIP

Almost all the pubs are shut at the weekend as is the norm in the City of London, so a weekday it must be. If you can start early (the Counting House opens at 11, the Crosse Keys as early as 9), or during the afternoon, you'll have more space to enjoy the pubs.

Statue of the Duke of Wellington on Cornhill

An excellent refurbishment and conversion by Fuller's was rewarded by a City Heritage Award, the first time that this accolade has been won by a public house. There are plenty of interesting fixtures and fittings to admire, among which the enormous glass domed skylight is an outstanding feature. The place offers a full range of Fuller's regular and seasonal beers, such as London Pride, Chiswick Bitter and ESB. It's worth a climb to the gallery to admire the splendour of the building from a height. Food is available throughout the day.

Leave the Counting House via the rear door leading to St Peter's Alley, one of numerous little alleyways that have survived in the City. Head past the tiny garden and this alley will quickly disgorge you into Gracechurch Street, right opposite the striking entrance to Leadenhall Market. This will be the quarry after the next pub, which is a few yards down the street to the right. You won't miss the **Crosse Keys** on account of its sheer size:

Decorative detail from Leadenhall Market

another former bank, this one built in 1912 for the Hong Kong & Shanghai Bank, this impressive Wetherspoon conversion opened in 1999 and occupies some 8,000 square feet – massive even by JDW's standards. It's named after the former *Crosse Key Inn* which was destroyed by the Great Fire of London in 1666. The building has a very high ceiling with glass-domed skylights, substantial marble pillars and a striking circular central bar in marble. One of the best parts of this Grade II-listed building is the elegant wood-panelled room at the rear. You'll be unlucky not to find a beer or two to suit you in here, for although the numbers on at any time are variable the choice of guests is usually one of the largest in Wetherspoon's London estate.

Cross the street and double back to the entrance to Leadenhall Market. On a site with a long history as a market, the current building, the work of the City's architect Sir Horace Jones, who was also the architect of Billingsgate and

The gallery of the Counting House provides a good view

room, Old Tom's, has branched out with its own more eclectic range of beers. Local guests, most frequently Sambrook's Wandle Ale, are supported by three on keg from the Meantime brewery, and a few interesting bottled offerings. Tempting-looking 'grazing plates' of cheese and meats are available too. On a more esoteric note, the Lamb has been a film location for both *Brannigan* starring John Wayne and *Winds of War* starring Robert Mitchum; and younger drinkers may know that more recently it was Diagon Alley in the *Harry Potter* films.

Head out of the market by taking the mall opposite the Lamb (so, turn right, as if you hadn't entered the pub) which will bring you out onto Lime Street. Bear right, and cross Fenchurch Street into Philpot Lane. At the end of this street, turn right into Eastcheap, and now just a few steps along, by the sandwich bar and bus stop, right again into the little covered alley, Talbot Court, leading to the **Ship 4**. Not so far from

Smithfield Markets, dates to 1881. For most of its life it was a meat, game and poultry market, and although the latter survived into the 20th century, it's a cleaner and more sanitised place, though still highly impressive, today. Walk down the covered arcade past the *New Moon* to the junction of malls which is dominated by the **Lamb Tavern 3**. This magnificent building on three floors dates back to the reconstruction of the market. The interior still has some venerable old fittings: look out for the fine tiled panel depicting Christopher Wren explaining his plans for rebuilding London, and some decent etched glasswork to doors and windows. After being a freehouse until 1985 the Lamb is now owned by Young's, so expect beers from their stable; but in the past few years the atmospheric little downstairs cellar

the Monument, the pub's 'new' name dates back to the rebuilding after the fire, when it apparently became patronised by salty types from the river. These days of course it's city workers who are the patrons, but tucked away as it is, it's often possible to find a spot, especially in the little upstairs room, when other local places are brimming. Don't expect a seventeenth century survivor, but it's a handsome building with a traditional interior, and has one of the larger range of beers in the Nicholson's chain, so you'll be able to pick up something interesting on the beer front from a wide array of handpulls. This pub is the last serious call for food, which is available all day.

When it's time to 'jump ship' (groan!), return to Eastcheap and turning left, continue down to the end and bear left again into Mark Street. Head up to the first turning on the right, and just around the corner you'll see the sign for the tiny **Ship** 5, jammed between two dismal modern office blocks. The exterior, narrow but elaborate, features two arched doorways flanking a

East India Arms

central window. Ornate grape motifs decorate the elevation below the first floor bay window.

Inside, there's a small bar (but there's a dining room upstairs too), and once you've had your fill of the huge collection of dubious ties adorning the interior, your attention can turn to the ales on offer: up to four, the house beer is rebadged Caledonian 80/-, whilst Deuchars IPA is pretty regular. Check the pub's facebook page for advance warning of the guest(s).

The next pub isn't called the Ship, but it does retain the nautical connection. To get there, look for the lane (New London Street) a few yards up on the left beyond the Ship, and head up the steps at the end of this bringing you outside Fenchurch Street station. Walk around the handsome brick façade of the station and up to Fenchurch Street itself at the junction. Look right, and the distinctive red brick elevation of the **East India Arms** 6 is right in front of you. There has been a pub on this site for almost 400 years. The current Grade II-listed building dates from the 1820s, and is one of only two London pubs celebrating the East India Company, although the name is not the original. The little drinking

The second Ship on our route has an elaborate frontage

East India Arms: popular with city workers

booths have been lost and the opened out interior is minimally furnished today, although not unattractive. The bar counter, around which the floorboarded drinking area wraps, is topped with an unusual glass gantry bearing the name of the pub's present owners, Shepherd Neame, whose beers you'll find on the four handpumps.

This is the final full entry on this walk; if Fenchurch Street station is of no use to you, continuing east along Fenchurch Street will lead to Aldgate Underground station in five minutes; alternatively, a similar walk in the opposite direction will bring you to Monument/Bank. If you're game for another pub, take the next turning right (Lloyd's Avenue), and at the railway bridge bear 45 degrees left onto Crosswall. At the second junction turn left again onto Minories, and a few yards up on the opposite side is the **Peacock 8** . Fans of the Streamline Moderne style of Art Deco will drool over the remarkable exterior of Ibex House which hosts the pub in one corner. It's in the same style as the more well-known Daily Express building on Fleet Street. In addition, the Peacock offers a decent range of well-kept ales: expect to find at least a couple, sometimes more, beers on, with local breweries like Hackney, Redemption and East London among the attractive offerings. From here, Aldgate station is directly north along Minories, and Tower Gateway is a few minutes south.

> **LINK** The *Dispensary*, first call on Walk 11, is about a ten minute walk via Aldgate High Street and Aldgate East station.

PUB INFORMATION

1 Counting House
50 Cornhill, EC3V 3PD
020 7283 7123
www.the-counting-house.com
Opening Hours: 11-11; closed Sat & Sun

2 Crosse Keys
9 Gracechurch Street, EC3V 0DR
020 7623 4824
Opening Hours: 8am-11 (midnight Fri; 7 Sat); closed Sun

3 Lamb Tavern
10-12 Leadenhall Market, EC3V 1LR
020 7626 2454
www.lambtavernleadenhall.com
Opening Hours: 11-11; closed Sat & Sun

4 Ship
11 Talbot Court, EC3V 0BP
020 7929 3903
Opening Hours: 10-11; 11-5 Sat; closed Sun

5 Ship
3 Hart Street; EC3R 7NB
020 7481 1871
Opening Hours: 11.30-11.30; closed Sat & Sun

6 East India Arms
67 Fenchurch Street, EC3M 4BR
020 7265 5121
Opening Hours: 11.30-8.30; closed Sat & Sun

TRY ALSO:

7 Cock & Woolpack
6 Finch Lane, EC3V 3NA
020 7626 4799
Opening Hours: 11-11; closed Sat & Sun

8 Peacock
41 Minories, EC3N 1DT
020 7488 3630
Opening Hours: 12-midnight; closed Sat & Sun

Ibex House – haute Art Deco and home to the Peacock

Legal London – Temple to Holborn

WALK INFORMATION

Start: ⊖ Temple

Finish: ⊖ Holborn

Distance: 1.1 miles (1.8km)

Key attractions: Inns of Court; Prince Henry's Room (tel: 020 7936 4004); Royal Courts of Justice; Churches of St Dunstan's and St Clement Danes; Lincoln's Inn Fields; Soane Museum

The pubs: Edgar Wallace; Devereux; Old Bank of England; Knights Templar; Seven Stars; Ship Tavern; Holborn Whippet

Squares and gardens outside Middle Temple

A south to north meander through three of the four Inns of Court takes us through an attractive area of the capital largely untouched by noisy traffic and modernisation, except at the end. There are tranquil gardens, lawns and squares, with classy pubs never too far away to break up the tour. The 'Inns' themselves though have nothing directly to do with drink! They are the collective name for the four ancient 'honourable societies' that have the exclusive right of admission to the Bar, that is, the right to practice law. If you're doing the culture as well as the pubs, a visit to the stunning 16th century Middle Temple Hall with its wonderful hammerbeam roof is highly recommended but access is limited and it's as well to check ahead. The pubs are a mixture of the classy (even the recent conversions) and venerable, with a brash new youngster to shake you up at the end. They are close together, so feel free to miss one or two out unless you're ticking them off.

Start at Temple Underground station on the Embankment and exit into Temple Gardens adjacent to the station (if the gates are shut bear left then right into Temple Place and rejoin the route at Milford Lane). On the way you will pass several statues, notably those of philosopher John Stuart Mill, and of Lady Somerset, a 19th-century champion of temperance who would no doubt frown upon us

if only she knew. Exit and cross the road to the old red phone box opposite and walk up Milford Lane to the steps ahead, taking us up into Essex Street. The street is named after the Earl of Essex, Robert Devereux, and two of the best surviving pubs in

TIMING TIP

This is a walk best done in the week since some of the Inns of Court as well as many of the pubs, are closed at weekends.

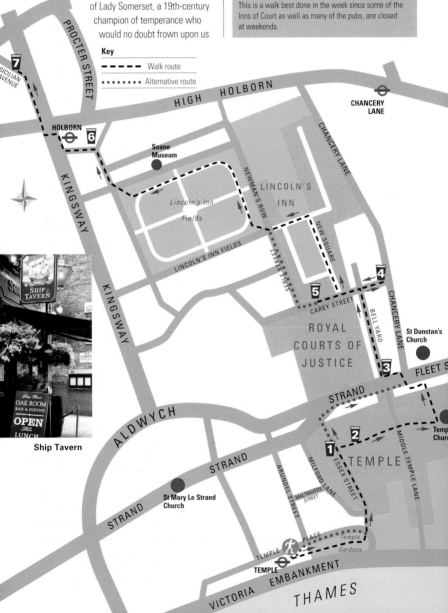

Key

– – – Walk route

······· Alternative route

Ship Tavern

LEFT: **The imposing enterance to the Devereux** RIGHT: **Milford Lane from Temple Gardens**

this little area used both to carry his name. The first call was formerly known as the *Essex Head*, but now it's called the **Edgar Wallace** 1 after the celebrated journalist, novelist and playwright. Revitalised over the past few years it's now a fine pub for the discerning ale drinker offering eight interesting ales, which you can expect to be in very good condition. The 'retro' ads on the wall, notably for seventies hip tipple Babycham, are worth a look. Food is available but it does get busy at lunchtimes (there's more seating upstairs).

Leaving the pub take the narrow lane, Devereux Court, heading east, and you'll see the **Devereux** 2 in a matter of yards. This place was formerly the Grecian Coffee House, opened in 1702, and frequented by Isaac Newton and Edmund Halley. Robert Devereux's mansion, Essex House, inherited from his stepfather Robert Dudley, an intimate friend of Elizabeth I, also stood in the vicinity. Devereux himself fell from grace and was beheaded in 1601 for high treason. The pub itself is an early-Victorian listed building, intimate and pleasantly decorated with an oak-panelled bar and carved wooden corbels. As regards beers, there are now five handpumps, with changing offerings, although both Fuller's London Pride and Sharp's Doom Bar make frequent appearances.

Leaving the pub, go through the gates opposite into the precincts of the Middle Temple (if the Temple gates are closed, later in the evening, go back to the Edgar Wallace and turn right to arrive on the Strand, then turn right again). The name of the Temple derives from the Knights Templar, a religious order of military monks formed in 1119 to protect pilgrims *en route* to the Holy Land. Their red cross on a white background can be seen in the grounds. The most interesting parts of the Temple today are the church, first built by the knights and consecrated in 1185; and the Middle Temple Hall (with its adjacent gardens) further east. However, much of the Temple was destroyed in the Blitz and the majority of what we see today is a postwar reconstruction, in classical Georgian style.

Walk through the arch opposite, dated 1677, across the small square, Brick Court, and through Pump Court arch to reach Temple Church. Unless visiting the church (worthwhile, but there's an admission charge); you've booked a trip to Middle Temple Hall and Gardens; or you wish to amble around the rest of the Inn, turn sharp left (north) here, keeping left of the church to exit on Fleet Street. Before continuing the pub tour you may enjoy a short detour to view Prince Henry's Room, a fine Jacobean building pretty much above the exit from the Temple, with a splendid plasterwork ceiling in the wood-panelled first-floor room. Admission is free but it may be worth phoning ahead. If there is time, wander across the street to the church of St Dunstan's-in-the-West with its distinctive 1830s octagonal tower and lantern. The clock tower adjacent is far older and was erected in thanksgiving for deliverance from the Great Fire of 1666. The splendid clock is presided over by Gog and Magog who strike the bell every hour.

LEFT: **Middle Temple Lane** RIGHT: **The superb Old Bank of England**

The imposing **Old Bank of England** 3 is across the road just left of the exit from the Temple. This impressive Grade I-listed building, itself dwarfed by the Law Courts immediately behind, has only been a pub since 1995 but was erected in 1886-8 as the Law Courts' branch of the Bank of England. It was designed in the then-trendy Italianate style. Ironically, an historic pub, the *Cock*, was moved across Fleet Street to make way for the new bank. History abounds here as this was also the spot where Demon Barber Sweeney Todd and his partner in crime Mrs Lovett prepared their pies containing the victims of his barbershop massacres – if you believe the legend. Read about this on the steps on the way into the pub. Inside, Fuller's have spent a small fortune: there are new paintings and murals, and large columns rise up to the high ornate plaster ceiling from which hang three very large brass chandeliers. The central stillion itself almost reaches the ceiling. For a good view you can climb to a gallery where there is further seating. Along with the *Counting House* in Cornhill, this pub must rank as one of London's very best bank conversions, and you can enjoy the place with a glass from the full range of Fuller's beers.

Leaving the Old Bank look across to the erection in the middle of Fleet Street, with a griffin atop. This marks the site of the old Temple Bar, the western gate to the City of London. It now stands in Paternoster Square by St Paul's. Its narrow portals became an obstruction to traffic, but not before it had assumed some notoriety as a place where (as Dickens put it in *A Tale of Two Cities*) severed heads of criminals were 'exposed on Temple Bar with an insensate brutality and ferocity worthy of Abyssinia or Ashantes', presumably *pour encourager les autres* to behave…

Take Bell Yard, the alleyway immediately to the west of the building, and walk up alongside the edge of the Royal Courts of Justice, the nation's main civil courts. This imposing Victorian Gothic building, designed by G E Street, was opened by Queen Victoria in 1882 and is faced with Portland stone. At the top of Bell Yard runs Carey Street named in memory of the wealthy seventeenth-century nobleman and landowner Nicholas Carey. Once home of the bankruptcy courts and known colloquially as 'Queer Street' (although this archaic reference is now obscure), the street has also had connections with glitterati from Thomas More to David Bowie, who worked briefly here. There are also two more pubs, very different but both well worth a visit. A few yards to the right you'll see the imposing **Knights Templar** 4 , a fine Wetherspoon's bank conversion. Whilst not quite in the same league as the Old Bank in terms of adornment, it's still mightily impressive. The once-dazzling orange décor has mellowed a bit now… On the beer side of things, the usual Wetherspoon's choices sit alongside several interesting guest beers all dispensed from a long array of handpumps – you won't want for choice (or quality) here. Naturally it gets very busy at peak times. Now retrace your steps in the other direction along Carey Street, passing the gated entrance to the Lincoln's Inn (see below) to one of London's classic old pubs, the **Seven Stars** 5. Originally built at the end of Elizabeth I's reign in 1602, it is one of the few buildings to have escaped the Great Fire in 1666 and recently renovations revealed genuine 400-year-old timbers. However, the current timbered ground-floor frontage probably dates from the mid to late-Victorian period. The exterior betrays the pub's expansion to the right. The etched and gilded glass in the doorways advertises 'General Counter' and 'Private Counter' but this small pub is now a single space. Inside you'll see some lovely old mirrors and woodwork. The atmosphere today owes all to landlady Roxy, truly one of the *femmes formidables* of the London pub scene and, like her food, the stuff of legends. Following the sad demise in 2011 of Tom Paine, the pub's resident moggy, his successor Ray Brown has assumed ownership in the same manner in no time at all! More importantly on the five handpumps there's a reliable range of beers with the ever-present Dark Star Hophead and offerings from Adnams alongside other guests.

If the New Square gate to the Lincoln's Inn was open, retrace your steps again and turn left into the Inn. If it is closed, go on past the Seven Stars to the corner of Serle Street and turn right; the gate into the Inn from Serle Street is open longer on weekdays, so it may still be possible to go in and look at the Inn if you wish. The Inn is closed to the public at weekends. Unlike the Temple, Lincoln's Inn miraculously escaped wartime destruction, so retains its old buildings; the whole place is a haven of tranquillity, and is indubitably the most attractive of the four Inns. Don't miss, about halfway up, the handsome Hogarth Chambers, the 15th-century Old Hall beyond, and Lincoln's Inn chapel adjacent. It was the bells here which were immortalised by John Donne, a one-time preacher at Lincoln's Inn: '... never send to know for whom the bell tolls; it tolls for thee.'

When you've seen enough, aim for the exit through the Serle Street gate (across to your left, by the unmistakable Great Hall). This gives out onto London's largest square, Lincoln's Inn Fields. If you're passing here at night (when the gates are locked and you'll need to walk round the square to the diagonally opposite corner) you'll maybe come across the queues of homeless waiting for the soup kitchen which is a relic of the days when the square was a night-time home to rough sleepers. By day it's a tranquil place with numerous imposing plane trees presiding over the lawns. Several notable buildings face it, and two worthy of mention are the Old Curiosity Shop, still quite quaint looking, in the south western corner; and rather grander, the Soane Museum on the north side. The celebrated architect (1753-1837) designed the house to live in, but also as a setting for his antiquities and *objects d'art*; and he established the house as a museum to which 'amateurs and students' could have access. Today it's one of London's most worthwhile attractions, and it's still free.

LEFT: **The Seven Stars – one of London's classic old pubs** RIGHT: **The cosy Ship Tavern**

The minimalist Holborn Whippet

Having arrived at the far (north west) corner one way or the other, take Gate Street which runs off to the right towards High Holborn. Where it narrows into little more than an alleyway, you'll find our next stop, the **Ship Tavern** [6]. It stands on a site which has been licensed for getting on for 500 years, and although still pretty small it was apparently once just half the size! Inside the latest refurbishment has been done very well to enhance the pubby feel. The beer range is probably better than ever too, with six handpumps on the bar. The two Theakston's offerings are probably a remnant of the pubs days as a William Younger's house, but in addition expect St Austell Tribute, Deuchars IPA and a couple of changing guests. Food is available all day, both down below and upstairs in a more formal setting.

The last official stop on this lengthy pub trawl takes us to one of the newer kids on the block of the London pub and bar scene at the time of writing. Turn right out of the Ship and take the next narrow alleyway, New Turnstile, through to High Holborn just short of the Underground station and the junction with Kingsway/Southampton Row. Negotiate the traffic lights to end up on the diametrically opposite corner, and head up Southampton Row for just a couple of minutes. You'll come upon Sicilian Avenue. This unusual little pedestrian street, developed as long ago as 1905 in a very elegant Italianate style, is an interesting setting for the second venture of the people who brought you the *Euston Tap*. The **Holborn Whippet** [7] is thankfully bigger than the Tap, but is still hardly spacious, although clever use has been made of what they have. The fittings are in the main modern, minimalist and functional, but it has an agreeable vibe to it. The retro dividing door with 'public bar' on the glass is a nice touch. Like the Euston Tap, there's an excellent and ambitious beer range, with half a dozen cask ales and even more 'craft' keg offerings; expect to see some of the best new British brewers like Arbor, Bristol, and Magic Rock. There's also a good foreign beer range. The draught beers are dispensed from a clever brick pillar with lots of taps sticking out of it.

The name? Well, they claim that this was once an area renowned for its whippet racing. Mmm, I think that's a bit of a cock and bull story myself...

You know where the Underground station is.

PUB INFORMATION

[1] Edgar Wallace
40 Essex Street, WC2R 3JF
020 7353 3120
Opening Hours: 11-11; closed Sat & Sun

[2] Devereux
20 Devereux Court, WC2R 3JJ
020 7583 4562
Opening Hours: 11-11; closed Sat & Sun

[3] Old Bank of England
194 Fleet Street, EC4A 2LT
www.oldbankofengland.co.uk
020 7430 2255
Opening Hours: 11-11; closed Sat & Sun

[4] Knights Templar
95 Chancery Lane, WC2A 1DT
020 7831 2660
Opening Hours: 9am-11.30 (midnight Thu & Fri); 11-5 Sat; closed Sun

[5] Seven Stars
53-54 Carey Street, WC2A 2JB
020 7242 8521
Opening Hours: 11 (12 Sat)-11; 12-10.30 Sun

[6] Ship Tavern
12 Gate Street, WC2A 3HP
www.theshiptavern.co.uk
020 7405 1992
Opening Hours: 11-11 (midnight Sat); 12-10.30 Sun

[7] Holborn Whippet
25-29 Sicilian Avenue, WC1A 2QH
www.holbornwhippet.com
020 3137 9937
Opening Hours: 12-11; closed Sun

The new owner of the Seven Stars, Ray Brown

July '14

Through Soho – the heart of the West End

WALK INFORMATION

Start: Piccadilly Circus

Finish: Tottenham Court Road

Distance: 1.2 miles (2km)

Key attractions: Phoenix Garden (www.thephoenixgarden.org); Soho Square; Charing Cross Road bookshops

The pubs: Crown, Ship, Dog & Duck, Three Greyhounds, Angel, Tottenham

Originally farmland, and then a hunting ground, legend has it that Soho got its name from hunters crying out 'Soo hoo!' as they rode through the fields. The rich finally gave up on Soho after a cholera outbreak in 1854. It's a colourful area which has had a long association with immigrants, the music scene and, during the mid twentieth century in particular, the brothels and sex shops attracted by the relatively cheap rents. Today it's full of cafes, bars and restaurants, retains much of its bohemian atmosphere, and the area around Old Compton Street is still the city's main gay district. This route also takes in one of my favourite Central London gardens. The selected pubs are, in the main, Victorian buildings, some of which retain some fine internal fittings, making the route a worthwhile one for lovers of architecture as well as good beer, although the latter is generally pricey.

Soho Square

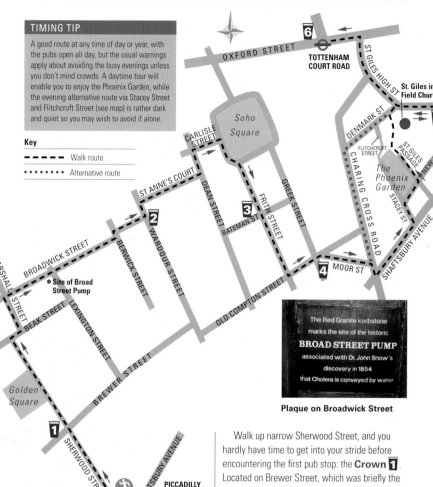

TIMING TIP

A good route at any time of day or year, with the pubs open all day, but the usual warnings apply about avoiding the busy evenings unless you don't mind crowds. A daytime tour will enable you to enjoy the Phoenix Garden, while the evening alternative route via Stacey Street and Flitchcroft Street (see map) is rather dark and quiet so you may wish to avoid if alone.

Key

- - - - Walk route

•••••• Alternative route

The Red Granite kerbstone marks the site of the historic **BROAD STREET PUMP** associated with Dr. John Snow's discovery in 1854 that Cholera is conveyed by water

Plaque on Broadwick Street

Start at Piccadilly Circus Underground station, and use exit 1 which brings you out with the onward route, Sherwood Street, directly ahead, and the traffic island with its famous statue behind you. Chances are that even if you're not a Londoner you'll be familiar with the statue of Eros atop the Shaftesbury Monument Memorial Fountain, erected in 1893 to commemorate Lord Shaftesbury, the Victorian politician and philanthropist. It was apparently the first statue in the world to be cast in aluminium, and has become something of a London icon.

Walk up narrow Sherwood Street, and you hardly have time to get into your stride before encountering the first pub stop: the **Crown** 1. Located on Brewer Street, which was briefly the home of famous Scottish philanthropist David Hume and also the site of the Hickford Rooms, once the main concert halls of London, this Nicholson's pub occupies a very handsome building on a corner site. As with most Nicholson's houses the external and internal décor is smart but respectful of the gravitas of the building. The floorboarded L-shaped drinking area wraps around the servery, and offers a range of seating areas, mainly circular brass-topped tables and comfy bench seating. Alongside the three regular ales: the house Pale (brewed by St Austell), Fuller's London Pride, and Windsor & Eton's Knight of the Garter, there are three other rotating guests. Upstairs, alongside the facilities, is the more formal Hickford Room, used as a restaurant.

The Crown occupies a prominent corner site

We're now heading up narrow Marshall Street, and turning right into Broadwick Street we're heading towards the centre of Soho. Passing the *John Snow* pub on the right there's an interesting little piece of history here. The pink granite kerbstone marks the site of the Broad Street pump where Dr. Snow, in an early example of applied geography demonstrated with a map that an outbreak of cholera in Soho was the result of contamination of the water from this pump. Prior to this it was thought that cholera was an airborne disease. The pub itself has been very nicely restored even down to replaced screens by Samuel Smith and you may wish to have a peek inside, but be aware that this is the pub which gained some notoriety in 2011 when a gay couple were ejected from the premises after allegedly kissing inside, prompting some entertaining protests which have wide coverage on the internet.

Head directly north from the Crown up Lower James Street, passing the rather disappointing Golden Square on your left. Dickens had it about right in *Nicholas Nickleby* when he noted it 'not exactly in anybody's way to or from anywhere'. Except, of course, we are very much on our way somewhere, for Dickens didn't enjoy the choice of ales we have now, nor of course could he have realised that close by here Carnaby Street would become the centre of London fashion in the swinging sixties. To take a peek, it's a short detour left and first right when we reach the T-junction with Beak Street, but looking rather sorry for itself these days. Culture vultures note that Canaletto lived briefly at No. 41, (see the blue plaque) but our route bears right, then left at the *Old Coffee House*, which appears in Walk 5 and is certainly worth a visit if you have the stamina (see description on page 39). Try not to be put off by the awful ground floor exterior: what a contrast to the Crown! It's much better inside.

Continue along Broadwick Street towards the Dutch-gabled pub at the end, the *Blue Posts*. It is claimed that the name referred to posts marking the boundaries of the Soho hunting ground, but mapping their locations hardly adds credence to this story, and the alternative explanation, that they were places where sedan chairs, an early form of taxi if you like, could be hired, may be

The Ship

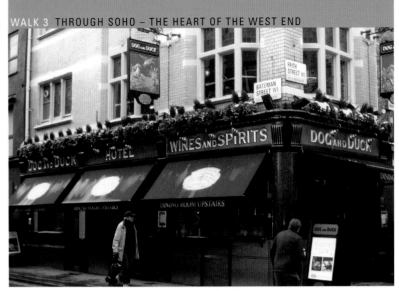

The Dog & Duck is the architectural highlight of the walk

more plausible. Today there are still five pubs in the district that carry this unusual name. The exterior of this one, with its Watney's lamps and frosted windows, looks very 60s and indeed you may well be tempted in for a quick visit. Rest assured, that the demon ales produced by this one-time *béte noire* of CAMRA are no longer to be found inside! To your right is Berwick Street with its market, but to continue the trail, carry on along Broadwick Street keeping the Blue Posts on your right to reach Wardour Street in a few yards.

This is one of Soho's main thoroughfares, and is remembered by many for the golden years of the Marquee Club at No. 90, which hosted many of the great names of rock music from the 60s to the 80s. Closer to hand, indeed almost opposite, is the next official pub on the walk, the **Ship 2**. This is one of Soho's best pubs and, fittingly for the area, is very keen on its music. Those who belong to the aforementioned Marquee era can wallow in nostalgia here, for music from that period is frequently played, sometimes rather loudly. The place has an attractive interior with etched glass and mirrors although most of what you see in is a post-war restoration following considerable wartime damage. This is a Fuller's house, so of course expect their range of beers.

Just north (turn right on exit) of the Ship is St Anne's Court, and cutting through this narrow passage leads out onto Dean Street. Turn left, and

at the next junction (with Carlisle Street by the *Nellie Dean of Soho* which itself has a range of real ales) bear right (the home of *Private Eye* is a few yards down on the left) to reach Soho Square. The attractive oasis was laid out in the late seventeenth century but it is best known for the attractive gardener's hut at the centre, although this isn't as old as it looks. It's believed that the current structure was a 1920s folly built primarily to conceal an electricity sub-station. Head anticlockwise (turn right) around the square and take the next exit which is Frith Street. On the first junction, 100 yards down, stands what is arguably Soho's best pub, at least as regards its décor, the **Dog & Duck 3**. Dating back to 1897, this splendid little pub has a distinctive exterior with polished granite facings, which probably date from a 1930s makeover. Don't miss the floor mosaic as you go into the fine interior, which has some notable Victorian tilework (look out for the yellow tiles sporting the two animals, underneath the large advertising mirrors). The Victorian pub would undoubtedly have had several divisions as evidenced by the former doorways and was probably opened out in the thirties when some of the internal fittings were renewed. A semi-enclosed snug at the rear still remains. This is another pub which has now passed into the Nicholson's chain, and as such it has a wider range of ales than before with the usual Nicholson's regulars and some interesting guests on the half dozen handpumps.

Continue down Frith Street passing the famous Ronnie Scott's jazz club on the right, and take the first left, Old Compton Street. There's no chance of missing the next pub, the **Three Greyhounds** 4 on the next corner, as it has a striking four-storey mock Tudor exterior. The name probably references the old hunting ground here. Inside it's far smaller than you might expect, but despite this there are no less than four separate doorways (not all used today) so the original layout must have been very intimate! Yet another Nicholson's house now, the place offers the almost standard fare for this route of Nicholson's regulars and around three interesting guests kept in good condition, alongside the house food menu.

Turn right out of the pub, and keeping the American diner on your left walk down to Cambridge Circus in fifty yards. Cross Charing Cross Road and walk down the left (north) side of Shaftsbury Avenue, although only for another 100 yards or so before taking Stacey Street, the first left. In daylight hours the wonderfully informal little Phoenix Garden, which is a short way along on the right, can be taken in *en route*. To get to the entrance, take first right and then left, keeping the garden on your left. The Phoenix Garden opened in 1984 and was created by the local community working together as the Covent Garden Open

Spaces Association. The site was bombed during the Blitz of London, and post-war, the damaged buildings were cleared and it was used as a car park. This is the last of several similar gardens on vacant plots once managed by the association, and it's a lovely little oasis of tranquillity full of wild flowers and secluded seats. Continue by bearing left out of the garden and taking the path through the edge of the churchyard to emerge on St Giles High Street by the church of St Giles.

If it's after dusk and the garden is closed, an alternative route to St Giles High Street is either up to the end of Stacey Street and right via another alleyway, Flitchcroft Street; or a more well frequented and better-lit alternative is to walk instead up the Charing Cross Road northwards and bear right down Denmark Street (see map). In each case just a few yards to the right from the frontage of the parish church is the **Angel** 5. Now that one of the sixties-style frosted windows has been replaced with clear glass, the place is no longer quite the secret it once was: one can now see into the main bar, and a very traditional affair it is too, as you'd expect from Samuel Smith. A recent spruce-up has changed little else in this three room pub which still retains two separate street entrances. Perhaps the highlight is the small rear saloon, accessed via the unusual enclosed

LEFT: **Three Greyhounds** RIGHT: **Phoenix Gardens is a lovely oasis**

St Giles church

more iconic (indeed it was listed in 1995), was completed in 1966. As of early 2013 the area is a navigational nightmare thanks to the works for the Crossrail project, but hopefully, dear reader, it will be easier by the time you head back past St Giles Church and bear round to the left on Oxford Street. If all else fails just make for Tottenham Court Road Underground station, for right adjacent, on the north west corner of the junction, stands the **Tottenham** 6 . This, the last-remaining pub on whole length of Oxford Street, was built in 1892 in a Flemish Renaissance style to the designs of architects Saville & Martin. The interior is a long, narrow space, and retains much to admire despite some opening out, as its Grade II* listing testifies. There is some impressive tile and mirror work, especially in the rear part where there is a tiled frieze with swirling foliage, an ornate mahogany-surround fireplace, mirror and mahogany panelling. The less said about the tacky coloured glass in the skylight, the better! Far better are the glazed paintings representing the seasons; and the carved mahogany panelling with large mirrored sections and small bevelled mirror sections at the top. It's yet another Nicholson's pub, serving the usual mixture of around half a dozen staple beers and guests (and a similar food regime) to other Nicholson's houses earlier in this walk.

side carriageway that also leads to a secluded little rear patio. There's also a tiny rear garden which closes quite early in the evening. As with all Sam Smith's pubs, the sole real ale is Old Brewery Bitter; unpretentious food is also available.

The final stop on this route involves negotiating the road network around and under Centre Point to reach the junction of Tottenham Court Road and Oxford Street. The tower block itself, one of London's earliest and still one of the

---

PUB INFORMATION

1 Crown
64 Brewer Street, W1F 9TP
020 7287 8420
www.nicholsonspubs.co.uk/
thecrownbrewerstreetlondon
Opening Hours: 10-11 (11.30 Fri
& Sat); 12-10.30 Sun

2 Ship
116 Wardour Street, W1F 0TT
020 7437 8446
www.shipsoho.co.uk
Opening Hours: 11-11; closed Sun

3 Dog & Duck
18 Bateman Street, W1D 3AJ
020 7494 0697
www.nicholsonspubs.co.uk/
thedogandducksoholondon
Opening Hours: 111-11 (11.30
Fri & Sat); 12-10.30 Sun

4 Three Greyhounds
25 Greek Street, W1D 5DD
020 7494 0953
www.nicholsonspubs.co.uk/
thethreegreyhoundssoholondon
Opening Hours: 12-11.30
(midnight Thu; 12.30am Fri); 10-
12.30am Sat; 10-11 Sun

5 Angel
61-62 Saint Giles High Street,
WC2H 8LE
020 7240 2876
Opening Hours: 11-11;
12-10.30 Sun

6 Tottenham
6 Oxford Street, W1D 1AN
020 7636 8324
www.nicholsonspubs.co.uk/
thetottenhamoxfordstreetlondon
Opening Hours: 11-11;
12-10.30 Sun

**The exterior of the
Tottenham, Oxford Street**

Covent Garden & theatreland

WALK INFORMATION

Start and finish:
Charing Cross or
Embankment

Distance: 1.5 miles (2.4km)

Key attractions: London
Transport Museum; Covent
Garden Market; St Paul's
Covent Garden; Royal Opera
house; Theatreland

The pubs: Coal Hole; Nell of
old Drury; Cross Keys; Lamb
& Flag; Salisbury; Harp

The West End district of Covent Garden is one of London's success stories. In the 1970s, it was threatened with a dismal office-led redevelopment after the departure of the fruit and vegetable market, but a spirited campaign by local residents managed to fight off the developers. Our walk starts on land reclaimed from the Thames in Victorian times, before circumnavigating the old Covent Garden market hall, piazza and associated buildings. These include the expanded Royal Opera House; the Theatre Royal, Drury Lane; Inigo Jones' St Paul's church and the London Transport Museum. The pubs include several worthy of their place in CAMRA's inventory of Real Heritage Pubs. If you are not a regular visitor to London you may well want to spend some time sightseeing in this interesting area. If you can, this is a route to do outside the peak evening periods.

TIMING TIP

Watch out for the limited hours (including mid-afternoon and all-day Sunday closure) at Nell of Old Drury.

Start at Charing Cross station and, unless it's evening, look for the exit by the *Beer House* close to platform 1. This will lead down, via steps, to Villiers Street below. The most pleasant route to the first pub stop is via the Victoria Embankment Gardens to the right, but these close at dusk; if they're shut, the easiest alternative is simply to head up onto the Strand (see map) and walk to the right. The gardens were created in 1874 on the reclaimed land following Joseph Bazalgette's construction of the Victoria Embankment

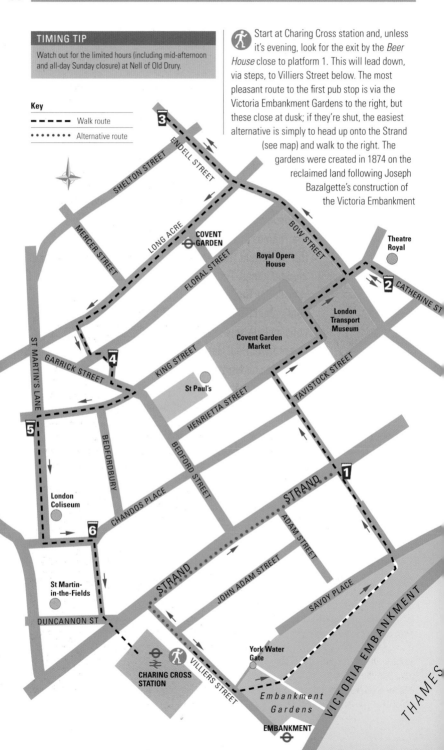

Key

– – – Walk route

• • • • • Alternative route

The Coal Hole, formerly part of the Savoy

between 1865 and 1870. One striking curio is the York Water Gate. Built for George Villiers, Duke of Buckingham, in 1626, the gate served as the riverside entrance for his mansion, York House, which stood between the Strand and the River Thames. It was one of several waterside steps which are now some distance from the river. The word Strand itself is a German word for 'beach': the road broadly followed the north bank of the Thames at one time.

Either leave the gardens on the left (north) by the statue of Robert Raikes, the founder of the Sunday Schools movement, in which case the onward route is directly opposite. Alternatively, walk along to the far end of the gardens and exit onto quiet Savoy Place, the tradesmans' entrance to the famous hotel, commissioned by Richard D'Oyly Carte of Gilbert & Sullivan fame and designed by Thomas Collcutt. Walk back to your left and look for Carting Lane, then walk up the sloping street towards the steps which lead up onto the Strand. By now you'll be upon the first pub stop of the walk, the **Coal Hole** 1 . With a name commemorating the coal-heavers of the Thames, this is part of Collcutt's Savoy complex but was opened in 1904 as the New Strand Wine Lodge. The name is still visible on the front fascia. Here, Art Nouveau features mingle with elements of the 'Olde England' revival. There is a good deal of dark panelling, leaded windows and original decoration. Under the beamed ceiling a plaster frieze depicts maidens picking grapes

and there is a decorated fire surround towards the rear where the gallery is a converted office. These days the pub is in the Nicholson's chain, and alongside the house Pale Ale (brewed by St Austell) you can expect to find an excellent choice of up to ten ales, with plenty of guests alongside favourites like London Pride. The small basement snug is used as a wine bar.

From the Coal Hole make your way across the Strand and up Southampton Street opposite. Ahead lies a cobbled square hosting the old Covent Garden market building dating from the 1830s and now a mecca of entertainment, shops and cafés. It was saved after a spirited campaign in the 1960s, when residents and workers took on the planners and won, although ironically the gentrification of the area and the exodus of the old fruit and vegetable market has since driven out the former community. Bear right around the market building unless you fancy a bit of sightseeing (for instance, Inigo Jones's handsome church of St Paul's is at the other end of the piazza), passing the London Transport Museum in the south eastern corner of the square. Take the first turn right (Russell Street) and cross straight over Bow Street by the *Marquess of Anglesey*. Take the next right by the corner of the Theatre Royal (Catherine Street) and a few yards down here on your right, opposite the striking façade of the theatre, is the dinky little **Nell of Old Drury** 2 . It's a handsome building with a distinctive bow window, and a clientele

Nell of Old Drury

LEFT: **The foliage-covered Cross Keys** RIGHT: **The Salsibury: the architectural high point of the walk**

consisting largely of tourists, after-work drinkers and of course, theatregoers. Because of this it gets busy at certain times. Expect Hook Norton's Old Hooky and Sambrook's Wandle on draught.

Return to Bow Street, turning right by the Marquess of Anglesey. This street is probably best known as the home of the first formal police station in London, although the colloquial term 'Bow Street Runners' refers to a forerunner force (before the founding of the Metropolitan Police) attached to a nearby magistrates' office. Where Bow Street reaches Long Acre, continue more or less straight ahead into Endell Street and walk up here until, at the point where it narrows and becomes one-way, you'll come across the very distinctive exterior of the next call, the **Cross Keys** ③ . Striking not just for its elaborate decoration (notably the two golden cherubs holding the crossed keys of Saint Peter, keeper of the gates of Heaven) but also on account of a heavy covering of foliage. The two together make quite an impression, even before entering. Inside is a fascinating collection of bric-a-brac, ranging from copper kettles to musical instruments and even a diving helmet. There are also brewery mirrors, a large collection of portraits and

pictures, including a good watercolour landscape, and two notable clocks. Leased by East London brewers Brodie's, this pub has a good range of its beers alongside Sambrook's Wandle and perhaps another guest. There's a range of food served during the day.

To continue on this anti-clockwise circuit around the market, retrace your steps down to Long Acre and turn right. Head along this shopping street for a few minutes looking out for Stanfords, the famous book and map shop, at No 14. If you want to drop in, leave by the rear door (or alternatively, take the passage left immediately beyond the shop), emerging into narrow Floral Street. Bear left here and take the narrow alley, Lazenby Court, a few yards on the right, to arrive at another famous London pub via the back passage, as it were. Watch your head as you go through the archway with the **Lamb & Flag** ④ on your immediate right. Entering the pub this way, rather than from Garrick Street at the front makes it easier to appreciate the late 17th century origins of this pub, with well-worn boards and panelling, and a lot of atmosphere to savour if you call at one of the few quiet times. The rear room is particularly characterful. Don't miss the array of little brass plaques named for various customers, not all of them celebrities. The pub has now been acquired by Fuller's and offers a wide range of their own beers as well as guests on the eight handpumps. Sandwiches and snacks can be had downstairs, whilst more substantial, good value meals are available in the Dryden Room upstairs (see box).

Looking back at building upon exit via the main front door, the front space with the two doorways has been opened out in recent times. There was a small lounge to the left, hence the sign above pointing right to the public bar. The smart brick frontage is of course, a relatively modern addition. Finally, those with a penchant for pub names will maybe recognise the flag as the red cross of the Knight's Templar, a military order of monks and the founders of the Temple (see Walk 2), carried on the Pascal Lamb of God.

Walk down the lane to Garrick Street and crossing over, bear right by the *Round House* and along brick-paved New Row. At the end, almost opposite, you will see the splendid exterior of the **Salisbury** 5 across the street. From a pub architecture perspective the Salisbury is the high point of the walk and it is pleasing to see the pride which the management take in the pub's heritage. Rebuilt in 1892, and then called the Salisbury Stores (note the double 'S' in the etched windows), this building fully conveys the sense of glamour of the late Victorian pub. The exterior is pretty stunning and repays close

THE DRYDEN CONNECTION

The poet John Dryden was beaten to within an inch of his life outside the Lamb in 1679 for writing uncomplimentary words about Charles II's mistress. This violence would become a regular feature of the pub's life as the years went on. In the early 19th century, the pub gained the nickname the 'Bucket of Blood' because of the bare-knuckled prizefights outside and in the rear room. In fact the whole area was a notorious slum in which fights were commonplace. Today the only fight you will be involved in is the one to get to the bar if you arrive at the wrong time!

inspection before venturing in. Inside, something of the divided-up plan survives with the small, screened snug on St Martin's Court. The original counter survives and you can mark the position of a now vanished partition by noting the change from wood to marble. The bar-back is also very fine, as is some, though not all, of the glass. Perhaps the tour de force is the row of bronze Art Nouveau nymphs holding electric lamps. The regular beers come from familiar brewers: St Austell Tribute, Timothy Taylor Landlord, and Wells Bombardier; and in addition there are guests. Food is available until mid evening, although here in the heart of Theatreland there are plenty of eating options, some maybe less busy, in the area.

Leaving the Salisbury, turn right down St Martin's Lane past the rejuvenated Coliseum

The Lamb & Flag offers eight real ales in convivial surroundings

theatre to the junction at the end, with the National Portrait Gallery and St Martin's church right and ahead, respectively. We turn left, along William IV Street as far as the next junction where Chandos Place bears half left, and a few yards along is the excellent **Harp** . This small and narrow pub, which has little Irish about it despite the name, is as good as it gets for the real ale drinker in London as the impressive array of CAMRA and other awards testify. Now an independent free house, there are ten handpumps serving a mouth-watering range of cask beers in tip top condition; many of them are sourced locally as the Harp is a strong supporter of CAMRA's LocAle initiative. There's also a range of bottle conditioned and keg craft beers, whilst the traditional cider and perry drinker is also catered for. The other attraction of the Harp is the dedication of the owner and licensee Binnie Walsh, and her enthusiastic staff. Binnie, although born in Ireland has worked in the London pub trade for some 40 years, and in addition to scooping the national CAMRA Pub of the Year award in 2011 – the first time a London pub has picked up the accolade – she was also awarded the 2010 annual CAMRA John Young Memorial Plaque for her services to real ale in the capital. Her professional influence pervades the place strongly.

The Harp has lovely stained glass windows which open in good weather, whilst the interior

The Harp – as good as it gets for drinkers in London

has stools around the wall below a wide shelf, above which are a collection of paintings. Upstairs is a smaller lounge which, like the main bar, is often full of appreciative patrons, so don't automatically expect a seat. In fact the crowds often spill out onto the pavement, such is the pub's popularity. It's primarily a pub for drinking, although the award winning O'Hagan's sausages are available.

Public transport options upon leaving include numerous buses from Trafalgar Square (return to the bottom of St Martin's Lane and aim for the church), or head down to Charing Cross station by taking the lane opposite the Harp.

PUB INFORMATION

1 Coal Hole
91-92 Strand, WC2R 0DW
020 7379 9883
www.nicholsonspubs.co.uk/
thecoalholestrandlondon
Opening Hours: 10-11(midnight
Fri & Sat)

2 Nell of Old Drury
29 Catherine Street, WC2B 5JS
0207 836 5328
www.nellofolddrury.com
Opening Hours: 12-3, 5-11.30;
12-midnight Sat; closed Sun

3 Cross Keys
31 Endell Street, WC2H 9BA
0207 836 5185
www.crosskeyscoventgarden.com
Opening Hours: 11-11;
12-10.30 Sun

4 Lamb & Flag
33 Rose Street, WC2E 9EB
020 7497 9504
www.lambandflagcoventgarden.
co.uk
Opening Hours: 11-11;
12-10.30 Sun

5 Salisbury
90 St Martins Lane, WC2N 4AP
020 7836 5863
Opening Hours: 11-11 (11.30
Thu; midnight Fri); 12-midnight
Sat; 12-10.30 Sun

6 Harp
47 Chandos Place, WC2N 4HS
020 7836 0291
www.harpcoventgarden.com
Opening Hours: 10-11.30 (midnight Fri & Sat); 12-11 Sun

West One – Regent's Park to Soho

WALK INFORMATION

Start: ⊖ Great Portland Street or ⊖ Regent's Park

Finish: ⊖ Oxford Circus or ⊖ Piccadilly Circus; or buses from Regent Street

Distance: 1.2 miles (2km)

Key attractions: Regent's Park and Zoo; Royal Institute of British Architects; Oxford Street; Liberty's; Soho

The pubs: Dover Castle; Cock; Argyll Arms; Clachan; Shaston Arms; Old Coffee House

This linear walk takes us from the southern end of Regent's Park towards Oxford Circus, finishing up in Soho. Expect to find good quality pub interiors, alongside some fine Georgian and Edwardian architecture, especially along and to the west of the north-south axis of Great Portland Street. The first pub is one of London's hardest to find, whilst the architectural highlight is undoubtedly the fine Argyll Arms where the trail crosses the shopping mecca of Oxford Street.

Regent's Park, part of architect John Nash's plan for this area commissioned by the then-Prince Regent (later George IV) in the early nineteenth century and now home to London Zoo, lies directly to the north of our start point, and offers a great opportunity to stretch your legs before tackling the pubs.

Argyll Arms

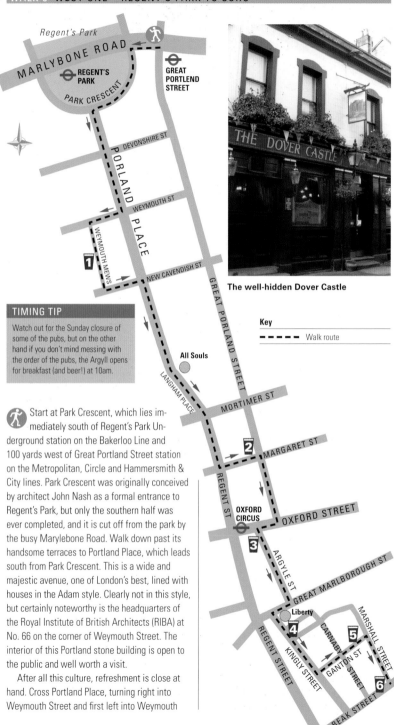

The well-hidden Dover Castle

Key

– – – – Walk route

TIMING TIP

Watch out for the Sunday closure of some of the pubs, but on the other hand if you don't mind messing with the order of the pubs, the Argyll opens for breakfast (and beer!) at 10am.

Start at Park Crescent, which lies immediately south of Regent's Park Underground station on the Bakerloo Line and 100 yards west of Great Portland Street station on the Metropolitan, Circle and Hammersmith & City lines. Park Crescent was originally conceived by architect John Nash as a formal entrance to Regent's Park, but only the southern half was ever completed, and it is cut off from the park by the busy Marylebone Road. Walk down past its handsome terraces to Portland Place, which leads south from Park Crescent. This is a wide and majestic avenue, one of London's best, lined with houses in the Adam style. Clearly not in this style, but certainly noteworthy is the headquarters of the Royal Institute of British Architects (RIBA) at No. 66 on the corner of Weymouth Street. The interior of this Portland stone building is open to the public and well worth a visit.

After all this culture, refreshment is close at hand. Cross Portland Place, turning right into Weymouth Street and first left into Weymouth

The newly-restored Cock

Mews, where halfway down on the right is the well-hidden **Dover Castle** 1 . Dating back to 1750, it has apparently held a licence since 1777. The somewhat bland exterior is more than compensated for within, where the old wood-panelled interior, whilst partially opened-out, retains its appealing atmosphere and there is some etched glass from its partitioned days. Comfortable seats and leatherette benches are the order of the day, and there's an open fire in the main room. The rear snug is a gem and almost has the atmosphere of a gentlemen's club. If you are a visitor to London, consider yourself lucky to have found the place. It's one of the most concealed of all London pubs, and many would-be patrons have given up. It's in the extensive London estate of über-traditional Yorkshire brewery Sam Smith, and so the only cask ale, as usual, is their Old Brewery Bitter.

Return to Portland Place by walking to the far end of Weymouth Mews, turning left, then right; walk down to the southern end of the street, past the distinctive church of All Souls, Langham Place. The road now becomes Regent Street and leads us directly towards Oxford Circus. Just before we get there, bear left onto Margaret Street and along to the next pub, the **Cock** 2 . This is another Sam Smith's pub. Built at the start of the 20th century, it certainly looks the part

inside and out, especially now that Smith's have returned it to something approaching its original splendour. Accordingly, much of what you see is not original, but the result of a Victorian-style refit. The attractive tiled floor, and the screens inside dividing the rooms are good examples of this, as are the 'snob screens': the array of little swivelling glass panels on the bar counter. These were present on a number of Victorian bar counters, and were installed to afford punters more privacy. Very few originals survive. For all that, the comfortable interior is very well done and makes up for the paucity of cask beer choice, which as usual in Sam Smith's pubs, is Hobson's choice, the Old Brewery Bitter.

Come out of the pub and walk straight down to Oxford Street, about 100 yards away. Wading through the shoppers, cross the road and turn right for a few yards before heading left into the pedestrianised Argyll Street just before the traffic lights. Note the distinctive Leslie Green tiled former entrance to the Underground station on the corner. Just a few yards further down is a pub which surely must be the architectural highlight of this walk, the **Argyll Arms** 3 . It's named after one of the Duke of Marlborough's generals who was also a local landowner. Given its location so close to the bustle of Oxford Street, the survival of the stunning exterior and interior

The Clachan offers up to eight real ales

of this pub, built in 1868 and remodelled circa 1895, is quite remarkable. The striking exterior, with those distinctive curved windows, leads to a mirror-lined and terrazzo-floored corridor. In turn, compartments open up on the right with splendidly etched and cut screenwork. These small compartments are now very rare in pubs and are not to be missed here; these are the best originals of their kind left in London. The bar-back is original, and note the tiny landlord's office halfway down. To the rear of this large pub is a spacious room where the staircase is worth looking at for its ironwork. Nicholson's have gone to town on the beer range here over the past few years: there's a fine array of no less than sixteen beer engines, in two sets (one set is in the rear room) and although they are not all continually in use, you can expect upwards of five changing guests along with three regulars. An all-day food menu complements the beers.

Continue down Argyll Street to Liberty's half-timbered building at the bottom. This imposing edifice was constructed in 1922-3, coinciding with the Tudor revival's influence on pub design. It was made of timbers from *HMS Impregnable* and *HMS Hindustan* and still houses the famous Arts and Crafts movement store, which was founded in 1875. Turn right and then first left into Kingly Street. Here, well-hidden in this quiet little side street parallel with nearby Regent Street, is the imposing façade of the **Clachan 4**. This is another late Victorian rebuild, circa 1898, which has managed to keep some of its original fittings, including some rich wood-carving and structural ironwork. Look for the pretty tiling, including a floor mosaic advertising the pub's unusual name, in the entrances. Note also the cosy raised seating area at the back of the pub, which could conceivably once have been the landlord's parlour. The pub was formerly known

All Souls church, Langham Place

as the Bricklayers and owned by Liberty, who had plans to turn it into a warehouse. Once again it's in the Nicholson's chain with up to five rotating guests supporting the three regulars, London Pride, Nicholson's Pale and (usually) Windsor & Eton Knight of the Garter.

From the Clachan, walk further down Kingly Street as far as the *Blue Posts* pub on the corner of Ganton Street, noting the rather handsome exterior with its leaded and stained glass. Turn left to reach and cross the pedestrianised Carnaby Street, now only a shadow of its former Swinging 60s self. Just a little further on the left and sporting a loud red paint job, is the next port of call, the **Shaston Arms** 5 . Stepping inside this inviting and intimate little pub, with its screened drinking booths and dark woodwork, one could be forgiven for thinking that this was one of London's hidden vintage pubs. In fact, it has been a pub for less than twenty years, having been skilfully converted via a wine bar from shop premises. There are modern booths along one side, and a back room with skylight, so it's a bit bigger than it appears from outside. It is part of the Hall & Woodhouse estate so you'll find Badger Bitter and Tanglefoot, plus a H&W seasonal ale, on handpump.

The intimate Shaston Arms

Leaving the Shaston, turn left and then take the right turn into Marshall Street. Continue south, crossing Broadwick Street to reach the final pub of this walk on the following corner with Beak Street. The **Old Coffee House** 6 looks frankly awful from outside with what looks to me like some seventies restaurant-style window job at ground floor level, but don't let that put you off. Inside the place could hardly be more traditional-looking, and definitely is an old pub,

Liberty's imposing façade

Inside the Old Coffee House

although the name stems from the 18th-century tradition of using coffee houses as political and business meeting places.

Today the cosy interior retains an old bar counter (with hatches to service the beer engines) and even vestiges of an old spittoon under the footrail. Large old brewery mirrors adorn the rear walls along with all manner of other ephemera. The real pull of the place however is the beer, as this is, at the time of writing, one of only three Brodie's tied pubs (the others both feature in this book). As such expect an extensive range of their beers, five on hand-pump and another five on keg. If you like your beers well-hopped and zesty you've come to the right place. Food is available here if you're planning to eat at the final stop on this walk.

For the nearest Underground stations, retrace your steps to Oxford Circus for the northern termini, or walk down Lower James Street, almost opposite the pub, for about five minutes in the same direction to reach Piccadilly Circus. Regent Street and buses are two minutes away to the right along Beak Street.

> **LINK** From the Old Coffee House you can join Walk 3, omitting the first pub, by retracing your steps up Marshall Street and turning right into Broadwick Street.

PUB INFORMATION

1 Dover Castle
43 Weymouth Mews, W1G 7EQ
020 7580 4412
Opening Hours: 12-11;
closed Sun

2 Cock
27 Great Portland Street,
W1W 8QG
020 7631 5002
Opening Hours: 12-11
(10.30 Sun)

3 Argyll Arms
18 Argyll Street, W1F 7TP
020 7734 6117
Opening Hours: 10-11 (11.30 Fri
& Sat); 12-10.30 Sun

4 Clachan
34 Kingly Street, W1B 5QH
020 7494 0834
Opening Hours: 10-11 (11.30 Fri;
10.30 Sat & Sun)

5 Shaston Arms
4-6 Ganton Street, W1S 7QN
020 7287 2631
shastonarms.co.uk
Opening Hours: 12-11;
closed Sun

6 Old Coffee House
49 Beak Street, W1F 9SF
020 7437 2197
Opening Hours: 11-11;
12-10.30 Sun

Political London –
Westminster & St James's

WALK INFORMATION

Start: Westminster

Finish: Piccadilly Circus

Distance: 2 miles (3.2km)

Key attractions: Westminster Abbey; Houses of Parliament & Palace of Westminster; Cabinet War Rooms; St James's Park; Buckingham Palace; St James's Palace

The pubs: St Stephen's Tavern; Speaker; Sanctuary House; Red Lion (Craven Passage); Golden Lion; Red Lion (Duke of York Street)

A very good walk for the beer tourist, offering plenty to see in addition to the interesting pubs. Many of the sights will be familiar but there will probably be something new here even for many Londoners. Starting at the very heart of the capital, close to some of its most iconic sights, the route winds into St James's, one of London's richest areas and one of its first true suburbs. From the latter part of the seventeenth century onwards, it was laid out in grid fashion as an exclusive residential area and remained as such until after World War Two. Today it's more associated with commerce, although many of the gentlemen's clubs survive here alongside some well-known London institutions such as Christie's the auctioneers. Unlike Westminster, St James's is a relatively unfrequented area for visitors, but finishing with one of London's best small pub interiors, you're unlikely to be disappointed, unless you turn up on a Sunday!

St James's Park

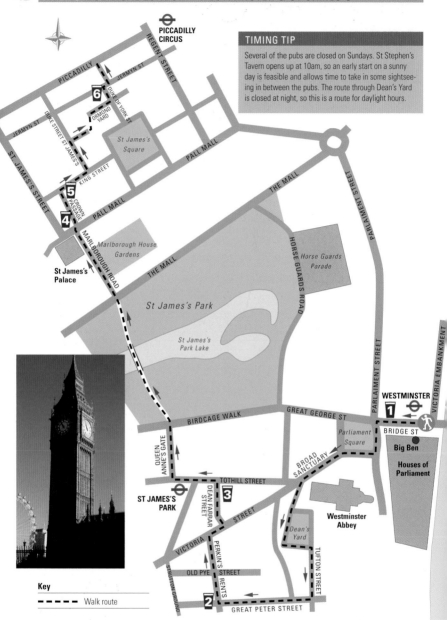

TIMING TIP

Several of the pubs are closed on Sundays. St Stephen's Tavern opens up at 10am, so an early start on a sunny day is feasible and allows time to take in some sightseeing in between the pubs. The route through Dean's Yard is closed at night, so this is a route for daylight hours.

Start the walk by the Bridge Street exit from Westminster Underground station. The first thing that greets you upon emerging from the station is the magnificent 'Big Ben' opposite, correctly named St Stephen's Clock Tower but recently renamed the Elizabeth

Tower in honour of Queen Elizabeth II's Diamond Jubilee. Behind this are the massed tourist sights of Westminster Hall, Westminster Abbey and Charles Barry's classic gothic Palace of Westminster. Once you've drunk in that little list, attention can turn to the first pub stop of

St Stephen's Tavern

the day, a few yards along to the right; and the **St Stephen's Tavern** has an interior which is not out of place in such exalted company. Surprisingly the pub had been closed for over a decade before it was acquired by Hall & Woodhouse and reopened in 2003 after an expensive refurbishment. Built in 1875, it takes its name from the clock tower across the road. The interior has been well restored with much to attract the eye; for example, the high bar-back with some very fine mirrors, an ornate coffered ceiling with chandelier, some attractive light fittings and a Victorian bar counter. Some of the window glass has survived too, particularly the very appealing 'Public Bar' door glass in the Bridge Street entrance. The exterior appearance is pretty good too as befits such a key location, with one of those wonderful big lamps hanging over each of the two main entrances. All sorts of the great, good and not so good have drunk here from the 'other places' across the road, but these days you're far more likely to be sharing the bar with tourists. Up to four beers from the Hall & Woodhouse portfolio, including Tanglefoot and a seasonal guest, are on tap.

The onward route involves crossing Bridge Street at the Parliament Square lights, and walking alongside the (now heavily guarded) entrance to the Palace of Westminster, and crossing again to walk alongside first St Margaret's parish church, itself with a long history stretching back to the 12th century; and behind, Westminster Abbey. I'm not even going to try to encapsulate the history of this building – there are plenty of good guides available, but leave adequate time to justify the admission fee if you're planning to take in the Abbey *en route*.

Walk along to the tall, slender scholars' war memorial facing the West Front of the Abbey and look for a sentry box beside an archway in the castellated frontage on the left – this is normally open during daylight hours so head through here into secluded Dean's Yard, which hosts the buildings of Westminster School and most of the remaining precincts of the former monastery of Westminster. The green in the centre is where the pupils have a right to play football, and indeed they have some claim to have invented the game as we know it today. Aim for the smaller archway at the diametrically opposite corner of Dean's Yard, leading out into Tufton Street straight ahead. Walk up as far as Great Peter Street, and turn right to follow it across Marsham Street and for a further 200 yards until you spot the distinctive **Speaker** on the

The Speaker

corner of the oddly-named Perkin's Rents. This friendly one-bar corner pub, whose exterior appearance has a bit of the Edinburgh tenement about it, is a peaceful haven for locals, civil servants and MPs (and like most bars in the area, it has its own division bell to summon MPs to the chamber). There are caricatures of past prime ministers and lesser MPs on the

walls. It has built a reputation for well-kept and interesting beers, three changing guests supporting Taylor Landlord and Young's Bitter. A decent range of Belgian bottled beers is available too alongside home-made food from sandwiches up to a daily main meal. No music or TV will intrude upon your conversation in this pleasant haven.

If you're after some food on the go, I would strongly recommend continuing up Great Peter Street to Strutton Ground, the second on the right, with its sandwich bars and cafes. Otherwise head up Perkin's Rents, directly north from the pub, to meet Victoria Street. This was part of an area known as the Devil's Acre (a term first coined by Dickens) in Victorian London, on account of the appalling housing conditions and outbreaks of cholera and typhoid.

The Red Lion in Crown Passage

Cross over carefully and head up Dean Farrar Street between the office blocks a little to your right. Fork right almost immediately and walk along to the next junction where sitting grandly on the corner is the **Sanctuary House 3** . The name derives from the almonry of Westminster Abbey which was here or hereabouts. Almoners were monks who were vested with the duty of providing food, drink and shelter to the poor and ailing. Since 1997 this has been a Fuller's hotel sitting atop a well-regarded pub serving a wide range of their ales, staples and seasonals. The décor is traditional with polished wood floors, benches and bar stools, and bar meals are available most hours.

Walk up Tothill Street to the left after leaving the Sanctuary House, towards St James's Park Underground station under the bulk of 55 Broadway, one of the few celebrated buildings in London to be known principally by its address. It was built by noted architect Charles Holden (he of Underground stations on the Northern Line and elsewhere: see Walks 26 and 27) as the headquarters for the Underground Group, the forerunner of the London Underground. Bear right here at the *Old Star* public house into Queen Anne's Gate, and then use the pedestrian crossing to St James's Park.

St James's Park is the oldest of London's royal parks and started life as a hunting ground for Henry VIII, though the present park was landscaped by John Nash in the early nineteenth century. Walk straight across to the bridge which affords attractive views of the London Eye to the right, and Buckingham Palace to the left through the trees. Keep on the same bearing to the exit, and cross the Mall, which, unless it's Sunday when it's closed to traffic, will be busy, so use the controlled crossing. Take the street opposite, Marlborough Road, past St James's Palace, most of which is closed to the public as it is Prince Charles's private London pad. The palace was also the principal London residence of monarchy until Buckingham Palace was selected by Queen

Victoria in 1837. Across the street is Queen's Chapel, one of Inigo Jones's classical churches. All this culture and you may be ready for the next drink, so at the end of Marlborough Road as you emerge onto Pall Mall (named after a French pre-cursor to croquet), look for an archway opposite in Quebec House. This is Crown Passage and home to an atmospheric little alleyway of shops and a pleasant pub, the **Red Lion** 4. The frontage of the pub suggests a venerable age, perhaps the eighteenth century, and a rather presumptuous sign reads, 'London's last village pub'. The cosy, panelled interior, however, is probably a legacy of the 1930s, and although the pub is very small it would have been subdivided at one time as the two doorways suggest. All in all it is a civilised place away from the well-beaten tourist trail. Adnams Bitter and St Austell Tribute are the offerings at the bar. Don't expect to dine here but sandwiches are available.

Upon leaving the Red Lion and continuing up Crown Passage, you emerge onto King Street. A few doors down to the right there is the second of three lions on this walk, this time

the **Golden Lion** 5. Built by the prolific pub architects, Eedle & Meyers, in 1897-9, it sports a very attractive façade with bow windows, whilst the interior is small, solid and handsome, with a sturdy bar counter and gantry, wooden floors and seating on stools. Young's, London Pride and Greene King IPA were available as well as Harvey's Sussex Best Bitter on my last visit.

As you leave the pub look across the street and you'll spot the home of Christie's, the famous auctioneers, who have been here since 1823. Before tak-ing the next turning on the left, Duke Street St James's, if you continue on the south side of the road as far as No. 33, and look across the street you should spot London's oldest blue plaque, at first floor level on No. 1C opposite. It com-memorates the brief residence here in 1848 of Napoleon III, first President of the French republic and its last Emperor.

Cross the street and head up Duke Street St James's as far as the narrow entrance into Ma-son's Yard on the right by No. 12. This tiny square is now dominated by the newest of the White Cube galleries, on the site of a former electricity

Westminster Abbey: St Stephen's Tavern's imposing neighbour

Inside the Red Lion on Duke of York Street

sub-station. Earlier the square was home to the Indica bookshop and gallery (at No. 23) which in its colourful history was where John Lennon met his future wife Yoko Ono for the first time at an art exhibition in 1966. As you head from the narrow exit to Mason's Yard in the far corner, by No. 9, the house on the right of the alley, No. 13, was despite its unprepossessing appearance today, the location of the former Scotch of St James club which attracted regulars like the Rolling Stones, The Who and Eric Clapton, not to mention being the venue which Jimi Hendrix first

played after arriving in London, also in 1966. The covered alley leads out into Ormond Yard, and at the end bear left to arrive at the final pub on this walk, yet another lion. This **Red Lion** 6 is one of the most splendid of the surviving Victorian pubs in London, and indeed in Britain. Although the building was constructed in 1821, both the pub's frontage and its interior are later in date. This is a veritable late Victorian cathedral of glass, mirrors and woodwork. The richness of the deeply-cut mirrors here are particularly impressive, as they glint and sparkle in the light. Yet, despite the size, it is clear that the building had several internal divisions in the past, hence three doors at the front, each of which would have led into a separate compartment. A quasi-corridor leads to the rear room which is separated from the small front space by an island servery. It can get quite crowded at lunchtimes and early evenings; but it quietens down later on. Since being acquired by Fuller's it offers a wide range of their beers including a rotating seasonal. The extensive menu is available on the pub's website. A real London classic to finish this route!

To get to transport, bear left on exit and turn right onto Jermyn Street by St James's church. This street has long been, and indeed still remains an epicentre of gentlemen's fashion, with shirts a speciality. The cut-through almost opposite leads a few yards up to Piccadilly, with the Underground station about five minutes walk away to the right.

PUB INFORMATION

1 St Stephen's Tavern
10 Bridge Street, SW1A 2JR
020 7925 2286
ststephenstavern.co.uk
Opening Hours: 10-11.30;
12-10.30 Sun

2 Speaker
46 Great Peter Street, SW1P 2HA
020 7222 1749
Opening Hours: 12-11; closed
Sat & Sun

3 Sanctuary House
Tothill Street, SW1H 9LA
020 7799 4044
www.sanctuaryhousehotel.co.uk
Opening Hours: 10-11
(10.30 Sun)

4 Red Lion
23 Crown Passage, SW1Y 6PP
020 7930 4141
Opening Hours: 11-11;
closed Sun

5 Golden Lion
25 King Street, SW1Y 6QY
0207 925 0007
Opening Hours: 11-11; 12-5 Sat;
closed Sun

6 Red Lion
2 Duke of York Street, SW1 6JP
020 7321 0782
www.redlionmayfair.co.uk
Opening Hours: 11.30-11;
closed Sun

Red Lion on Duke of York Street

Back-street Belgravia

WALK INFORMATION

Start: Victoria

Finish: Sloane Square

Distance: 1.7 miles (2.5km)

Key attractions: Hyde Park; Albert Hall; Victoria & Albert Museum; Knightsbridge shopping; Belgrave Square

The pubs: Horse & Groom; Grenadier; Nag's Head; Star Tavern; Antelope; Duke of Wellington; Fox & Hounds. Try also: Wilton Arms

It's difficult to believe that Belgravia's smart streets of stuccoed houses occupy land once known as the 'five fields', a marshy wasteland which was a hangout of highwaymen and other ne'er-do-wells. The crossing of the River Westbourne (the same steam which a little to the north was dammed to form the Serpentine) was known as the Bloody Bridge after their activities. The area was drained and laid out for the Earl of Grosvenor in the 1820s by Thomas Cubitt (1788–1855), one of the earliest and most important of London's speculative builders. Today an average house on fashionable Chester Square will set you back about £7m. Belgravia's residents don't like unnecessary change, including tacky refurbishments; so the pubs on this top quality stroll are much the same as they were when the first edition came out – generally classy, tastefully decorated and urbane.

The Nag's Head

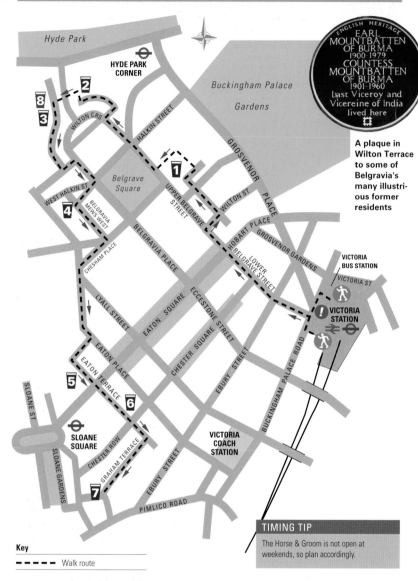

ENGLISH HERITAGE
EARL
MOUNTBATTEN
OF BURMA
1900-1979
COUNTESS
MOUNTBATTEN
OF BURMA
1901-1960
Last Viceroy and
Vicereine of India
lived here

A plaque in Wilton Terrace to some of Belgravia's many illustrious former residents

Hyde Park

HYDE PARK CORNER

Buckingham Palace Gardens

WILTON CRS
HALKIN STREET
GROSVENOR PLACE

8
3
2
1

Belgrave Square

WEST HALKIN ST
BELGRAVIA MEWS WEST
UPPER BELGRAVE STREET
WILTON ST

4

BELGRAVIA PLACE

HOBART PLACE
GROSVENOR GARDENS
LOWER BELGRAVE STREET

CHESHAM PLACE

LYALL STREET
EATON SQUARE
ECCLESTONE STREET

VICTORIA BUS STATION
VICTORIA ST

VICTORIA STATION

EATON PLACE
EATON TERRACE
CHESTER SQUARE STREET
EBURY STREET

5
6

SLOANE ST

SLOANE SQUARE

CHESTER ROW
GRAHAM TERRACE
EBURY STREET

VICTORIA COACH STATION

BUCKINGHAM PALACE ROAD

SLOANE GARDENS

7

PIMLICO ROAD

Key

– – – – Walk route

TIMING TIP

The Horse & Groom is not open at weekends, so plan accordingly.

Exit Victoria station, if possible, by the side exit to Buckingham Palace Road, or turn left and left again from the front exit. Carefully cross the busy road and head down Lower Belgrave Street, towards Belgrave Square. When Thomas Cubitt, who also laid out Kemp Town in Brighton and built Osbourne House on the Isle of Wight for Queen Victoria, developed the area from the 1820s onwards, he was building for the

well-connected, the success of which is testified by the high blue plaque quotient today; but in so doing he excluded pubs from everywhere in Belgravia except the mews, those little backstreet alleys hidden from immediate view. So it's no surprise that our first few pubs here are mews pubs off the beaten track. Pass Eaton Square with St Peter's church on your right. Originally designed in a classical style by the architect

Horse & Groom

Henry Hakewill about 1825, the church was the victim of an arson attack in 1987 which destroyed the roof and the interior. It was rededicated in 1992 following a widely-praised restoration. Bear right immediately beyond St Peter's, and left into cobbled Wilton Mews. You'll see the first pub of the day coming into view across the next junction. The **Horse & Groom** ☐ was opened in 1864 with the then clientele being the stable and mews workers of the gentry. Today

it's a pleasant Shepherd Neame house with a small wood-panelled bar; outside tables appear in decent weather. Expect Shep's Master Brew and Spitfire, plus a seasonal guest. There's a full food menu including sandwiches. The pub is reputed to have been a favourite haunt of Beatles manager, Brian Epstein.

Continue along Groom Place following it round to the first left, and left again into Chapel Street. This in turn leads in a few yards to Belgrave Square with its profusion of mature trees. Turn right and, at the end of the square, cross the roads and continue directly ahead into Wilton Crescent before taking another mews turning, Wilton Row, first right. Following this quiet little street brings you to one of the city's most sequestered pubs, the **Grenadier** ☐. Licensed from around 1820, it is quite likely that Wellington's guards from the nearby barracks used the place, but whether the Iron Duke himself did is open to question, since he was Prime Minister by 1828 and had switched military matters for politics before this time. Certainly an old photograph in Mark Girouard's *Victorian Pubs* suggests a far humbler past than the smart building of today. The small front bar with its well-worn floorboards and atmospheric seating would have originally been divided up, as

The Grenadier

LEFT: **Adnams beers at the Nag's Head** RIGHT: **The Star Tavern – one of the 'magnificent seven'**

the side door suggests, and the once private rooms to the side and rear of the bar counter are now dining rooms, though without loss of character. Note the now very rare pewter bar top, and the old fashioned handpulls, now redundant. Those on either side, however, offer four ales, Taylor Landlord, Fuller's London Pride, and two guests, often including Woodforde's Wherry. Food is available throughout the day.

Leave the pub by the side alley, Barrack Yard, and keep left into another mews. If you follow this round to the left again, you should be able to exit onto Wilton Place. If, for any reason, the gates are closed simply return to Wilton Crescent and turn right and right again into Wilton Place. Cross over into Kinnerton Street, another mews, and almost directly ahead is the **Wilton Arms** 8, which is worth a visit if you have time and capacity. It's another Shepherd Neame house, open daily, with Master Brew, Spitfire and the brewery's seasonal guests. Just a few yards down the street to the left, however, is an altogether rarer beast, the **Nag's Head** 3 . This is a lovely old-fashioned pub, which was built in the 1830s and first licensed as a beer house shortly afterwards. The name reminds us that horses and carriages for the rich of Belgravia were stabled in the mews, and this would have been a basic beerhouse for the stableboys and footmen who lived hereabouts. There are wood-panelled walls, floorboards, a fireplace with a range, and perhaps the lowest bar counter in London. As with so many pubs, new drinking areas have been brought into use by extending into once private quarters; in this case the pub has been

extended up to a rear mezzanine and down into the basement, but without detriment to its quirky character. That character derives from the guv'nor who has been here a long, long time. It's Belgravia's only genuine free house but Kevin favours Adnams beers: you have a choice of three. There's an interesting collection of old penny-arcade machines, but I'm glad to say, no modern ones in this staunchly traditional boozer. Finally, I'm happy to say that Kevin operates a zero-tolerance policy for mobile phones or other electronic gadgetry – you have been warned!

Continue down Kinnerton Street to Motcomb Street and turn left to the junction with Wilton Terrace. Before turning right down to the other corner of Belgrave Square, note the blue plaque on the first house left, indicating that Earl Mountbatten of Burma and his wife, Edwina, lived here. Turn right again at the square into West Halkin Street before taking the mews on the left, coming upon the **Star Tavern** 4 almost immediately, a pleasant surprise indeed. The attractive frontage is matched by a welcoming interior, although I preferred the shabby benches to the plusher post-refit ones. Again it's an early 19th-century building that once would have been divided into several rooms. It is now popular with a range of customers and retains an upstairs bar as well as the main drinking areas below. Since 1951 it's been a Fuller's house, so expect their beers. It's one of CAMRA's 'magnificent seven', to have appeared in every edition of the *Good Beer Guide* to date. Legend has it that this was also the place where the Great Train Robbers planned their heist.

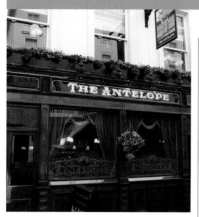

The Antelope

Continue down the mews to the German Embassy at the end and reach Chesham Place. If you've had your fill by now, you can return to Victoria rail and tube stations in 10 minutes by turning left then right and continuing straight down Belgrave Place. However, to continue our tour, turn right and at the junction half left into Chesham Street, merging into Eaton Place and almost immediately taking next right into West Eaton Place. Follow the road round, and in a couple of minutes

you will reach the **Antelope** [5]. On the outskirts of Belgravia and close to Sloane Square, the Antelope was, like the Nag's Head, also built for the household staff working in the grand houses, though there had apparently been a pub here before Cubitt developed the area. Note the two separate entrances, a sign that it was originally divided into several bars. Some vestige of this layout can still be seen inside, although some of the areas, like the room on the left, have only been recently converted into use from private quarters. The rear area has an attractive tiled fireplace and floorboards. Fuller's beers are on offer, plus one guest. A recent development is a new upstairs dining room with food until 3pm at lunchtimes and 9.30 in the evenings.

Leaving the Antelope, you can see the next stop across the street ahead of you, so there's not much opportunity to walk off any excesses! Continue down the street across the main road and reach the **Duke of Wellington** [6], on a prominent corner site, with benches outside. This is yet another early Victorian pub, but reportedly it was originally opened as a library for employees of the Belgravian gentry. The modernised interior, with

LEFT: **Duke of Wellington** RIGHT: **Drinkers enjoying a leisurely afternoon at the Fox & Hounds**

Fox & Hounds

To finish, continue down Eaton Terrace as far as Graham Terrace, the next road on the right, and turning here you will see the **Fox & Hounds 7** just ahead. Or at least, you may need to look behind a splendid floral display, as I did on my last visit. In 1999, this former Charrington's pub was the last pub in London without a spirits licence. This quaint custom dated back to the Beer Act of 1830 and was at one time very common, put into place with the hope of luring the populace away from spirits.

Credit where it's due: Young's, who currently own the pub, have, in my opinion, improved the ambience with their most recent refurbishment, creating a homely and cosy atmosphere in the long, narrow interior. Would that their other refits had been as sensitive as this. Another welcome development is the availability of a guest beer on one of the pub's three handpumps.

several prints of the Iron Duke around the walls, now has a single drinking area around a horseshoe bar. The television can be rather obtrusive if switched on but the pub is a pleasant enough locals' pub, with a range of up to five well-kept beers from the Shepherd Neame portfolio.

From here, the easiest public transport option is to walk to the other end of Passmore Street and take bus 11, 211 or 239 to Victoria. Alternatively continue to the end of Graham Street and turn right into Holbein Place, it's then a walk of about five minutes to Sloane Square Underground station.

PUB INFORMATION

1 Horse & Groom
7 Groom Place, SW1X 7BA
020 7235 6980
Opening Hours: 11.30-11
(midnight Thu & Fri); closed
Sat & Sun

2 Grenadier
18 Wilton Row, SW1X 7NR
020 7235 3074
Opening Hours: 12-11.30
(10.30 Sun)

3 Nag's Head
53 Kinnerton Street, SW1X 8ED
020 7235 1135
Opening Hours: 11-11;
12-10.30 Sun

4 Star Tavern
Belgrave Mews West, SW1X 8HT
020 7235 3019
Opening Hours: 11 (12 Sat)-11;
12-10.30 Sun

5 Antelope
22-24 Eaton Terrace, SW1W 8EZ
020 7824 8512
Opening Hours: 12-11 (11.30
Fri); 11-5 Sun

6 Duke of Wellington
63 Eaton Terrace, SW1W 8TR
020 7730 1782
Opening Hours: 11-11;
12-10.30 Sun

7 Fox & Hounds
29 Passmore Street, SW1W 8HR
020 7730 6367
Opening Hours: 11-11;
12-10.30 Sun

TRY ALSO:

8 Wilton Arms
71 Kinnerton Street, SW1X 8ED
020 7235 4854
Opening Hours: 11-11;
12-10.30 Sun

Gems around Smithfield

WALK INFORMATION

Start: ⇌ ⊖ Farringdon, or ⊖ Chancery Lane

Finish: ⇌ ⊖ Farringdon

Distance: 1.4 miles (2.3km)

Key attractions: Smithfield Market; Old Bailey; St Bartholomew's church; Charterhouse

The pubs: Olde Mitre; Viaduct; Hand & Shears; Red Cow; Jerusalem Tavern

This is a walk full of interest in a lesser-known part of London. It circumnavigates the great structure of Smithfield Market, still the largest meat market in the land, and passes the great ecclesiastical treasure of St Bartholomew's church. There are other notable landmarks, not to mention a variety of excellent pubs. Most of these are closed at weekends so it's a walk to enjoy during the week.

St Peter's brewery's only London house, the Jerusalem Tavern

Start at the newly refurbished Farringdon station on Thameslink National Rail and the Underground. Upon exit from the station turn right and walk down to the Farringdon Road by the *John Oldcastle*. The name of this Wetherspoon pub recalls the eponymous tavern which once stood in the former grounds of Sir John's nearby mansion. Oldcastle is thought to have been the model for Shakespeare's character Falstaff. Turn left, then first right onto Charterhouse Street, before turning right again into the curious Ely Place with its gated and guarded entrance. To get to this point from Chancery Lane Underground station, head eastwards down High Holborn to Holborn Circus, and Ely Place is the first turning left after crossing into Charterhouse Street.

The first pub on this walk is one of the hardest to find in London, although since Fuller's acquired it they have taken to placing advertising boards at the end of the tiny alley where it lies hidden, removing much of the mystique! Turn into gated Ely Place and aim for the passageway between numbers 9 and 10. In fact, given its history the **Olde Mitre** 1 might well feel like a separate kingdom. The original tavern is said to have been built in 1546 for the servants of the nearby palace of the Bishops of Ely, and technically the pub was for years part of the county over which they presided. Until the late 1970s Cambridgeshire was the licensing authority for the pub! The nearby palace, the oldest Roman Catholic church in the city, was demolished in 1772 along with the pub, although the latter was rebuilt soon afterwards. The preserved trunk of a cherry tree, which allegedly marked the boundary of the Bishop of Ely's property, can still be detected in the corner of the small front bar of this very atmospheric hostelry. The interior you see today, replete with wood panelling throughout, dates back to an interwar refitting, and a rare outside gents' toilet completes the scene. The larger back room has a cosy snug. In addition to Fuller's beers, the six handpumps dispense several guest ales, usually including Deuchars IPA and other Caledonian beers; and Adnams Bitter. Expect a draught cider too. The popular and long-serving licensee, 'Scotty' to the regulars, is still in situ, and the pub goes from strength to strength, collecting CAMRA awards almost annually. Not to be missed!

If you continue on the narrow passageway upon leaving the Olde Mitre, you emerge onto Hatton Garden, centre of the London jewellery trade. Turn left to reach Holborn Circus with St Andrew's church, rebuilt by Wren after the Great Fire, on the busy intersection. Be careful crossing Charterhouse Street before turning next left on the continuation of High Holborn, now named after the viaduct over Farringdon Street below. Constructed during the 1860s over the valley of the Fleet River, it was the first 'flyover' in London and didn't come cheap. Just beyond is the street-level entrance to what was Holborn Viaduct station, which once had a connection to the Metropolitan line at Farringdon before becoming a terminus until the re-opening of Snow Hill

CHANCERY LANE

HOLBORN

Olde Mitre

Key

- - - - Walk route
••••••• Alternative route

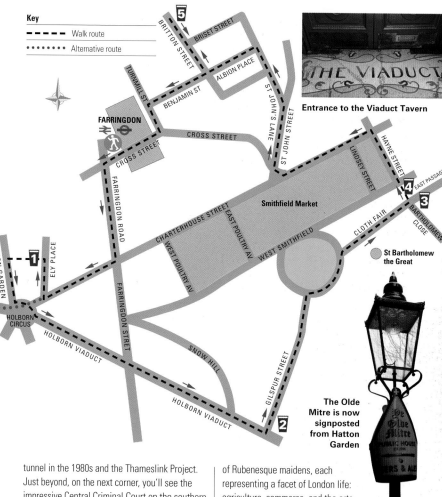

Entrance to the Viaduct Tavern

St Bartholomew the Great

The Olde Mitre is now signposted from Hatton Garden

tunnel in the 1980s and the Thameslink Project. Just beyond, on the next corner, you'll see the impressive Central Criminal Court on the southern side of the street, with its gilded statue of justice with her sword and scales. Until 1902, this was the site of the infamous Newgate prison.

Time for another stop, and right opposite stands the handsome Grade II-listed **Viaduct Tavern 2** with its impressive curved frontage. Although remodelled at the turn of the century, the pub dates back to about 1870, taking its name of course from the viaduct you've just crossed. The four doorways suggest a once typically divided Victorian pub, although predictably the partitions have gone. However, many of the other original features have survived, the most prominent being the three large Victorian paintings

of Rubenesque maidens, each representing a facet of London life: agriculture, commerce, and the arts. The latter painting was either shot or, according to some stories, bayoneted by a drunken soldier in World War I, and still carries the wound. Nowadays, the paintings are glazed to prevent further damage to the canvas. Between each of the paintings is one of several cherubic face reliefs that are a feature throughout the pub. Look out for the cut and gilded glass-work, especially towards the rear of the pub, where a little publican's office, once common but now a rare survivor, can also be seen. The widely-circulated story that the pub's cellars were once cells of Newgate prison seems improbable given that Newgate was rebuilt around 1770 and

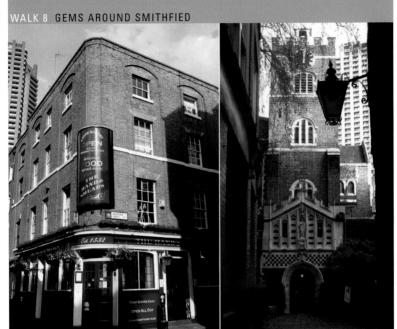

LEFT: **The Hand & Shears** RIGHT: **The church of St Bartholomew the Great is well worth a visit**

was on its last legs when the Viaduct was built. Anyway, it's still worth a call! The pub is another fairly recent acquisition of Fuller's brewery so expect their beers including a seasonal guest.

Walk north up Giltspur Street towards Smithfield Market. This is a famous spot in the history of London, with a market having existed here since the twelfth century. Older still was the famous Bartholomew Fair, which was a cloth fair originally founded to fund the famous Bart's hospital nearby. The site was also used for jousting and was notorious as a place of execution during the Reformation. In the nineteenth century, Smithfield established itself as the largest meat market in England and the current market hall with its ironwork and glass roof was built to a design by Sir Horace Jones in 1868. Like most London markets it's only a shadow of its former self, but at least it's not yet a chintzy boutique mall or a collection of wine bars. To the right of the small open space in front of the market hall, down a narrow passage to the right of the *Butcher's Hook & Cleaver*, is what remains of the splendid church of St Bartholomew the Great. A detour to visit the church is highly recommended. The Priory church was founded in 1123 by Prior

Rahere as part of a monastery of Augustinian Canons, but was dissolved in 1539 and the nave of the church demolished. What remains is the impressive chancel, parts of the transepts and one side of the cloisters. The interior must surely still be the most atmospheric of all London's parish churches.

Fortified spiritually, we can now walk down the narrow and attractive Cloth Fair just a bit beyond to the right, where the poet John Betjeman used to live, before we encounter the **Hand & Shears** **3** on a corner site. This handsome pub has kept an interior which is still faithful to the style that countless unassuming London pubs would have once had, but is now a significant Central London surviving example of what is basically a Victorian layout. The woodwork is plain and simple; and remarkably, there are still three separate bar areas plus a small snug partitioned off by simple screenwork. The plain floorboards and wooden panelling are entirely in keeping with this delightfully simple former working-men's beerhouse. Staple beers are from Courage, and Adnams is often among the limited guest range, but you're here as much to take in the atmosphere as the beers. Anyway, a step across the street and you'll have more beers than you can shake a stick at: to get there, simply cross the road and go through the archway to arrive immediately at the **Old Red Cow** 🄰 on Long Lane. A pub that has seen a few ups and downs over the years, it has recently been given a very welcome facelift especially on the beer front. The exterior is tastefully smartened up but it's far smaller inside than first impressions might suggest, and you may have to fight your way to the small bar but for once it'll be well worth it. Expect three cask ales which could be from anyone, anywhere, but likely to be interesting; however, it's for their 'craft' keg beers that the Cow is gaining a good reputation via one of the best selections in the area. Arbor, Camden Town, Magic Rock and Kernel are among the well-regarded brewers who make regular appearances here. The informative web site gives an up-to-date lowdown on the latest beers on, with tasting notes and an opportunity to suggest guest brews. There is an upstairs bar, again hardly large, and sometimes hired out privately, but worth a look if it's rammed down below. The kitchen is open all day but food is on the pricey side with even burgers starting at £13 at the time of writing.

Cross into Hayne Street opposite. Emerge by Charterhouse Square and cross the road to walk along the left of the square, maybe detouring again to look at the enticing group of buildings on its northern side. This Oxbridge-looking building is

The newly-refurbished Old Red Cow

Charterhouse, founded as a Carthusian monastery in 1370. It passed through successive owners after dissolution by Henry VIII, coming into the possession of Thomas Sutton in 1611. He it was, being fabulously wealthy, who established both the Charterhouse Hospital for aged men, and Charterhouse School for the education of the sons of the poor. By the early 19th century, Charterhouse had become a leading public school. Interestingly the writer William Makepeace Thackeray (1811-63), was not impressed by his education there; he wrote that he 'was lulled into indolence... [and] when I grew older and could think for myself I was abused into sulkiness and bullied into despair'. Although the public school with which the name is perhaps associated most closely moved out to Surrey in 1872, the building still functions as an almshouse. Guided tours are Wednesdays only, from April-July at 2.15pm. Call 020 7253 9503 for details.

Returning to the task at hand, head through the gate at the north-western corner of the square and pass the *Fox & Anchor*, a recently smartened-up fin-de-siècle building with its Art Nouveau exterior, including some fine Doulton tiling. On account of the very high beer prices I'm not going to recommend it in this book, but wealthy readers could sneak in without me knowing...

The ornate roof of Smithfield Market

The cosy interior of the Jerusalem Tavern

Continue down to Charterhouse Street opposite the northern side of the meat market, and turn sharp right into St John Street, and then branch into narrower St John's Lane, consulting your map if need be. Turn left into Albion Place, and right at the end into Britton Street. Here is the final pub in this walk, the little **Jerusalem Tavern** 6. The name comes from the Priory of St John of Jerusalem, founded in 1140, which once stood in St John's Lane, but the building itself has only been a pub for about fifteen years. It was built in 1719-20 by Simon Mitchell, originally as a merchant's house. The interior, reached via a lobby room, has lots of atmosphere, and displays some eighteenth century panelling. Note also the 'four seasons' tile panels from the same period in the front lobby. The other noteworthy thing here is the beer; this is the only London house of the St Peter's brewery of Suffolk whose fine ales are dispensed from wall casks, and from a wide range of bottles on sale.

Turn back towards Albion Street but bear right opposite into Benjamin Street to reach Farringdon station in less than five minutes.

> **LINK** To join the latter part of Walk 12, turn right from the Jerusalem Tavern and walk up to the Clerkenwell Road. Turn left, and continue for 5-6 minutes, crossing the Farrindon Road, and turn right into Eyre Street Hill for the *Gunmakers*.

PUB INFORMATION

1 Olde Mitre
1 Ely Court, Ely Place, EC1N 6SJ
020 7405 4751
Opening Hours: 11-11; closed Sat & Sun

2 Viaduct Tavern
126 Newgate Street, EC1A 7AA
020 7600 1863
viaducttavern.co.uk
Opening Hours: 8.30am-11pm; closed Sat & Sun

3 Hand & Shears
1 Middle Street, Cloth Fair, EC1A 7JA
020 7600 0257
Opening Hours: 11-11; closed Sat & Sun

4 Old Red Cow
71-72 Long Lane, EC1A 9EJ
020 7726 2595
www.theoldredcow.com
Opening Hours: 12-11 (midnight Fri & Sat)

5 Jerusalem Tavern
55 Britton Street, EC1M 5UQ
020 7490 4281
Opening Hours: 11-11; closed Sat & Sun

Hand & Shears

A Central London pub heritage tour

WALK INFORMATION

Start: Blackfriars

Finish: Holborn

Distance: 1.25 miles (2km)

Key attractions: Rich internal pub fittings and architecture; Sir John Soane's museum (www.soane.org); Lincoln's Inn Fields; Dr Johnson's house (www.drjohnsonshouse.org)

The pubs: Black Friar; Olde Cheshire Cheese; Cittie of Yorke; Princess Louise. Try also: Punch Tavern; Tipperary

One of the key objectives of the first edition of CAMRA's *London Pub Walks* was to promote London's rich heritage of pub interiors which, until fifteen years ago, had received very little attention or documentation. A good many of the pubs recommended in this new edition have features of architectural and/or historic interest, but this route, along with Walk 16, offers concentrated dose of riches as far as heritage is concerned, and all the entries appear on CAMRA's inventory of 'Real heritage pubs'. Devotees of this subject should acquire a copy of *London Heritage Pubs – an inside story* by Jane Jephcote and Geoff Brandwood, where there is more detail on what to look for.

The Princess Louise boasts arguably London's finest tile and mirror work

As well as the 'core' entries for this walk there are links to other quality pubs which appear on other routes; and two or three further pubs with some features of interest. Several of the pubs on this walk are in the estate of Yorkshire brewer Samuel Smith where the only real ale available is the frankly unexciting Old Brewery Bitter; but the excellence of the fittings and fixtures makes a visit worthwhile, and if it's your first time, frankly unmissable.

Start at the nicely revamped Blackfriars station with its excellent access via both Underground and Thameslink rail services (if arriving via the latter onto Blackfriars Bridge, exit on the north bank of the Thames). If you want to stretch your legs before starting the walk, why not take a stroll along the South Bank from, say, Waterloo, and cross via Blackfriars Bridge? The station exit at the north end of Blackfriars Bridge lies directly across the road from the first pub stop of the walk, and with its highly distinctive shape the **Black Friar** 1 is hard to miss. In fact the view from across the street here shows the exterior at its best, with a huge black monk surveying the traffic carnage from the apex of the building. This Grade II*-listed pub was originally built circa 1875 on the site of a 13th-century Dominican Priory; this religious heritage gave the area its name and was the inspiration for the pub's design. Once safely across the road, the

TIMING TIP

Some of the entries, including the optional additions, are closed at weekends, especially Sunday, so if you can, aim for a weekday, although Saturday sees most of the key entries open.

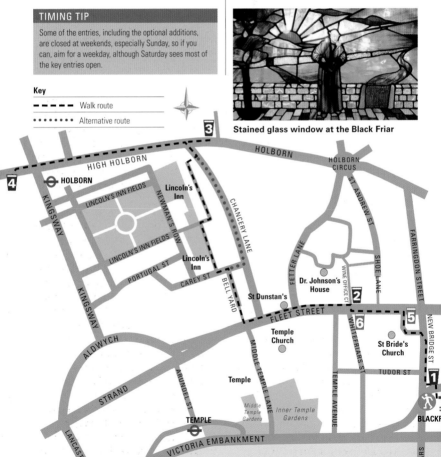

Stained glass window at the Black Friar

Key

– – – – Walk route

• • • • • • Alternative route

The interior of the Black Friar is not to be missed

exterior is worth closer examination. A plaque outside reminds us that some 30 years ago, the Black Friar nearly followed thousands of other fine pubs into oblivion, but was saved following a spirited campaign led by the redoubtable John Betjeman. Look also for the copper signs directing customers to the former saloon bar at the left hand extremity.

The numerous doorways remind us that once there were several separate spaces – and even today with these all interconnected it's still easy to see, once inside, that the further one moves around to the left, the more

Copper sign outside the Black Friar

sumptuous the décor, culminating in the astonishing chapel-like snug in the far interior. And it is the interior, dating from an Art-Nouveau refit from 1905 onwards, that makes this pub so remarkable; and at that time, when austerity was replacing the glamour and confidence of the late Victorian period, exuberant design of this kind was very rare. Royal Academy sculptor Henry Poole used high quality materials such as marble and alabaster, while adorning the pub with the imaginary antics

of the local Dominican friars. Look for the witty captions like 'Don't advertise, tell a gossip!' The crypt-like snug, dating from 1917, is especially notable, but the management have recently seen fit to allocate this area to diners, the only thing I can really find to criticise here. The main bar would originally have been partitioned with screens, but these have now gone.

It's not only the architecture that is worth sampling here: the beer list is better than ever, with London Pride joined by a changing range of interesting guests from Nicholson's list on the other seven taps. This is a great pub, best enjoyed outside the busy lunchtime and early evening periods.

One of London's most famous buried rivers, the Fleet, still dribbles into the Thames under Blackfriars Bridge; and as you walk up New Bridge Street directly away from the river upon leaving the Black Friar, you're following the old river valley up towards Holborn Viaduct where the valley was spanned nearly 150 years ago by what was effectively the first flyover in London.

LEFT: **The quaint little Tipperary** RIGHT: **Wren's St Bride's - the 'wedding cake' church**

Just before reaching the traffic lights at Ludgate Circus, use the controlled pedestrian crossing to switch to the west side of the road by Bridewell Place. Walk north and take the next turning left, Bride Lane, a narrow road which takes you onto Fleet Street via an atmospheric little short cut. As you bear right and walk up the slope (once the old terrace of the River Thames), there's interest all around: on the right, the *Crown & Sugarloaf* is a good quality renewal by Samuel Smith of what was once the western half of the Punch Tavern, just around the corner. It features some fine glass and woodwork. The **Punch Tavern** 5 itself, accessed by turning right onto Fleet Street, is of historical interest as it was on these premises in 1841 that *Punch* magazine was supposedly conceived. Staff of this satirical magazine met here for 150 years until it folded in 1992. If you have time it's worth dropping in as it retains some fine early features, particularly the

Mr Punch, of course, in the lobby of the Punch Tavern, Fleet Street

splendid tiled entrance corridor with mosaic floor, presided over by paintings of Mr and Mrs Punch. Inside, there are two fine skylights and a nicely proportioned bar-back boasting some rich etched glass. Geologists in particular will appreciate the bar top in pink marble and the attractive fireplace. The pub is now aimed at affluent city workers, with prices to match; beers are from national brewers such as Timothy Taylor and Adnams.

Back on Bride Lane, take the steps opposite the Crown & Sugarloaf leading up to an alley between the back of the *Old Bell* and the imposing St Bride's church, which traditionally had close connections with journalists and printers. The church has the highest Wren steeple in London and was apparently the inspiration for the traditionally tiered wedding cake. The spire was built in 1701-3 and withstood the Second World War Blitz although the rest of the church was destroyed in December 1940 and later rebuilt.

The Old Bell was reputedly constructed to refresh the builders at work on the church. Despite alterations, it still has an atmospheric interior with plenty of wood and glass, and there is a striking floor mosaic in the entrance to the back door. The alley brings you onto Fleet Street, where turn left. Look out on the opposite side of the road for two of the finest monuments to the long-gone days of Fleet Street's newspaper culture. Number 135, the old *Daily Telegraph* building, was a very bold building for such a conservative newspaper, but was architecturally outflanked shortly afterwards by the glass curtain wall of the old *Daily Express* HQ just to the east, nicknamed the 'Black Lubyanka' by *Private Eye*. Another little pub with some features of heritage interest worth a visit (particualrly if you haven't been before) is a little further along on the left, and so overshadowed by modern office blocks that the narrow frontage is easy to miss. The **Tipperary** 6 claims to be the earliest Irish pub in London, a boast backed by the words on its exterior board: that it was acquired and refitted by J G Mooney & Co of Dublin in 1895. The well-worn remains of the Mooney name appears on a slate at the entrance and shamrocks are found in the mosaic flooring. Starting life as the *Boar's Head*, the pub was renamed the Tipperary in 1918 to commemorate the Great War song. The ground floor bar is a long narrow room with wood panelling, inset mirrors, and an imposing bar-back. It is now owned by Greene King and real ales on offer include their IPA.

Fleet Street used to run more or less along the Thames' shore, and the area retains many of the alleys and courtyards typical of medieval cities. It is in one of these that the next pub is found, with the hanging lantern sign visible across the street to the right, on looking across from the Tipperary. To reach the **Olde Cheshire Cheese** 2 in one piece, use the crossing and head right for a few yards to an alley with the distinctive name of Wine Office Court. Here stands the atmospheric entrance to an important survivor in the social history of the urban tavern, with its exterior pendant lantern giving the date of 1667, the year after the Great Fire. Inside, the original pub retains a domestic-style layout that is very rare in London pubs. Two rooms lead off the entrance corridor, conjuring up a sense of homeliness with

their large fireplaces, and the vintage panelling is possibly the oldest of any London pub. It's easy to imagine the right-hand room without its Victorian bar counter, a remainder of a time when bar counters did not exist and drinks were brought to customers at their table in jugs or pitchers from the cellar. The Cheese stems from the tavern rather than the alehouse tradition, as it sold mainly wine and food and thereby catered for the upper and middle classes. The rear left-hand room continues in that tradition, with a long history of use as a dining room, going back at least to the days of Dr Johnson who was reputedly a patron here. In the dining room, hangs a Reynolds portrait of the sturdy lexicographer with the following inscription beneath:

'The Favourite Seat of Dr. Johnson … born 18th Septr, 1709. Died 13th Decr, 1784. In him a noble understanding and a masterly intellect were united with grand independence of character and

The Olde Cheshire Cheese

The Cittie of Yorke's great timber hall is unique in English pub design

unfailing goodness of heart, which won him the admiration of his own age, and remain as recommendations to the reverence of posterity. "No, Sir! There is nothing which has yet been contrived by man by which so much happiness has been produced as by a good tavern."'

Perhaps the best of the many poems penned in praise of this venerable house is that 'Ballade' written by John Davidson (1857-1909) the Scottish poet, one stanza of which reads:

> *I know a house of antique ease*
> *Within the smoky city's pale,*
> *A spot wherein the spirit sees*
> *Old London through a thinner veil.*
> *The modern world so stiff and stale,*
> *You leave behind you when you please,*
> *For long clay pipes and great old ale*
> *And beefsteaks in the 'Cheshire Cheese.*

The Cheese also has cellar rooms and an upstairs eatery but the two ground floor rooms are the kernel of the old tavern. Other curios are the old fly screens with 'OCC' inscribed on them, and above the doorway to the bar room there is an old warning: 'Gentlemen only served in this bar'.

Beyond the staircase, a 1991 extension has significantly increased the area of the pub; which is a good thing, for it gets very busy, with tourists popping in to gaze in awe. Despite this, the main bar room is frequently quiet enough to enable one to appreciate the wonderful panelling and glazing unimpeded. The Cheese is owned by Sam Smith of Tadcaster, so expect their OBB on handpump.

If it's a weekday you might wish to take in another classic London pub, the *Olde Mitre*, the full description for which appears in Walk 8. To get there, follow Wine Office Court, and take the first right onto Shoe Lane, following it north until it becomes St Andrew Street which brings you to Holborn Circus; then regain the main route at the Cittie of Yorke by walking west along High Holborn. Another cultural diversion is a visit to Dr Johnson's house at 17 Gough Square – turn right out of the Olde Cheshire Cheese, then first left. Otherwise return to Fleet Street and turn right to join the route of Walk 2: Legal London, at the church of St Dunstan's-in-the-West.

Follow the route as set out on that walk, past the lavishly refurbished *Old Bank of England*, and up Bell Yard to Carey Street. The *Seven Stars*, 100 yards to the left, and fully described in

Walk 2, is another Premier division heritage pub which would take its place alongside the entries described here. During weekdays, until 7pm, whether or not taking in the Seven Stars, turn left along Carey Street and then right through the gate by No. 57 (where the youthful David Bowie once worked) into Lincoln's Inn New Square, walking right through the Inn into Old Buildings at the north-eastern end, where a gateway exits into Chancery Lane. This was named after the Inns of Chancery, which were attached to and, for a while, training institutions for the Inns of Court. If the New Square gate to Lincoln's Inn is closed, turn right on Carey Street, passing the *Knights Templar*, and then left into Chancery Lane.

At the top of Chancery Lane, turn right on High Holborn, crossing to the north side, and walk along a few yards until you reach the striking clock protruding from the **Cittie of Yorke** 3. Named after a pub that occupied a site across the road until the 1970s, this is the finest survivor of a pub style popular during the interwar years, which tried to evoke a return to an Olde England of medieval banqueting halls. Despite the apparent antiquity of the place the ground-floor pub dates back only as far as 1923, when it was rebuilt as a Henekey's wine bar. Enter via a corridor and to the left is a panelled mock-Tudor room. A cellar bar, which is a remnant of a much older building, is sometimes open and also worth a look. However, it is the rear room, built in the style of a great timber hall with a high-pitched roof, which is the jewel here. There is little like it in any English pub, with its arcade under clerestory windows, an array of small railway carriage-style booths and, above the servery, a walkway to serve the huge casks which at one time contained wine. Don't miss the fine old early 19th-century triangular stove in the centre of the room, another unique fixture with an unusual flue that exits downwards. The pub is owned by Samuel Smith's of Tadcaster, so the only real ale on sale here is Old Brewery Bitter. Good food is available most of the day from a modern servery

RIGHT: **The Princess Louise** RIGHT: **Lincoln's Inn Fields and the eponymous Inn**

at the near end of the room, but this is a pub to enjoy first and foremost for its architecture.

Upon leaving, a few yards detour to the left will enable you to view, across the road, Staple Inn, the rickety-looking half-timbered buildings which is the only surviving Inn of Chancery. The onward route continues west along High Holborn, first to the junction with Kingsway by Holborn Underground station, and straight across here to the final pub on this walk just 100 yards further on the left. And the **Princess Louise** 4 is a fitting finale to this

The striking Cittie of York

route, for since the fine restoration carried out by Samuel Smith in 2007 this late Victorian building is arguably the finest surviving authentic Victorian pub interior in the capital. Named after one of Queen Victoria's daughters, the pub, rather plain on the outside, has some of the best mirror and tile work in any pub, a testimony to the skills of the celebrated firms of R. Morris and W.B. Simpson respectively. The rich mirrors represent a technique known as French embossing which was applied with tremendous results

here by Morris. The wonderful stillion with its pendant lights, probably the work of W. H. Lascelles, must surely be one of the finest survivors of this kind and it can still enjoyed without the intrusion of a glasses gantry on the counter to obstruct the view. The rich lincrusta ceiling, attractive bar counter and appropriate seating are all pleasing. In contrast to most modern restoration work, the quality of wood and glass in the replaced screens which faithfully divide the interior into separate booths just as in the original pub, is superb. The same goes for the new floor mosaic work in the newly recreated corridors running down each side of the interior. Yet again Samuel Smiths deserve praise for returning this now treasured building (which once was in a rather sorry condition) to its former glory, even if they only offer their own single real ale, as usual in their London estate.

From here it is but a minute's walk back along High Holborn to Holborn Underground station, on the Piccadilly and Central lines; or, if you prefer, buses to virtually all parts.

PUB INFORMATION

1 Black Friar
174 Queen Victoria Street, EC4V 4EG
020 7236 5474
www.nicholsonspubs.co.uk/ theblackfriarblackfriarslondon
Opening Hours: 10-11.30 (midnight Fri & Sat); 10-11 Sun

2 Olde Cheshire Cheese
145 Fleet Street, EC4A 2BU
020 7353 6170
Opening Hours: 11 (12 Sat)-11; 12-4 Sun

3 Cittie of Yorke
22 High Holborn, WC1V 6BN
020 7242 7670
Opening Hours: 11.30-11; closed Sun

4 Princess Louise
208 High Holborn, WC1V 7EP
020 7405 8816
Opening Hours: 11.30-11; 12.00-10. 30 Sun

TRY ALSO:

5 Punch Tavern
99 Fleet Street, EC4Y 1DE
020 7353 6658
www.punchtavern.com
Opening Hours: 7.30am-11 (midnight Thu & Fri); 11-7 Sat & Sun

6 Tipperary
66 Fleet Street, EC4Y 1HT
020 7583 6470
Opening Hours: 12-11 (6 Sat & Sun)

Notting Hill, Bayswater & Portobello Market

WALK INFORMATION

Start: Notting Hill Gate

Finish: Paddington

Distance: 2.4 miles (3.8km)

Key attractions: Kensington Gardens; Whiteley's Shopping Centre; Portobello Road Market; Hyde Park; Notting Hill shops

The pubs: Uxbridge Arms; Windsor Castle; Churchill Arms; Cock & Bottle; Prince Edward; King's Head; Cleveland Arms

As late as the 1950s, Notting Hill was still described by some as a slum, while the insalubrious bedsits of the area became home to West Indian migrants. The Pembridge Road area saw Britain's first race riots in 1958, in response to which the now celebrated Notting Hill Carnival was born. Today the area has been gentrified to a great degree, especially in the posher south-eastern side of Notting Hill, touching Kensington and Bayswater, where this walk takes us. Despite the high tourist quotient around Bayswater there are still a good number of pubs where a decent pint comes before fancy food. That said, you'll be able to eat well at most of the places on this rewarding walk, finishing at one of my favourite Central London pubs. If you're up for the market first, it's a good option to do a shortened tour by heading down to the nearby Cock & Bottle from Portobello Road and taking it from there. If you're doing the whole round, there's an option to use the bus halfway through the route.

The Churchill Arms

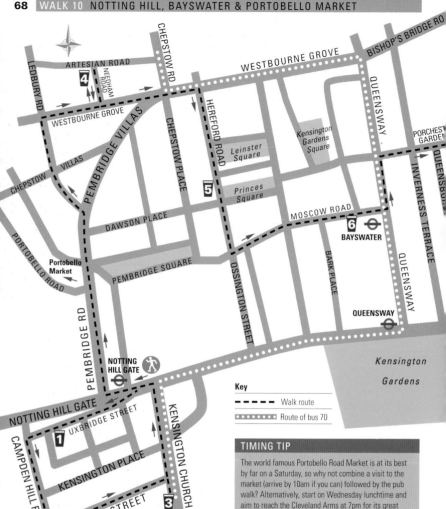

Key

- - - - Walk route
∘∘∘∘∘∘∘∘ Route of bus 70

TIMING TIP

The world famous Portobello Road Market is at its best by far on a Saturday, so why not combine a visit to the market (arrive by 10am if you can) followed by the pub walk? Alternatively, start on Wednesday lunchtime and aim to reach the Cleveland Arms at 7pm for its great value curry night.

Start at Notting Hill Gate Underground station and exit onto the southern side of the road. If you've arrived before noon, there are plenty of cafes, bric-a-brac shops and other attractions along Notting Hill Gate and Pembridge Road, which also leads to the Portobello Road Market. To start the day's drinking head south down the narrow, short Farmers Street right at the junction, opposite Pembridge Road, and bear right into Uxbridge Street. Here just yards away from busy Notting Hill Gate is the secluded **Uxbridge Arms** **1**, a smart little wood-

panelled Enterprise Inns house unknown to the vast majority of the trippers heading for the market. It's very comfortably furnished but the reliable quality of the beers here is what draws drinkers. Expect a choice of three: currently Fuller's London Pride, Harveys Sussex Best, and St Austell Tribute. You can sit outside in good weather on this quiet street.

Continue down to the end of Uxbridge Street and turn left into pleasant Campden Hill Road. It's a mere five minutes' walk to the next stop: the attractive **Windsor Castle** **2**, occupies

Antique shop on Portobello Road

a bold corner plot and displays a fine old-fashioned pub sign. A good quality 1930s refit has survived very well: this divided the interior layout into three main rooms, a layout more typical of the Victorian pub. In fact the mahogany bar-back in the 'Campden Bar' is the sole survivor from the Victorian era. If you can get here at a quiet time you can walk around and admire the timber panelling and screens, and some curious low doorways between the separate rooms, which were probably inserted for cleaners. The public area has been extended, notably by a new restaurant at the rear with views of the pub's garden; but the character of the old core of the pub has not been compromised too much. They have expanded their beer range now too, the three regulars include Windsor & Eton's Knight of the Garter, and there are two guests from the M&B list. If you're out for the day and want to eat properly this is as good as anywhere to do it, unless you love Thai food, in which case hold your horses…

Coming out of the Windsor Castle, drop straight down adjacent Peel Street, with its attractive Campden Houses estate of flats on the left, to reach Kensington Church Street at the bottom. Now, turn right and walk along to the

next corner, where, sporting what must surely be the best display of plants adorning any London pub, sits the **Churchill Arms 3**. A real local institution, this grand old pub caters for a loyal and appreciative clientele, although at Fuller's bar prices you'd need to well-heeled to be a regular here. It was built in the Victorian era but given a complete internal refit around 1930. The separate rooms have been merged into a U-shaped drinking area, but there is a characterful little

Windsor Castle

Back bar in the Cock & Bottle

of the Churchill. Take bus 70 (every 8-15 minutes) to the Artesian Road stop in Chepstow Road (see map) and walk down to the first corner. If you're walking, head back to Notting Hill Gate using your map; take Pembridge Road/Gardens as far as Chepstow Crescent, turn left up here, keep on until you reach Westbourne Grove, turn right, first left into Needham Road and the **Cock & Bottle** 4 is on the far corner. Of early Victorian origin, this attractive corner pub on a handsome terrace retains traces of its former multi-room layout, together with some snob screens, although these are modern. The jewel here though, is the splendid bar back with its unusual shape and remarkably ornate detailing. The nice little illuminated stained glass panels with the swan motifs commemorating the pub's former name are probably of inter-war origin, as is the proper old-fashioned urinal in the gents: I still think we need all these listed before they are lost! The beers: the experienced guv'nor keeps a good pint, offering four ales, including Harveys Sussex Best and usually one from Hog's Back brewery. It remains a good, no-nonsense boozer in an area afflicted with a lot of frothy tourist-trap pubs. Lunchtime food is available on weekdays only.

Return to Westbourne Grove and turn left, passing the upmarket shopping parade and taking the second right into Hereford Road, which puts us firmly into Bayswater with its hotels and general air of affluence. Just past Leinster Square, and still on Hereford Road, we arrive at our next port of call, the spacious **Prince Edward** 5, on the right. Considering the location, and the fact that tourists from nearby hotels make up a good deal of its trade, the pub is still fairly unpretentious. The drinking area is

room on the way to the restaurant. The walls are panelled and there are a couple of pretty tiled fireplaces. The snob screens on the bar are interesting; they were widespread in the 19th century, conferring the privacy Victorians wished for; but it's very possible that these are reproductions from the mid twentieth century. As mentioned, this is a Fuller's house and usually offers the whole range of their beers, but a good proportion of the clientele also come to enjoy the popular Thai restaurant at the right hand side of the pub. Food is served in an atmospheric rear conservatory, which has a glass roof hidden in a mass of foliage, the plants creating a splendid jungle-like canopy. If you wish to join the diners on your route, it may be advisable to book ahead.

Having almost reached the halfway point of this tour, you may well feel like a longer stroll to walk off any surplus before drawing a second wind. It's a little over ¾ of a mile to the next stop. However, if you prefer a far shorter walk, the bus stop is forty yards to your right upon coming out arranged around an island bar, and dining (the kitchen is open throughout the day) tends to take place in the rear area. The more unspoilt part fronting Needham Road retains a wooden dado. This is Hall & Woodhouse pub and the normal offerings are their K&B Sussex, Badger Best, and Tanglefoot.

Suitably fortified, it's once again an easy walk to the next pub. Continue down Hereford Road to Moscow Road. This street of attractive early nineteenth century houses but may have been named in honour of Tsar Alexander's visit to England in 1814. Turn left and a five-minute stroll brings us to the **King's Head** 6. A smart but tasteful looking corner pub inside and out, as befits a location just a stone's throw from Queensway, the interior is spacious and comfortable, with not too much sunlight, just as a proper pub should be. Note the three sets of doorways suggesting the former partitions. Fuller's London Pride is the anchor ale here but the management obtain most of their beers from the Society of Independent Brewers (SIBA) which means you can look forward to

a varied and interesting choice on the other four pumps. Moreover, if you can show a valid CAMRA membership card, you'll get 10% off the pump prices. You can also eat in here until 10pm.

The last pub of the day is a little more of a walk, about ½ a mile; but it's very well worth it. If you've had enough by now though, Bayswater Underground station is just down on Queensway at the end of Moscow Road. Otherwise turn left onto Queensway and then right at the *Prince Alfred* into Porchester Gardens. Follow it almost directly ahead into Leinster Place and then right into Leinster Gardens. This whole area was laid out in the later Victorian period, and although an area where war damage was extensive, most streets have survived intact, including some private squares. We pass one of these, Cleveland Square, soon after turning left into the street of the same name. This street continues beyond the next junction as Chilworth Street, but by then the final pub of the day, the **Cleveland Arms** 7 will be in your sights. The promise of the handsome frontage with

Cleveland Arms

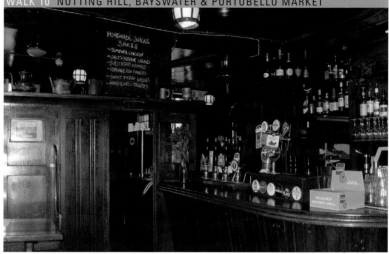

Inside the Windsor Castle

good tilework, wood and glass is more than fulfilled once inside; it's not a large pub but it's welcoming, unpretentious and homely, with that undefinable pubby character that characterises the best British boozers. Some interesting ephemera (mainly of the transport variety) adorn the walls, whilst there's a variety of seating areas in the main room and the partially opened-out rear room with its pool table. Like many pubs in this guide, they have installed more handpumps since the first edition came out to meet the rising expectations of the great beer-drinking public: three regulars (Greene King IPA, Harveys Best and Taylor Landlord) are joined by a pair of rotating guests in this popular free house. You'll get very good value for money with both drinks and food here and if you take advantage of the excellent Wednesday curry nights from 7pm, you'll guarantee a good finish to a long and hopefully rewarding pub walk.

Your best option transport-wise is to continue down to the far end of Chilworth Street and at the T-junction turn right onto Eastbourne Terrace which runs down the west flank of Paddington stations, for mainline and Underground services, and bus routes.

PUB INFORMATION

1 Uxbridge Arms
13 Uxbridge Street, W8 7TQ
020 7727 7326
Opening Hours: 12-11
(10.30 Sun)

2 Windsor Castle
114 Campden Hill Road, W8 7AR
020 7243 8797
www.thewindsorcastlekensington.co.uk
Opening Hours: 12-11
(10.30 Sun)

3 Churchill Arms
119 Kensington Church Street,
W8 7LN
020 7727 4242
Opening Hours: 11-11 (midnight
Thu-Sat); 12-10.30 Sun

4 Cock & Bottle
17 Needham Road, W11 2RP
020 7229 1550
Opening Hours: 12-11.30
(10.30 Sun)

5 Prince Edward
73 Princes Square, W2 4NY
020 7727 2221
www.princeedward-nottinghill.
co.uk
Opening Hours: 11-11

6 King's Head
33 Moscow Road, W2 4AH
020 7229 4233
Opening Hours: 12-11
(10.30 Sun)

7 Cleveland Arms
28 Chilworth Street, W2 6DT
020 7706 1759
Opening Hours: 11-11.30 (midnight Fri & Sat); 12-10.50 Sun

SIBA
local beer
Society of Independent Brewers
2012

Aldgate to Shoreditch via Brick Lane

WALK INFORMATION

Start: ⊖ Aldgate East

Finish: ⊖ Shoreditch High Street or ⇌ ⊖ Old Street

Distance: 2 miles (3.2km)

Key attractions: Whitechapel Market; Whitechapel gallery; Brick Lane; Christ Church; Fournier Street; Spitalfields City Farm; Old Truman Brewery

The pubs: Dispensary; Pride of Spitalfields; Carpenters Arms; Well & Bucket; Barley Mow

Brick Lane is one of the most famous streets in the East End. Its name comes from the brick and tile makers who used to live in the area, but the area has been home to successive waves of immigrants, for example Huguenot silk weavers (whose arrival prompted the development of the handsome Georgian houses of the Fournier Street area), and Jewish refugees. More recently, Bangladeshis migrated here in large numbers from the 1970s onwards. Hand-in-hand with this story goes the history of anti-racist struggle culminating in the 'Battle of Brick Lane' in 1978 and the murder of garment worker Altab Ali. Happily things are far more harmonious today.

Brick Lane

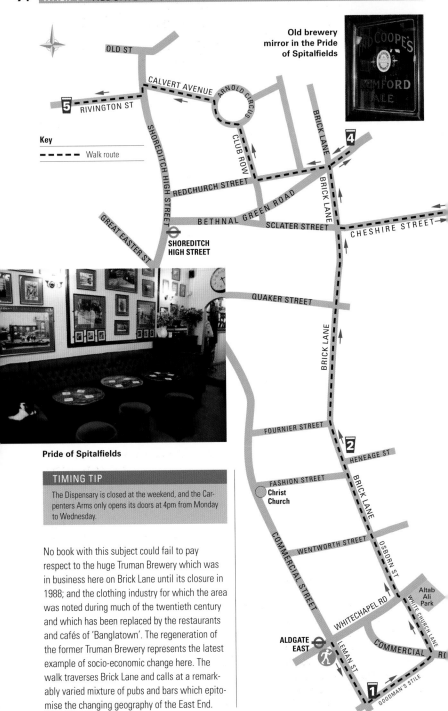

Old brewery mirror in the Pride of Spitalfields

COOPE'S ROMFORD ALE

Key

- - - - - Walk route

OLD ST

CALVERT AVENUE

ARNOLD CIRCUS

RIVINGTON ST

5

CLUB ROW

SHOREDITCH HIGH STREET

REDCHURCH STREET

BETHNAL GREEN ROAD

GREAT EASTERN ST

SHOREDITCH HIGH STREET

BRICK LANE

4

SCLATER STREET

CHESHIRE STREET

QUAKER STREET

BRICK LANE

FOURNIER STREET

HENEAGE ST

2

FASHION STREET

Christ Church

BRICK LANE

WENTWORTH STREET

COMMERCIAL STREET

OSBORN ST

WHITE CHURCH LANE

Altab Ali Park

WHITECHAPEL RD

COMMERCIAL RD

ALDGATE EAST

LEMAN ST

1

GOODMAN'S STILE

Pride of Spitalfields

TIMING TIP

The Dispensary is closed at the weekend, and the Carpenters Arms only opens its doors at 4pm from Monday to Wednesday.

No book with this subject could fail to pay respect to the huge Truman Brewery which was in business here on Brick Lane until its closure in 1988; and the clothing industry for which the area was noted during much of the twentieth century and which has been replaced by the restaurants and cafés of 'Banglatown'. The regeneration of the former Truman Brewery represents the latest example of socio-economic change here. The walk traverses Brick Lane and calls at a remarkably varied mixture of pubs and bars which epitomise the changing geography of the East End.

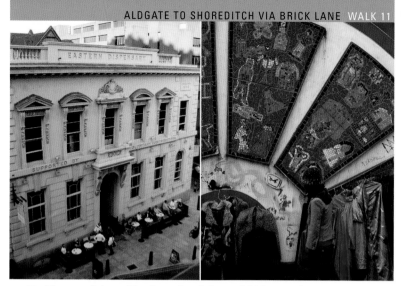

LEFT: **The Dispensary is housed in a former hospital** RIGHT: **Brick Lane market**

Start at well-connected Aldgate East Underground station. You need the southern side of busy Whitechapel Road, unless it's a weekend when our first stop is closed, and you're heading straight for Brick Lane; so look for the correct exit to save negotiating the busy street. It's not far to the first pub stop: Leman Street is the one-way street running south from the junction, and it's less than a five minute walk before you'll come across the first building of any antiquity hereabouts. The **Dispensary** ❶ is housed in a handsome former hospital built in 1858 as home to the Eastern Dispensary, a philanthropic institution with roots almost a century earlier still, and one of the first endeavours to provide medical treatment for the poor in East London. As the bold inscriptions on the front elevation make very clear, all this relied upon voluntary contributions. The listed building was re-opened in 2006 following a sympathetic renovation retaining much of the gravitas of the original: the tiled entrance gives onto a couple of small rooms to the right, a Portland stone staircase, and the main bar, left, which is smaller than one might have expected but which leads to a mezzanine floor set out primarily for diners. The real attraction for us is the beer range, with the house beer (by Growler) supported by four interesting guests, usually including a dark beer. There's a wide food menu served at lunchtimes and in the evenings.

Bear left on exit from the pub, turning into Goodman's Stile. The name relates, one assumes, to nearby Goodman's Fields which in turn is named for Roland Goodman, who once farmed the land here for a local nunnery. Cross over Commercial Road into narrower White Church Lane which brings you out on the Whitechapel Road with the little garden on the corner now named Altab Ali Park in memory of the victim of the 1978 race riots. Use the controlled crossing and head up Osborn Street opposite; this becomes Brick Lane, whose colourful history and lively street scene has already been mentioned. These days you may have to wave away numerous enthusiastic Bangladeshis keen to usher you in to eat, or indeed you might want to return here once the drinking is done. One architectural gem to look out for is on Fashion Street, the second turning on the left: the Moorish Market was an ambitious indoor market, a sort of early mall, opened by one Abraham Davis in 1905 with over sixty shops. It didn't really take off but the remarkable building survives and is now an educational institution.

Just beyond this, on the other side of Brick Lane, the next pub is well-hidden and, if you don't know it, quite a surprise in view of the all the multi-ethnic commerce along Brick Lane. The **Pride of Spitalfields** ❷ is just a few yards down Heneage Street, a turning on the right. From the outside the snowy white paintwork of

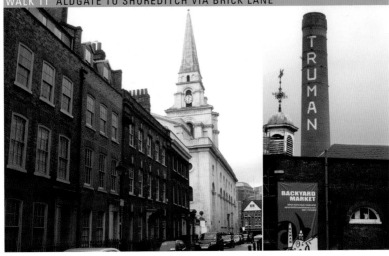

LEFT: **Fournier Street and Hawksmoor's Christ Church** RIGHT: **Old Truman Brewery**

this classic local makes it look like a bit of Greece transported to Banglatown, but inside it's as traditional as you could expect, and deservedly a firm favourite. The friendly and efficient service is a big plus as it often gets very busy, but it's worth almost any wait to sample the well-kept ales. The guv'nor keeps four beers as regulars: Fuller's London Pride and ESB, alongside Crouch Vale Brewer's Gold and Sharp's Doom Bar. The fifth handpump is allocated to a guest beer but appropriately for the locale, that's often from the nearby 'phoenix' Truman microbrewery. The walls are lined with interesting pictures of bygone East End life. There's food on weekday lunchtimes only.

There's plenty of interest as you continue northwards along Brick Lane. Don't miss Fournier Street, the next left as you continue northwards. Named after Huguenot refugee George Fournier, the houses mainly date from the 1720s and, ironically since the successive waves of immigrants were too poor to change them, they now form one of the best preserved collection of early Georgian townhouses in Britain, and these days some of the most desirable listed residences in London: you'll need at least

Doorway, Fournier Street

£2 million to buy into the street and join neighbours like Tracy Emin and Gilbert & George. The next sight to see is the Old Truman Brewery, presided over by the chimney still bearing the name of the old brewery. The ten-acre site has undergone extensive regeneration with a mix of businesses, retailers, galleries, and a market moving in. Brick Lane continues north (the Spitalfields City Farm is just Buxton Street, to the right), passing under the new bridge carrying the London Overground railway. Look out for Cheshire Street on the right shortly beyond, and head down here away from the bustle of Brick Lane.

A good five minutes stroll will bring you across the border into Bethnal Green, and to the next pub on this walk; and it's one with a bit of history. The **Carpenters Arms** 3 was once the most notorious pub in London, bought by notorious gangsters Reggie and Ronnie Kray and run by their mother Violet. Closed for years, the place was rescued by current landlords Eric and Nigel, former customers, who saved it from property developers intent on turning it into flats. They have repositioned the pub to suit the new demographic, and turned it

The newly-refurbished Well & Bucket

into a good beer destination. The three cask ales (Taylor Landlord, one from Adnams and a changing guest) are complemented by a variety of keg beers which includes a changing and often interesting guest; and a wide range of bottled beers which are advertised on the blackboard. For such a small pub there's a surprisingly good and varied menu: check the website for typical fare. There's a pleasant little rear courtyard which might offer some space if the two pub rooms are busy.

Return to Brick Lane and turn right to walk up to the junction with busy Bethnal Green Road. Bear right and, crossing the road at a safe point,

look for the **Well & Bucket 4** a short distance down on the left. The pub was established in an era when the local population still collected their water from the public well in Bethnal Green Road, hence the name. However, the lingering presence of cholera in the area made drinking beer a much safer option than drinking water! Part of the Truman estate, it was later acquired by Belhaven but after falling out of pub use for some fifteen years it was acquired by pubco Barworks; and after extensive restoration of what was left of the interior including the remaining fragments of the once-splendid tilework, it re-opened in February 2013. Great new artwork adorns the wall; and a splendid modern wall mirror hangs in convincing Victorian gin-palace style. The re-born pub has an island bar, comfortable seating all around, dim lighting and a back yard for outdoor drinking. There's also a vibrant little cocktail bar hidden away in the cellar. Four hand-pumps have been installed and the pub always has an interesting and varied selection of beers including some from local micros. Other interesting offerings are available on the keg taps and in the fridge. Fresh oysters are the pick of the food menu. Be warned that it's already proving popular and can be quite crowded at peak times.

The Carpenters Arms

The attractive street-corner Barley Mow

as laws came in to prevent the street sale of live animals. Walk clockwise around Arnold Circus at the top, and take the third exit onto Calvert Avenue, where you'll see gentrification in progress as you walk down to join Shoreditch High Street. Cross the busy road and, bearing slightly left, take the first right into Rivington Street. The final stop on this walk is about 200 yards down on the corner with Curtain Road. The **Barley Mow 5** is an attractive little corner pub with a traditional floor-boarded interior. It's been spruced up, along with the neighbourhood, but some features such as the bar back retain continuity with its former incarnations. Of the four ales on tap, the choice is safe and traditional: two from Fuller's, Courage Directors, and a guest. The food is Thai.

Upon exit, and to finish with, if you still have the energy, (if not, plenty of buses stop nearby, and Shoreditch High Street station on the Overground is not far down the street to the right) retrace your steps back down the road and by the modern *BrewDog* bar (no real ale) take the quieter right hand fork (Redchurch Street) on the northern side of the bar, and then third right into Club Row. Older readers will recall the infamous Club Row market, which finally closed in 1983,

To pick up transport, Shoreditch High Street station is a few minutes' walk south once back on the High Street; if the Underground is more use, Old Street is the nearest, a similar distance west, check your A to Z.

> **LINK** From Old Street, you can reverse Walk 30 from the *Old Fountain*.

PUB INFORMATION

1 Dispensary
19A Leman Street, E1 8EN
020 7977 0486
www.thedispensarylondon.co.uk
Opening Hours: 12-11; closed Sat & Sun

2 Pride of Spitalfields
3 Heneage Street, E1 5LJ
020 7247 8933
Opening Hours: 11-11; 12-10.30 Sun

3 Carpenters Arms
73 Cheshire Street, E2 6EG
020 7739 6342
www.carpentersarmsfreehouse.com
Opening Hours: 12 (4 Mon-Wed)-11.30 (12.30 Fri & Sat)

4 Well & Bucket
143 Bethnal Green Road, E2 7DG
020 3664 6454
Opening Hours: 12-11 (midnight Fri & Sat)

5 Barley Mow
127 Curtain Road, EC2A 3BX
020 7729 3910
Opening Hours: 12 (1 Sat)-11.30; 1-10.30 Sun

Pride of Spitalfields

From King's Cross into Clerkenwell

WALK INFORMATION

Start: 🚃 ⊖ King's Cross / St Pancras

Finish: 🚃 ⊖ Farringdon

Distance: 1.8 miles (2.9km)

Key attractions: Charles Dickens Museum (www. dickensmuseum.com); Karl Marx Memorial Library; British Museum; British Library (www.bl.uk); Old Clerkenwell village; St James's church; Spa Fields; Exmouth Market; Leather Lane Market

The pubs: Queen's Head; Pakenham Arms; Exmouth Arms; Gunmakers; Craft Beer Co. Try also: Calthorpe Arms; Old China Hand

Clerkenwell takes its name from the Clerk's Well in Farringdon Lane. Like many other inner London suburbs it was transformed by the Industrial Revolution. Brewing made use of the good water, while precision instruments, notably clock and gunmaking, became local specialities: Hiram Maxim invented the first machine gun in nearby Hatton Garden. Perhaps Clerkenwell's most interesting claim to fame is its strong communist connections, with both Marx and Lenin having lived and worked at some point around Clerkenwell Green. These days the area is very much on the up, and even in the few years since the first edition of *London Pub Walks*, much (generally tasteful) gentrification has taken place inside the area's pubs and bars; and beer choice is far better. Nearly all of the stops on this linear walk are 'new entries'.

However you arrive at the transport hub of King's Cross/St Pancras, make your way down to the front exits on the Euston Road, admiring the tremendous gothic hotel of Sir George Gilbert Scott, now restored to its former glory and function having survived years of dereliction and attempts to demolish it by British Rail. The new Eurostar terminal has been the impetus for a wholesale regeneration of what was a rather seedy area. Cross Euston Road and bear left at the busy junction along the Grays Inn Road, past the cheap eateries which still line the road here, and the rather grander Willings House, built for an advertising company but now a budget hotel. The third turning on the left is Acton Street and here's our first call of the day, the **Queen's Head 1** . It's a handsome Victorian pub inside and out. The appealing central bay window is flanked by two pairs of double doors which suggest the usual Victorian internal subdivisions, but today only the far door is in operation, leading into a single bar, a long narrow room. A recent change of ownership has brought a sensitive rearrangement and refurbishment of the interior, making the most of the heritage features, notably the floor and wall tilework; and retaining the 'proper' gents' urinals. Equally, the beer range and choice has improved no end, with three cask ales and a cider complemented by several craft beers on keg. The display of pump clips on the walls suggests that you're always likely to get something interesting in here these days. It might be early in the day to think about food if you're doing the whole route, but there's a tempting menu of meat and cheese boards and chunky sandwiches.

From the Queen's, return to Grays Inn Road and walk down to Frederick Street, the next left turn in a few yards, and head down here, bearing right into Ampton Place. This area of handsome villas makes a nicer stroll than the main road. Follow the cycle route to the left, and then turn right into Cubitt Street, named after the prolific nineteenth century master builder. This becomes Pakenham Street, and leads promptly to pub stop number two, the **Pakenham Arms 2** .

The Pakenham is now part of the small but enterprising Convivial pub group, and it now has no less than a dozen ale taps (along with up to four more for draught cider). It's an ambitious move, but early signs are that it's bringing in extra punters. The pub has a spacious interior and still opens early to cater for local posties who pop in from Mount Pleasant sorting office, the erection across the road that looks like a gigantic nuclear bunker (see box). Food is available – you can check out the menu on the pub's website.

KING'S CROSS/ST PANCRAS

GRAYS INN R

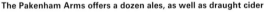
The Pakenham Arms offers a dozen ales, as well as draught cider

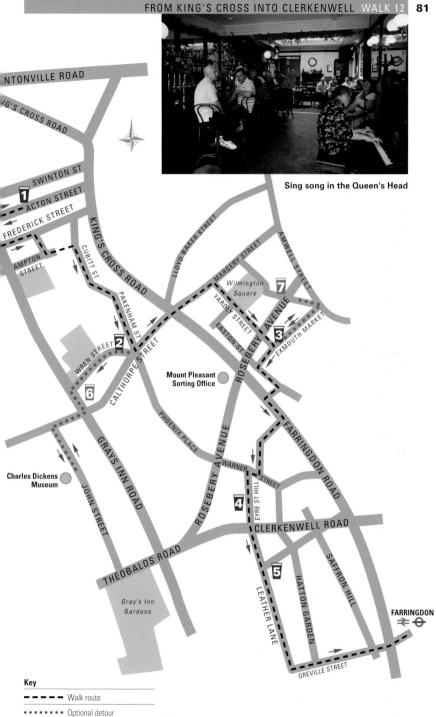

Sing song in the Queen's Head

The handsome tiled exterior of the Exmouth Arms

When the great author moved here in 1837 it must have been on the very northern fringe of the city – he lived here for only two years but wrote *Nicholas Nickleby* and *Oliver Twist* whilst here. It's the only one of some fifteen London addresses he had to have survived intact.

Retrace your steps, or use Calthorpe Street to return to the Pakenham.

Back at the Pakenham, head east (left) along Calthorpe Street crossing Farringdon Road into Margery Street.

Fellow lovers of interesting architecture may wish to make a short detour at this point: head instead into Lloyd Baker Street a few yards to the left of Margery Street. This attarctive estate was laid out by Thomas Lloyd Baker in the 1820s, with a series of extraordinary and very handsome individual houses. Granville Square was the scene of Arnold Bennet's novel *Ricey-man Steps*. You can do a circuit with your map, or return to Farringdon Road and continue up Margery Street.

Now take the first right into Yardley Street which takes you past the handsome houses set around Wilmington Square. The character of the walk changes abruptly however on reaching busy Rosebery Avenue, and just beyond the crossing, lively Exmouth Market with the next pub stop, the **Exmouth Arms 3** . With a handsome tiled exterior dated 1915, the Exmouth Arms epitomises the changes that have taken place in the district: the market has lost its earthiness and is now attracting a younger, trendier crowd with a lot more money. The pub itself is no longer a down-to-earth market boozer, but the recent refurbishment has a left it with a good mix of 'traditional' and 'trendy'. What's not in doubt is that the beer range and quality has taken a sharp turn upwards: four casks from small British ale breweries and around eighty bottled beers as

On leaving the Pakenham there are opportunities for a cultural (and an additional beery) diversion. If you take Wren Street by bearing sharp left out of the pub, you'll pass the pleasant St Andrews Garden and arrive in just a couple of minutes at the **Calthorpe Arms 6** . A Young's local in a Victorian building with a solidly attractive corner frontage in brick and tile, the Calthorpe made a small piece of history, being once used as a temporary magistrates' court after the first recorded murder of a policeman on duty, back in 1830. As is usual with Young's these days, I would say that the latest refurbishment, notably the soft patterned carpet, doesn't do the building any favours; but at least the beer is reliable!

You are very close to the Charles Dickens Museum here, which has re-opened following a £3m restoration and upgrade and is particularly to be recommended. To get there, cross into Guilford Street opposite and take the first left into Doughty Street. The Museum is at No. 48.

MOUNT PLEASANT SORTING OFFICE

Mount Pleasant probably takes its names from the higher ground hereabouts overlooking the valley of the River Fleet, which is now, of course, buried underground. In 1877 the former Clerkenwell prison on this site was closed and the Post Office acquired the site, although some of the old prison buildings survived until 1930. Operations grew rapidly, first with parcels, and later with the transfer of the London Letter Post Office here in 1900. By 1914 the volume of post had had reached almost six billion items a year! This was what stimulated the construction of the Post Office Underground Railway in that year. The site was rebuilt following extensive war damage and although mechanisation electronic recognition and new technology has reduced the volume of mail and the number of workers, it's still Britain's largest sorting office, and covers an area of 7.5 acres.

well as a wide range of over a dozen decent craft beers on keg. The management deserve credit for making this pub a destination, and it's now very popular among the local workers and residents, so much so that you may find it pretty full at times. All in all it's a welcome addition to the area's pub stock.

If you have serious stamina, a short optional detour will enable you to take in another interesting beer stop; walk further down Exmouth Market and take Tysoe Street, the first left at the end. Across the Clerkenwell Road on the corner is the **Old China Hand** [7]. The interior has lost some of its quirky charm from its O'Hanlon's days, but it's still worth a visit with one or two well-kept ales and decent range of bottled beers. CAMRA members get a good discount too… Retrace your steps to the Exmouth Arms.

Moving on, walk down to and cross Farringdon Road. Turn left, passing the *Eagle*, which is credited with being probably the first 'gastropub', before turning right into Bakers Row. Now at the end of this short street turn first right, then left, and in a short step you'll be walking up the hill (it's the old Fleet valley again) to the **Gunmakers** [4]. Described by one reviewer as 'a terrific Tardis of drinking pleasure' it's certainly small, but they know about their beers here. There are occasional beer festivals in the back room, but it's the front bar room which will appeal most to the visiting drinker: like other small bars offering food there is some tension between those eating and those 'merely' drinking – if you can arrange to drop by mid afternoon or at another less busy time you'll probably find it a more relaxing experience.

LEFT: **Calthorpe Arms** RIGHT: **The Gunmakers**

The Craft Beer Co has a great beer range

open for longer on the first corner is one of London's newer beer destinations, the **Craft Beer Co** 5.

There's no argument that this place offers one of the finest selections of beers, on draught and in bottle, that you'll find in any pub in London. Expect over a dozen cask ales plus many more on keg. Moreover they are interesting and well-kept; the chances are that if you are a beer geek you'll already know all about this place. All that said, I have to admit that as a pub fan, I'm not a great devotee of the place as somewhere to drink: it's nearly always very busy, and even when it isn't it somehow lacks the intimacy that a well-worn pub can offer. Make your own mind up, but as a final stop on a rewarding pub walk, it's well worth popping in.

To get to transport, continue down Leather Lane and take Greville Street on the left to reach Farringdon (Underground & Thameslink); or continue right to the end of Leather Lane for High Holborn buses and Chancery Lane Underground a few yards to the right.

Finding the last pub once you have left the Gunmakers is simplicity itself; carry up the hill and cross the Clerkenwell Road directly into Leather Lane. The down-to-earth street market operates until about 3pm on weekdays; but

▶ **LINK** ◀ Continue down Leather Lane and take Greville Street on the left, then first right into Hatton Garden for the *Olde Mitre* at the start of Walk 8.

PUB INFORMATION

1 Queen's Head
66 Acton Street, WC1X 9NB
020 7713 5772
www.queensheadlondon.com
Opening Hours: 4-11 Mon;
12-midnight Tue-Sat; 12-11 Sun

2 Pakenham Arms
1 Pakenham Street, WC1X 0LA
020 7837 6933
pakenhamarms.com
Opening Hours: 10.30am-
midnight (1am Fri; 12.30am Sat;
10.30 Sun)

3 Exmouth Arms
23 Exmouth Market, EC1R 4QL
020 3551 4772
www.exmoutharms.com
Opening Hours: 11-midnight
(1.30am Fri & Sat; 10.30 Sun)

4 Gunmakers
13 Eyre Street Hill, EC1R 5ET
020 7278 1022
www.thegunmakers.co.uk
Opening Hours: 12-11; closed
Sat & Sun

5 Craft Beer Co
82 Leather Lane, EC1N 7TR
07502 337339
www.thecraftbeerco.com
Opening Hours: 12-11
(10.30 Sun)

TRY ALSO:

6 Calthorpe Arms
252 Grays Inn Road, WC1X 8JR
020 7278 4732
Opening Hours: 12-11
(10.30 Sun)

7 Old China Hand
8 Tysoe Street, EC1R 4RQ
020 7278 7678
www.noordinarypub.com
Opening Hours: 12-2am

**The recently-refurbished
Exmouth Arms**

A gourmet's walk through Southwark & Borough

WALK INFORMATION

Start and Finish:
≥ ⊖ London Bridge

Distance: 1.75 miles (2.8km)

Key attractions: Borough Market; Southwark Cathedral; Rose Theatre Exhibition; Clink Prison Museum

The pubs: Market Porter; Charles Dickens; Lord Clyde; Royal Oak; Southwark Tavern; Sheaf (Hop Exchange). Try also: George

Southwark, south of the original London Bridge and home to Borough Market, has a long history dating back to Roman times. Before the seventeenth century Puritan purges, and despite the land being owned by the Bishop of Winchester, it was a thriving red light district, illegally until 1611, when brothels were licensed by Royal decree. Thanks to the coming of the railway and the recent gentrification of the riverside, Southwark's character has changed considerably. The market stems from the trade that came up to London from Kent, and thence derives the area's long association with the hop trade. The thriving modern market is the focus for this walk which also reaches further afield to make the most of some fine and varied drinking holes, which between them offer one of the best beer ranges in this book; and if you are an aficionado of Harveys of Lewes, this is the walk for you.

The George, London's only surviving galleried coaching inn

Start at the recently refurbished London Bridge station, and walk down the hill to Borough High Street, where the bulk of Southwark Cathedral competes with the railway bridges and viaducts for your attention. The cathedral is probably more attractive inside than out, with the Early English choir the most admired feature, while the nave is late Victorian.

Alongside the cathedral is the gentrified but still wonderful market with an atmosphere all of its own thanks to its location under the ironwork holding up the trains above your head. It's well worth factoring in half an hour to the walk to enjoy the stalls and maybe buy some of the goods on show. If it's cheese you're after, Neal's Yard Dairy is in Park Street across the road from the Market Porter (see below).

Our first refreshment call is adjacent to the market and the cathedral in Winchester Walk. Linked to Utobeer, the people running the beer stall in the market, the **Rake 1** has in its short life risen rapidly to take its place among the 'must do' beer bars of London. Another place which is little bigger than the proverbial Tardis, it's especially well-known for its remarkable range of bottled beers from around the world; but in addition, there are three handpumps and another six keg taps. The former dispense a changing array of rotating guest beers from quality brewers, with Oakham and Dark Star among the favoured visitors; the taps offer craft world beers. In short, the place is a world tour of beer under one roof, with knowledgeable and enthusiastic staff on hand to offer guidance should you require it. As such it's a big hit with overseas beer tourists as well as us natives so don't expect the place to yourself; indeed it's often hard to reach the bar especially if you go at busy times. Aim to get here soon after midday opening or mid-afternoon, however, and you should be alright. In either case the outdoor covered terrace doubles the drinking area, and leads to the gents.

Utobeer beer stall in Borough Market

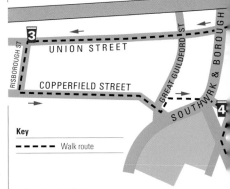

Key

- - - - - Walk route

Leaving the Rake, turn left and walk round the edge of the market to the **Market Porter 2**. This well-known and highly popular boozer rarely lacks for customers, so if and when you get to the bar you'll have earned your reward; and the reward is a wide choice of ever changing beers, which are chalked up on the blackboard to the right of the bar. The regular is Harveys Sussex Bitter, but you'll have up to a dozen to choose from in what is a permanent beer festival. The crowds keep on coming to enjoy them, and it's almost become a victim of its own success with the thankfully efficient staff having little time to draw breath at busy times. The interior, whilst much altered, still retains some character, whilst the outside sports an impressive display of colourful flowers in summer.

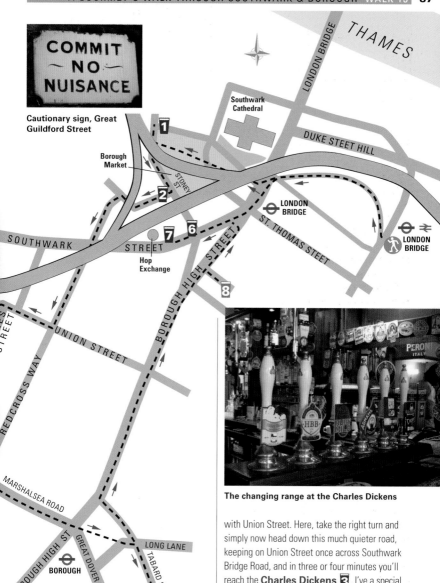

COMMIT
~ NO ~
NUISANCE

Cautionary sign, Great Guildford Street

The changing range at the Charles Dickens

with Union Street. Here, take the right turn and simply now head down this much quieter road, keeping on Union Street once across Southwark Bridge Road, and in three or four minutes you'll reach the **Charles Dickens** 3. I've a special soft spot for this back-street gem since it had just re-opened in its new incarnation at the time of the first edition of *London Pub Walks*; and I wondered if it would survive in this slightly out-of-the-way location. I needn't have worried, since it has become a real favourite with connoisseurs of good beer who make the trip to enjoy a changing range of interesting beers (with Adnams a fixture) in a traditional atmosphere. Cider drinkers are

Leave the Market Porter by Park Street, heading away from the market and the crowds, past the Neal's Yard cheese emporium. Head around the corner and first left into Redcross Street. Continue across busy Southwark Street and under the rail bridge to the next junction,

LEFT: **The Shard – Western Europe's tallest building – dominates the area** RIGHT: **The Lord Clyde**

well catered for here too, and you can eat at both lunchtimes and evenings. All the cask ales are at one fixed price, and CAMRA members can enjoy 50p off at the weekends on production of their membership card.

On leaving the pub, head up Risborough Street opposite the pub and turn left into Copperfield Street, which also retains the local Dickens connection. The attractive Winchester Cottages on the right were provided by the Church Commissioners and inspired by social reformer Octavia Hill; and the small garden opposite occupies the site of All Hallows Church, which was bombed in the Second World War. The building facing you at the junction ahead carries a stern admonition from a past era! Round the building on either side to reach the road junction beyond, and you should be able to see the pub sign of the next stop opposite, across the junction and directly ahead. The **Lord Clyde** presents a striking frontage with its distinctive tiled exterior; this bears the names of both the former owners Truman Hanbury Buxton, and the erstwhile publican. It's also unusual in that it dates back to a 1913 rebuild, a period from which we have few pubs; and its restrained internal fittings reflect the austerity of that era compared with the glitz of Victorian pub interiors. Unusually too, this resolutely traditional local retains two separate drinking areas, although there would have originally been more, as is apparent by

the number of doorways. The main bar still has its tapering tongue-and-groove counter, bar-back, an original fireplace and some of the original etched glass. The back room has a hatch to the servery. Above all it's a first rate pub, run by the same family for over 50 years and which represents the finest traditions of the Great British boozer, serving a top notch pint in a friendly atmosphere where conversation is the order of the day. There's a good choice of five well-known beers including the two London stalwarts, Fuller's London Pride and Young's Bitter. Hog's Back TEA is currently also a regular here. There's a full lunchtime menu on weekdays, with evening meals Wednesday to Friday.

From the main door of the Clyde, walk the thirty yards or so down to the Marshalsea Road and turn left, passing the Peabody flats before reaching the busy junction by Borough Underground station. The easiest and safest way to get to the next pub is to cross the Borough High Street by the controlled crossing so that you're standing under the tower of the church of St George the Martyr. The church stands on a small island with part of Tabard Street running behind it – the rest of Tabard Street runs away across Long Lane (with the island refuge in the centre) to your right; and that's where we're heading, so cross again and walk up past the older shops and new flats to the next corner where sits the **Royal Oak** 5 . This pub is housed in a mid-Victorian building, which was purchased and re-styled by Harveys of Lewes in 1997, their first London tied house, and still one of only two. The restoration has been done very well, in a robustly traditional style, even down to the two bars being separated by a parody of an off-sales counter. Expect a good range of Harveys fine ales here, including their seasonals, with the odd guest. Prices both for food and for beer have in relative terms steadily crept up but it's still a must-do pub and a regular winner of CAMRA awards.

Return to the Borough High Street, this time walking beyond the church down towards London Bridge. Borough High Street was used as a primary route into the City of London from the south for over 2,000 years and the place still retains some of its former character. The further part of the High Street, beyond the Union Street junction, is the more atmospheric, with high buildings, narrow frontages and deep plots, some with rear yards, a land use pattern adopted by the old coaching inns that once lined Borough High Street. Many of the yards are still in existence today, including King's Head Yard, White Hart Yard and George Inn Yard, which all survive in name if not form. Also noteworthy (at No. 67, on the right, just beyond the George), is the frontage proclaiming WH & H Le May's Hop Factors, a reminder of this area's long association with the Kentish hop trade.

If you're a Londoner, chances are you'll know of the **George** ⑧, London's only surviving galleried coaching inn. If you've seen it before, you can afford to miss it as there are more interesting

beer venues nearby; so it's relegated to 'try also' status on this walk. If you haven't seen it, it's a must – down the alley at No. 77. The George is only a vestige of its former self, as two sides of this old inn were demolished when the Great Northern Railway was built, and what remains is the south wing. This was not the first time it had been tampered with, as it was rebuilt in 1676 after a devastating fire swept through Southwark. The room at the west end of the building, as one enters the courtyard, is the real jewel, with panelling, fireplace and plain bench seating of considerable antiquity. Note the glazed servery with now rare examples of old fashioned 'cash register' style handpumps. The ground floor rooms to the east were not originally pub rooms and have, along with the modern bar, been more recently brought into use. The panelled upstairs rooms are well worth a look. The George is owned by the National Trust and leased to Greene King.

Just beyond the George on Borough High Street there's a road junction where Southwark Street joins from the left. Cross the two roads here to find yourself on the busy corner of Stoney Street at the edge, once more, of Borough Market. Look behind you and you'll get a decent view of the Shard, the striking new 95-storey office block which rises above London Bridge station. The last two pubs on this tour are almost adjacent here. The first, on the corner, is the **Southwark Tavern** ⑥. It's always been an attractive building with its glazed tilework in favour of the long defunct Meux brewery, along

The George – London's only surviving galleried coaching inn

Glazed tilework at the Southwark Tavern

with leaded windows, hop motifs and a bit of surviving stained glass. Of late the place has been made over internally but tastefully, and now offers a wide range of beers: six handpumps dispense three regulars, the most unusual being Leeds Pale Ale, and some changing guests; alongside these there's a lengthy list of beers on keg, and a bottled list featuring a decent range of Belgian beers. Besides the main bar there's an atmospheric basement with some small cubicles, well worth looking at.

A few yards further down Southwark Street is the remarkable Hop Exchange. Built in 1867, it provided a single market centre for hop dealers, in much the same way there was a Coal Exchange, Metal Exchange and a Stock Exchange. This is now the only survivor, and even here the building has lost a couple of floors and suffered the ignominy of being converted into a corporate hospitality suite and offices; but it's still highly impressive, both the external façade and the great hall within. But it's the cellar that will be of greatest interest at this particular time, for here is to be found the **Sheaf 7**. Until recently it was the Wheatsheaf, but following the re-opening of the original Young's *Wheatsheaf* (minus all its internal features of heritage interest) around the corner in Stoney Street, a name change by one or the other looked on the cards. The Sheaf is accessed down some steep stairs but thanks to the cast iron supports and barreled brick roof retains plenty of original character (unlike its reopened competitor). Part of the Red Car pub group, the Sheaf offers up to ten beers, with plenty of changing guests supporting (ironically) Young's Bitter and Fuller's London Pride. The house beer is brewed by Growler. Check the website for the current and forthcoming beer menu, not to mention the extensive food menu which stretches from sandwiches to full plates.

London Bridge station is close by. Just retrace your steps, pass the Southwark Tavern crossing Stoney Street, and the station is on the right.

PUB INFORMATION

1 Rake
14 Winchester Walk, SE1 9AG
020 7407 0557
utobeer.co.uk
Opening Hours: 12 (10 Sat)-11
(8 Sun)

2 Market Porter
9 Stoney Street, SE1 9AA
020 7407 2495
Opening Hours: 6-8.30, 11-11;
12-11 Sat; 12-10.30 Sun

3 Charles Dickens
160 Union Street, SE1 0LH
020 7401 3744
www.thecharlesdickens.co.uk
Opening Hours: 12-11 (6 Sun)

4 Lord Clyde
27 Clennam Street, SE1 1ER
020 7407 3397
www.lordclyde.com
Opening Hours: 11 (12 Sat)-11;
12-6 Sun

5 Royal Oak
44 Tabard Street, SE1 4JU
020 7357 7173
Opening Hours: 11 (12 Fri)-
11.30; 12-9 Sun

6 Southwark Tavern
22 Southwark Street, SE1 1TU
020 7403 0257
www.thesouthwarktavern.co.uk
Opening Hours: 11 (10
Sat)-midnight (1am Thu-Sat);
12-midnight Sun

7 Sheaf
24 Southwark Street, SE1 1TY
020 7407 9934
www.redcarpubs.com/The-
Wheatsheaf
Opening Hours: 11 (12 Sat)-11;
12-10 Sun

TRY ALSO:

8 George
George Inn Yard, 77 Borough High
Street, SE1 1NH
020 7407 2056
www.traditionalpubslondon.
co.uk/georgesouthwark
Opening Hours: 11-11

Kentish Town locals

WALK INFORMATION

Start & Finish:
Kentish Town; or Gospel Oak

Distance: 1.7 miles (2.7km)

Access: Northern Line, Barnet branch; Thameslink rail services from Luton, St Albans, St Pancras, London Bridge and Croydon

Key attractions: Hampstead Heath & Parliament Hill Fields; Camden Lock and market (1 mile)

The pubs: Pineapple; Junction Tavern; Southampton Arms. Try also: Assembly House; Bull & Last; Bull & Gate

Bar back at the Pineapple

This is a short but rewarding ramble in a varied area between Camden to the south and Highgate to the north. It's not an area for tourist sights, but it's easily accessible by train, and nearby are the contrasting attractions of Hampstead Heath and Camden Town. If you're keen to stretch your legs before tackling the pubs then take the Underground, and map, to Hampstead (or the Overground to Hampstead Heath) and enjoy a stroll across the Heath and Parliament Hill Fields, with fine views across London. This will bring you out at Gospel Oak and the Southampton Arms from where you can reverse the route. As for the pubs, unusually I have included just three core stops, all of which should meet the expectations of the discriminating imbiber. The three 'try also' entries will appeal for different reasons and can be added if you wish without significantly lengthening the route.

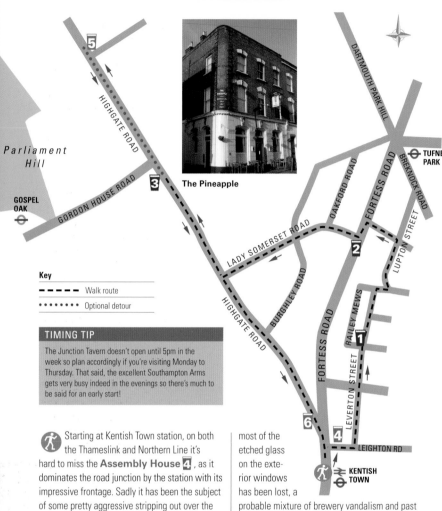

The Pineapple

Key

– – – – Walk route

• • • • • • Optional detour

TIMING TIP

The Junction Tavern doesn't open until 5pm in the week so plan accordingly if you're visiting Monday to Thursday. That said, the excellent Southampton Arms gets very busy indeed in the evenings so there's much to be said for an early start!

Starting at Kentish Town station, on both the Thameslink and Northern Line it's hard to miss the **Assembly House 4** , as it dominates the road junction by the station with its impressive frontage. Sadly it has been the subject of some pretty aggressive stripping out over the years, and the main bar is now a vast open space where once there would have been screens and partitions. Nonetheless there's enough of the former grandeur of this late Victorian drinking palace remaining to testify to its former glories and make it still worth a visit on architectural grounds. The best bits today, aside from the bar back with its decorated glazing, are undoubtedly at the far right hand end, *en route* to the former billiard room at the rear. The skylight over the billiard room remains and the surviving glass, French embossed and cut, is some of the best you'll find anywhere in London. This was the work of local firm, William James, and is a joy to behold. Sadly

most of the etched glass on the exterior windows has been lost, a probable mixture of brewery vandalism and past negligence by the local council. Owners Greene King have continued the attempt to reposition the pub upmarket in line with the area's gentrification; beer-wise they offer up to three guests as well as their in house-range of Greene King IPA and Abbot Ale, so you may pick up something interesting if you pop in.

Whether or not you visit the pub, walk eastwards along Leighton Road and take the first turning left into Leverton Street. Five minutes' walk up here brings us to one of Kentish Town's success stories in an area littered with the corpses of dead pubs. A vigorous local campaign in 2001-2 resulted in the listing of the **Pineapple 1** and the defeat of an application to turn it into flats. It's easy to see why local people hold the place in such high regard. Inside there is a central servery surrounded by a horseshoe-shaped drinking area with a couple of small lobbies *en route* to a pleasant conservatory and garden at their rear. Look out for the impressive mid-Victorian bar-back with etched and gilded mirror work and two old Bass mirrors on the pub walls. Meanwhile, behind the unpretentious benches, there is some old panelling. This all makes for a very relaxed ambience. Even though it's just a short distance away, this area feels like a different world from the hurly burly of Kentish Town and the Assembly House. Save the *Guardian* crossword until you get here! The beer range has expanded to five with one from Adnams and Sharp's Doom Bar being the regulars. The guests are often LocAles from the likes of Redemption and East London. Two beer festivals a year include one at Easter with a popular bonnet parade. Expect the beers to be in fine form, as the Pineapple was voted local CAMRA Pub of the Year for 2012.

Walk further up Leverton Street and on through the traffic-free area on Lupton Street ahead before turning next left into Ravelly Street which leads us onto Fortess Road. Just down to the left on the opposite side is the next pub, the **Junction Tavern** 2. At first glance this looks like another casualty of the gastrophication of our pub heritage, and without a doubt it's food and wine that dominate, but enter through the side door and you come into an attractive rear drinking area with lots of wood and, more importantly, an interesting range of beers. Four handpumps serve a rotating selection from the Enterprise Inns guest list, with Sambrook's Wandle Ale the regular. Moreover, the pub holds beer festivals in late May and October. The backyard has been converted into a conservatory and a small but very attractive garden. Be warned, during the week (Monday to Thursday) the pub is only open from 5pm.

Leaving the Junction, it's again a short walk to the next stop. Cut down Lady Somerset Road to the Highgate Road and turn right. Just past the railway bridge look out for the distinctive sign of the **Southampton Arms** 3. Since opening in late 2009 in its current incarnation this pub has made a tremendous impression on the London beer scene. It's a tiny pub stripped back to the basic elements of good beer and cider, and simple pub food (Scotch eggs, scratchings, sausage rolls, pork pies etc); but with friendly, efficient and knowledgeable staff serving one of the best beer selections you'll find in London it's little surprise it gets so busy. There are at least ten ales on tap and almost as many ciders, and all of them from independent brewers around the UK; the pub boats that it doesn't serve any mass-produced fare from the big breweries. The house beer is from Howling Hops, based at the Southampton's sister pub, the *Cock* in Hackney. With a vintage record player and a real fire for

LEFT: **The Victorian Assembly House is hard to miss**   RIGHT: **Etched glass in the Assembly House**

Southampton Arms: small but perfectly formed

those winter nights, what's not to like? Of all the numerous new alehouses springing up around London, this one is still one of the very best. But, be warned, take cash, they won't appreciate you waving plastic at them in here!

From the Southampton, there's an option to detour up the road for a few minutes to take in the **Bull & Last** 5. What you'll get is an upmarket foodie joint with a serious menu presided over by a 'young and passionate team' according to the website. You'll need some serious money to eat here but if you do, or even if you don't, the (pricey)

beers are sourced carefully and you'll almost certainly get some interesting offerings on the five handpumps. The pub's policy is to source locally so expect the likes of Redemption, Cronx and Red Squirrel among others. The décor is modern but tasteful and respects the Victorian corner building.

If you've come up here it might be tempting to take the 214 bus down to the centre of Kentish Town, which is also an option from the Southampton Arms although it's only a few minutes' walk south along the road before you pass the **Bull & Gate** 6 on the right just before the road junction, the Assembly House and the station.

The Bull & Gate is another 'try also' option included primarily for its architecture. The particularly ornate exterior is worthy of admiration, whether or not one steps inside, but the interior has its appeal too: this is another pub with an impressive bar-back sporting cut glass. Note also the classical pillars and archway between the two main drinking areas. The screened-off room to the left is another ex-billiard room, now a venue for live music. This is a down-to-earth workaday boozer to finish with, and the usual ales here are Fuller's London Pride and Sharp's Doom Bar.

Kentish Town station is just 100 yards away beyond the Assembly House (right upon exit).

> **LINK** Bus 214 from outside the Southampton Arms takes you to Highgate village in about five minutes for Walk 15.

PUB INFORMATION

1 **Pineapple**
51 Leverton Street, NW5 2NX
020 7284 4631
Opening Hours: 12-11
(10.30 Sun)

2 **Junction Tavern**
101 Fortess Road, NW5 1AG
020 7485 9400
www.junctiontavern.co.uk
Opening Hours: 5 (12 Fri; 11.30
Sat)-11; 12-10.30 Sun

3 **Southampton Arms**
139 Highgate Road, NW5 1LE
020 7485 1511
www.thesouthamptonarms.co.uk
Opening Hours: 12-11 (11.30
Fri & Sat)

TRY ALSO:

4 **Assembly House**
292-294 Kentish Town Road,
NW5 2TG
020 7485 2031
www.assemblyhouse.co.uk
Opening Hours: 12-11 (midnight
Fri & Sat; 10.30 Sun)

5 **Bull & Last**
168 Highgate Road, NW5 1QS
020 726 73641
www.thebullandlast.co.uk
Opening Hours: 12-11 (midnight
Fri & Sat; 10.30 Sun)

6 **Bull & Gate**
389 Kentish Town Road,
NW5 2TJ
020 7704 0187
www.bullandgate.co.uk
Opening Hours: 11-11.30

**Stunning mirror in the
Assembly House**

A hilltop tour of Highgate

WALK INFORMATION

Start & Finish: ⊖ Hampstead then walk via Hampstead Heath or ⊖ Archway and bus via Highgate Hill ⇌

Finish: ⊖ Highagte

Distance: 1 mile (1.6km)

Access: Northern Line, to ⊖ Hampstead. Also from ⇌ ⊖ Finsbury Park via Parkland walk, or ⇌ Alexandra Palace via Capital Ring Walk

Key attractions: Highagate village and cemetery; Hampstead Heath; Parkland Walk (www.parkland-walk. org.uk); Highgate & Queen's Woods; Waterlow Park; Kenwood House

The pubs: Flask; Prince of Wales; Gatehouse; Bull; Wrestlers

Deservedly one of London's best-loved urban villages, Highgate commands a hilltop site offering views across London. Historically, Highgate adjoined the Bishop of London's hunting estate. The Gatehouse pub in the centre of the village today marks the site of the toll-house where the road from London entered his land. In later centuries Highgate was associated with highway-man Dick Turpin, and of course is also renowned for its atmospheric Victorian cemetery in which Karl Marx is buried. The walk across the Heath from Hampstead is a highly recommended way to start this pub walk around Highgate; but a fine alternative is the Parkland Walk (and its Northern Heights Walk extension, part of the Capital Ring) which, using old rail lines, converge on Highgate Underground station from Finsbury Park, and from Alexandra Palace via Queen's Wood and Highgate Wood.

The Flask in Highgate

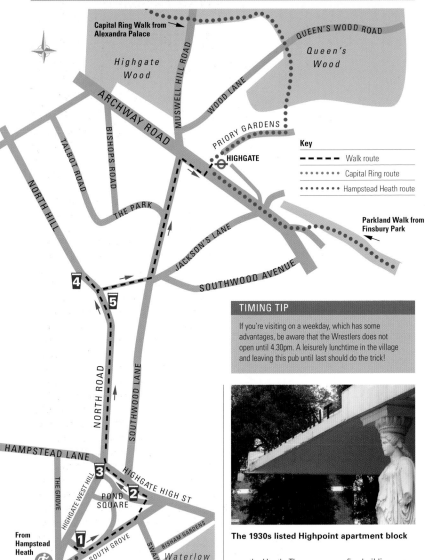

Capital Ring Walk from
Alexandra Palace

QUEEN'S WOOD ROAD

*Highgate
Wood*

*Queen's
Wood*

ARCHWAY ROAD

MUSWELL HILL ROAD

WOOD LANE

PRIORY GARDENS

HIGHGATE

Key

– – – – Walk route

• • • • • • Capital Ring route

• • • • • • Hampstead Heath route

TALBOT ROAD

BISHOPS ROAD

NORTH HILL

THE PARK

JACKSON'S LANE

SOUTHWOOD AVENUE

Parkland Walk from
Finsbury Park

4

5

NORTH ROAD

SOUTHWOOD LANE

HAMPSTEAD LANE

THE GROVE

HIGHGATE WEST HILL

3

HIGHGATE HIGH ST

POND
SQUARE

2

BISHAM GARDENS

From
Hampstead
Heath

1

SOUTH GROVE

SWAIN'S LANE

*Waterlow
Park*

To Highgate
Cemetery

TIMING TIP

If you're visiting on a weekday, which has some
advantages, be aware that the Wrestlers does not
open until 4.30pm. A leisurely lunchtime in the village
and leaving this pub until last should do the trick!

The 1930s listed Highpoint apartment block

As mentioned above there are fine walks
converging on the village from several
directions, but whether you arrive on foot, or by
bus, bike or car, make your way to the pretty green
between Highgate West Hill and The Grove, immediately south west of the village centre. This is the
way you'll approach the village if you've walked

over the Heath. There are some fine buildings on
both sides, something Highgate is famed for, and
jealously guarded by its active Civic Society. Their
website (www.highgatesociety.com) also gives
details of a circular walk around Hampstead and
Highgate taking in Kenwood House, Highgate
Cemetery and Waterlow Park. At a focal point of
the green, by the fork in the roads, the **Flask 1**
is a bit of a Highgate institution. It's easy to see
that the pub is an amalgamation of two buildings,
both of which have undergone great alteration.

LEFT: **The Gatehouse marks the fomer boundary between Middlesex and London** RIGHT: **Highgate**

The older, three storey part is eighteenth century, and retains the former servery with its glazed sashes. The left hand part is a later conversion of a former outbuilding. The interior retains some of its rambling character but hopefully new owners Fuller's will desist from any further 'improvements' and tarting up. The garden/patio outside is agreeable enough if not too busy, but the place gets packed at times. A wide range of Fuller's beers are available, including Chiswick Bitter, ESB and a seasonal; and there's a non-Fuller's guest. There are menus on the pub's website.

Now from the Flask's front door bear left, and follow South Grove past the bus stance and you will see the rear of the **Prince of Wales** 2 almost immediately. Either enter here, or walk around onto the High Street, maybe browsing some of the shops before entering via the front door. The Prince is a handsome brick building, certainly the most unspoilt pub in the village, with several distinct but interconnected drinking areas around

a central servery. It's exactly the sort of villagey pub you'd expect in Highgate, with bookish locals hopefully plotting the overthrow of capitalism in one of the quiet corners. Butcombe Bitter is a regular fixture here, along with three guests; on my last visit they had two from excellent North London micro Redemption. The Thai kitchen provdes the food, whilst there's an all-day Sunday roast.

Don't get too comfortable here, for just a stone's throw up the road, on the road junction with Highgate School opposite, sits a very significant Highgate landmark, the **Gatehouse** 3. The name refers to a former tollgate and archway over the road, for this was the former boundary between Middlesex and London. The earliest mention of the Gatehouse in licensing records is as early as 1670, and amongst the former glitterati who have drunk here were Byron, Dickens and George Cruickshank. The mock-Tudor style of the pub we see today goes back to the early twentieth century. The upstairs was previously used as a courtroom, but now it's a very successful fringe theatre. To top it all there is a resident lady ghost! As the pub is now part of the Wetherspoon empire you can expect the company stamp on the décor and fittings, with the normal good range of beers, and long food hours.

Leaving the Gatehouse, cross the road to your left and walk along North Road, to the north of the pub, with the school opposite. It's a few minutes' walk along the road to reach the last two pubs on this tour, and they stand almost opposite each other. On the left

The Prince of Wales is the most unspoilt pub in the village

The famous Horns in the Wrestlers, above the fireplace

hand side, the **Bull** 4 is a recently refurbished and revitalized gastropub, almost painfully smart on the outside, but included here for its on-site microbrewery producing some interesting and well-regarded beers. The small 2.5 barrel kit turns out two or three brews per week at present, and you can expect at least three beers on sale, which occasionally include a guest from another London brewer. In addition there are several keg taps serving a good list of both regular and guest beers, together with some Belgian bottles. You can eat here, but be warned that at weekends you'll probably be sharing with some noisy and precocious free-range children.

And now for something slightly more traditional. Beyond the Bull, North Road becomes North Hill. Architecture lovers may enjoy a detour along this street and back, since it's regarded as one of the best examples of architectural diversity in London. With or without this detour, and having

checked your watch and the opening times, you can safely set off for the last pub, the **Wrestlers** 5, almost opposite the Bull. Considered by many to be the finest pub in the village, it has stood on this site since 1547, although the current building dates to 1921. The star of the show is the atmospheric interior with its dark panelling and impressive fireplace which evidently survived the twenties rebuild. You can learn for yourself about the curious ancient ceremony of 'swearing on the horns' which apparently goes back to 1623, for the horns in question, and the procedure, are there above the fireplace. The beer menu has improved significantly since the first edition of this guide: London Pride and St Austell Tribute are the regulars, and they're joined by two changing guests with a local flavour. Supporting the cask ales are several 'craft' beers such as the hoppy and refreshing Brooklyn Lager and Chicago's Goose Island IPA. If you're finishing off here and looking to eat, there's a very extensive menu including Sunday roasts, again available on the pub website.

By now you will be replete and probably ready for a train home! Simply turn down the alley, Park Walk, immediately to the side of the pub, and on reaching the road at bottom turn sharp left and follow down the short distance to the Archway Road, where Highgate Underground station (on the Northern Line) is just to your right.

LINK A 214 bus from the centre of Highgate (via the *Southampton Arms*) or two stops on the Underground from Archway will deliver you to Kentish Town, right opposite the *Assembly House* and the start of Walk 14.

PUB INFORMATION

1 Flask
77 Highgate West Hill, Highgate,
N6 6BU
020 8348 7346
Opening Hours: 11 (12 Sat)-11;
12-10.30 Sun

2 Prince of Wales
53 Highgate High Street,
Highgate, N6 5JX
020 8340 0445
Opening Hours: 12-11 (midnight
Fri & Sat)

3 Gatehouse
1 North Road, Highgate, N6 4BD
020 8340 8054
Opening Hours: 9am-11.30
(midnight Fri & Sat; 10.30 Sun)

4 Bull
13 North Hill, Highgate, N6 4AB
020 8341 0510
thebullhighgate.co.uk
Opening Hours: 12-11.30
(midnight Fri & Sat)

5 Wrestlers
98 North Road, Highgate,
N6 4AA
020 8340 4297
www.thewrestlershighgate.com
Opening Hours: 4.30-midnight
(1am Fri); 12-1am Sat; 12-11 Sun

A North London 'inside story'

WALK INFORMATION

Start: ⇌ Stoke Newington

Finish: ⇌ Dalston Junction/ Dalston Kingsland

Distance: 3 miles (4.8km); 4.5 miles including Stag's Head (7.2km)

Access: From ⇌ London Liverpool St, or by London Overground services to Dalston Junction/Kingsland then northbound buses on A10

Key attractions: Exterior and interior pub architecture; Abney Park cemetery; Clissold Park; Metropolitan Benefit Society Alms Houses, Balls Pond Road

The pubs: Jolly Butchers; Rochester Castle; Rose & Crown; Lord Clyde; Scolt Head; Duke of Wellington. Try also: Stag's Head

One of CAMRA's campaigning priorities is pub heritage, which is always under threat. In London the enthusiastic members of the CAMRA London Pubs Group, led tirelessly by Jane Jephcote, have worked hard to research, promote and celebrate this heritage. Jane is the co-author of *London Heritage Pubs: an Inside Story*, the most authoritative and detailed publication on the subject; and she has kindly allowed me to make use of her research in this walk. This particular route, taking in an area of Stoke Newington and Dalston, has the added advantage that all of the pubs offer a very decent pint.

The route given here starts in Stoke Newington and works south towards the Regent's Canal, but of course, if you wish to finish in the Jolly Butchers for a protracted sampling of its lengthy beer menu, there's nothing to prevent you tackling the route in the other direction.

William Booth memorial, Abney Park

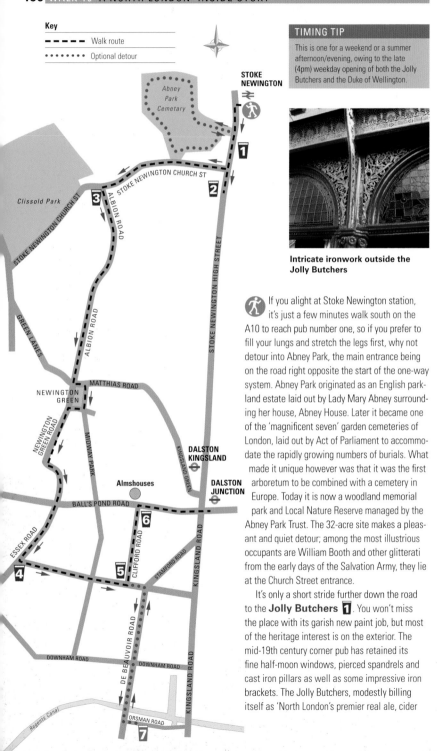

Key

– – – – Walk route

•••••••• Optional detour

STOKE
NEWINGTON

Abney
Park
Cemetery

1

STOKE NEWINGTON CHURCH ST

2

3

Clissold Park

STOKE NEWINGTON CHURCH ST

ALBION ROAD

STOKE NEWINGTON HIGH STREET

ALBION ROAD

GREEN LANES

MATTHIAS ROAD

NEWINGTON
GREEN

NEWINGTON
GREEN ROAD

MIDWAY PARK

DALSTON
KINGSLAND

KINGSLAND ROAD

Almshouses

DALSTON
JUNCTION

BALL'S POND ROAD

ESSEX ROAD

4

6

CLIFFORD ROAD

5

STAMFORD ROAD

KINGSLAND ROAD

DE BEAUVOIR ROAD

DOWNHAM ROAD

DOWNHAM ROAD

KINGSLAND ROAD

ORSMAN ROAD

7

Regents Canal

TIMING TIP

This is one for a weekend or a summer afternoon/evening, owing to the late (4pm) weekday opening of both the Jolly Butchers and the Duke of Wellington.

Intricate ironwork outside the Jolly Butchers

If you alight at Stoke Newington station, it's just a few minutes walk south on the A10 to reach pub number one, so if you prefer to fill your lungs and stretch the legs first, why not detour into Abney Park, the main entrance being on the road right opposite the start of the one-way system. Abney Park originated as an English parkland estate laid out by Lady Mary Abney surrounding her house, Abney House. Later it became one of the 'magnificent seven' garden cemeteries of London, laid out by Act of Parliament to accommodate the rapidly growing numbers of burials. What made it unique however was that it was the first arboretum to be combined with a cemetery in Europe. Today it is now a woodland memorial park and Local Nature Reserve managed by the Abney Park Trust. The 32-acre site makes a pleasant and quiet detour; among the most illustrious occupants are William Booth and other glitterati from the early days of the Salvation Army, they lie at the Church Street entrance.

It's only a short stride further down the road to the **Jolly Butchers** **1**. You won't miss the place with its garish new paint job, but most of the heritage interest is on the exterior. The mid-19th century corner pub has retained its fine half-moon windows, pierced spandrels and cast iron pillars as well as some impressive iron brackets. The Jolly Butchers, modestly billing itself as 'North London's premier real ale, cider and craft beer house' has reverted to what was once its old name after a pretty grim interregnum. The interior has been stripped out and replaced with… well, not a fat lot, in keeping with the modern

Putti or cherubs at the Rochester Castle

style. It also gets very busy with the hip Stoke Newington set, whose cheery chatter reverberates off all the hard surfaces. But to be fair there's a great beer list with some of Britain's best breweries showcased regularly here on the nine handpumps; and an extensive and appealing array of craft-keg 'world beers' on the even more numerous keg founts. Check the 'featured breweries' section of the website for a flavour of what to expect. In short, a temple of great beer, but far from the most comfortable or intimate place to enjoy them.

Walk a bit further down onto Stoke Newington High Street, beyond the junction with Church Street opposite, and look out for the imposing frontage of the next pub across the street at No. 143. Whereas the Jolly Butchers is basically a spruced up humble street-corner boozer, the **Rochester Castle** 2 is something far grander, architecturally at least, and it's worth lingering for a couple of minutes on the other side of the street to admire the elevation. Despite significant meddling this late Victorian pub still presents a striking appearance. The garlanded cupids frolicking around a cartouche

between the first and second floor bays are particularly attractive, but down at ground floor level, having crossed the street in one piece, there's some quality columns and tilework to admire. Inside Wetherspoon have retained the glazed tilework and pilasters, although some of the figurative bordered panels depicting the Seasons, had been hidden behind fruit machines when I was there. The bar counter has been shifted to one side and all the one-time partitions (note three sets of former doors) have of course gone. Expect the usual JDW fare of regulars and guests on the handpumps.

Return north to the junction with Church Street and head down here, maybe pausing briefly to admire the attractive exterior (including a pretty wrought iron panel above the door) at the *Three Crowns* opposite. You could take a bus (73, 393 or 476) for a couple of stops from the stop here, but it's not a bad walk, and there's a chance to peek into Abney Park again and look at William Booth's grave by the entrance. Either way, when you arrive at the striking Stoke Newington Town Hall, a very impressive Art Deco pile at the junction with Albion Road, look across the street to another impressive building, the **Rose & Crown** 3 . Running elegantly around the corner, this Truman's pub dating to the mid 1930s

LEFT: **The Rochester Castle** RIGHT: **Vitrolite ceiling panels in the Rose & Crown's lounge**

The Victorian Metropolitan Benefit Society's impressive almshouses on Balls Pond Road

has retained a great deal of original fittings and is one of the highlights of this walk in terms of pub heritage. The five external doorways around the sweep of the façade show the former internal divisions, whilst the clear glazed 'shop window' style on the corner itself actually dates back to the days of the off-sales department, and would have been used to display goods to take away. Note the metal pub signs and lamps outside. Moving inside, the pub has kept much of its 1930s layout since the screens which once would have divided the various rooms survive in their upper parts. The wood-panelled interior, with its gilded lettering above head height, is typical of the classic Truman's interwar style; whilst the bar counter with its doors to access the beer engines

Appealing bar in the Lord Clyde

is also original. Some pretty lamp shades and the ceiling Vitrolite panels are particularly remarkable survivors. Given all this respect for the past it seems entirely fitting that one of the three beers on tap is from the reincarnated microbrewery carrying Truman's name. The others are St Austell Tribute and a guest. Food is served throughout most of the day, with Sunday roasts.

Leaving the pub, Clissold Park is just across the street to the left, if you are looking for a half-way point rest from the rigours of the schedule.

The next pub stop is quite a walk to the south, so I would recommend jumping on a bus; pop back across the road to the bus stop opposite the Town Hall and catch a southbound 73 or 476. It's about eight stops. Alight at Northchurch Road, just a few yards beyond the **Lord Clyde 4** . (If you decide to walk it, check your map and A to Z, and ensure you take the right route when you get to Newington Green).

From a pub heritage viewpoint the Clyde is another of the best destinations on this walk, having now reverted to its former name and traditions after a period as Kenrick's bar. Note the unfinished brick courses above the single storey left hand end of the pub: according to the licensee this could be where plans to resume the completion of the remodelled pub after the Second World War were aborted, due presumably to lack of resources. Inside, the fittings are pure interwar, with a separate public bar to the left, the remains of an off-sales counter between this and the main room (the doorway survives too); the latter would once have been further subdivided, evidenced by the different extent of the old spittoon either side of the curved corner. Also surviving are the good bar counter and bar back, the latter a rather attractive affair carrying the name of Charrington's, the once-widespread purveyor of bland beer.

On the beer and food front, the place is a metaphor for the transformation of many formerly dismal North London boozers into attractive destinations for the new breed of discerning customer. Expect the ales here to be well-kept: Harveys Sussex is a regular here and one of the two guests is typically from a local supplier like London Fields. The food has attracted favourable reviews.

Walk along Englefield Road, (on the right, immediately outside the Clyde) and cross the Southgate Road and into the district of De Beauvoir Town. Named after a nineteenth century local landowner, there are some handsome Victorian villas in the part you're now walking through, which is now a Conservation Area. In little more than five minutes you'll reach the penultimate destination on this tour, the **Scolt Head 5**. A striking three storey building occupying a prominent plot, it sits on the apex of a triangle of roads. It was formerly the Sussex Arms but the new owners apparently have a

predilection for the Norfolk coast where Scolt Head Island is found. At least they didn't choose 'Fox & Newt' or something similar. Original fittings here are more sparse than at the previous two pubs but the pretty bar back survives, and the room around to the left may have been a former billiard room. The spacious interior does however have a homely pubby atmosphere, with an attractive open fire (note the painting of the eponymous island above the mantel) and a variety of seating opportunities. It's a bit of a foodie joint but there are three ales, currently Greene King IPA, Truman Runner and Crouch Vale's excellent Brewer's Gold.

At this point, if you wish to take in the Stag's Head, you need to continue on your former eastward journey along Englefield Road to the next junction, and turn right down De Beauvoir Road. Follow it down, admiring the pretty villas, and crossing the Regent's Canal into a more working-class area, take the first left into Orsman Street. The **Stag's Head 7** offers a couple of ales from national brewers like Greene King and Charles Wells, but has a lot of surviving internal features from its Truman's days, notably a well-preserved off-sales counter between the public and saloon bars. To finish at Dalston, return the way you came back to the Scolt Head.

LEFT: **Pretty bar back at the Scolt Head** RIGHT: **One of two metal inn signs at the Rose & Crown**

A little etched glasswork survives inside the Duke of Wellington

From the Scolt Head a very short walk up the Culford Road to the north will lead you to the last stop, the **Duke of Wellington** 6 , on the Balls Pond Road right opposite the impressive Victorian Metropolitan Benefit Society's almshouses. As to the pub, it's another one to go back its old name following a refit and slight repositioning to attract the new clientele of the area. It's retained the surviving bits of its Victorian past, notably some cut and etched glass. The screen which runs across the servery is a pleasing feature, whether original or not; and the bar counter is solidly attractive. In keeping with the high standards of beer quality and choice on this round, the Duke offers a very tempting range of ales, five on tap (Sambrook's Wandle always on, alongside four interesting guests from the SIBA list) and some interesting bottled beers (Kernel, Bristol Beer Factory, etc) in complement. You'll be able to finish the tour with food (including Sunday roasts) if you wish.

It's a few minutes stroll to the right down the Balls Pond Road to Dalston Junction/Kingsland for trains and buses.

PUB INFORMATION

1 Jolly Butchers
204 Stoke Newington High Street, N16 7HU
020 7241 2185
www.jollybutchers.co.uk
Opening Hours: 4-midnight (1am Fri); 12-1am Sat; 12-11 Sun

2 Rochester Castle
145 Stoke Newington High Street, N16 0NY
020 7249 6016
Opening Hours: 8am-midnight (1am Fri & Sat)

3 Rose & Crown
199 Stoke Newington Church Street, N16 9ES
020 7923 3337
www.roseandcrownn16.co.uk
Opening Hours: 11.30-midnight; 12-10.30 Sun

4 Lord Clyde
340-342 Essex Road, N1 3PB
020 7288 9850
www.thelordclyde.com
Opening Hours: 12-11 (midnight Sat; 10.30 Sun)

5 Scolt Head
107A Culford Road, N1 4HT
020 7254 3965
www.thescolthead.co.uk
Opening Hours: 12-midnight

6 Duke of Wellington
119 Balls Pond Road, N1 4BL
020 7275 7640
www.thedukeofwellingtonN1.com
Opening Hours: 3-midnight (1am Thu & Fri); 12-1am Sat; 12-11.30 Sun

TRY ALSO:

7 Stag's Head
55 Orsman Road, N1 5RA
020 8616 4129
stagsheadhoxton.com
Opening Hours: 12-11 (1am Fri & Sat; midnight Sun)

Tiled panel inside the Rochester Castle

East beyond the Lea Valley

WALK INFORMATION

Start: Lea Bridge Road, by *Princess of Wales*

Finish: ⊖ Leytonstone

Access: ⇌ Hackney Central then buses 48, 55, to Lea Bridge Road; ⇌ Hackney Downs then bus 56 to Lea Bridge Road. Or (Overground) to Homerton or Hackney Wick, then walk via Lea Navigation towpath. ⇌ Clapton is a short walk from the Lea towpath (see map)

Distance: 7 miles (11.2km) total (about 2 miles (3.2km) walking)

Key attractions: Hackney & Walthamstow Marshes; Bakers' Almshouses, Leyton;

The pubs: Anchor & Hope; Drum; King William IV; Birkbeck; North Star; Red Lion. Try also: Leyton Orient Supporters' Club

It wasn't long ago that London's eastern postcodes were a significant desert for the cask ale aficionado, and there was little reason to go out of one's way to cross the Lea Valley. Now that has changed, and this bus-assisted tour of E5, E10 and E11 will reward you with some excellent beer and food in a variety of very good pubs. The districts of Clapton, Leyton and Leytonstone were developed as working-class railway suburbs in the late nineteenth century. Even here, however, some of the pubs were exuberant and impressive in their architecture. Remnants of that are easy to see in the King William IV, Leyton, now the flagship home of Brodie's brewery, and the Red Lion at Leytonstone. The extensive open spaces along the Lea Valley around Hackney Marshes and the river towpath offer an excellent opportunity to stretch your legs before starting the pubs. It's also a route that you can attempt by cycle, if you're confident in traffic.

On the Lea Navigation near the Anchor & Hope

The walk starts at Lea Bridge Road, which is well-served by buses, close to the *Princess of Wales*. If you've arrived via Clapton station, Southwold Road, to your right, will take you to the Lea towpath, south of the footbridge. When I first visited the Anchor & Hope nearly thirty years ago the riverside here was dominated by the sheds of Latham's wood yard, to and from which barges made their way up and down the oily, polluted river. Now the industry has gone, replaced by the usual array of modern apartments no doubt occupying a 'stunning waterside location' as per usual, and the river is certainly far cleaner. Head upstream (north) on the wide towpath, noting for the return journey the footbridge after a short way, but keeping to the western bank. Just beyond the rail bridge, and with the expanse of Walthamstow Marshes on the opposite side, you'll spot the first pub of the day. Overlooked by interwar flats, the diminutive **Anchor & Hope** 1 looks slightly out of place among all the modern developments close by.

The Anchor & Hope

Nonetheless, the pub (one wonders whether the name with the two words in their more unusual order suggests a command rather than two nouns?) has long been a beacon of excellence in a beer desert, and in

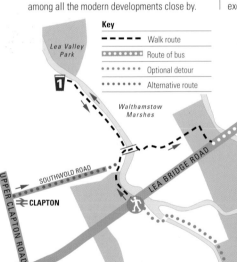

Key

- – – – Walk route
- ○○○○○○○○ Route of bus
- ・・・・・・・・ Optional detour
- ・・・・・・・・ Alternative route

Lea Valley Park

1

Walthamstow Marshes

SOUTHWOLD ROAD

CLAPTON

UPPER CLAPTON ROAD

LEA BRIDGE ROAD

LEA BRIDGE ROAD

CHURCH ROAD

LEA VALLEY WALK
Horseshoe Bridge
Enfield Lock 8 m
Broxbourne 13½ m
Leagrave 48½ m

CAPITAL RING
Springfield Park 1 m
Highgate Wood 2½ m
Hendon Park 14½ m
Richmond Bridge 32½ m

HACKNEY
MARSHES

TIMING TIP

Don't start this route too early as the Anchor & Hope is closed until 1pm (noon on Sunday). In addition the North Star only opens at 4pm, Monday to Thursday. If you can take in a visit to the CAMRA award-winning Leyton Orient Supporters' Club bar (open on match days) this will be a feather in your cap.

HOMERTON
¾ mile

HACKNEY
WICK
¾ mile

HOMERTON ROAD

that regard nothing has changed. We owe much to the legendary former landlord, Les Heath, who kept this basic beerhouse for fifty years. There's an interesting video interview of him at the pub's celebratory party on YouTube. He died in 2003, but not before he was awarded the MBE. The current young guv'nor Matthew has respected his legacy, and expanded the beer range to four handpumps. It's been a Fuller's house for a long while now and to their credit refurbishments have been carried out with a light touch, keeping the simple character of the small interior intact. In addition to staples London Pride and ESB, the beers can include guests from other brewers. All in all, a classic London boozer and not to be missed.

Bakers' Almshouses

Return down the towpath, and cross the river via the footbridge you passed earlier. Bear round to the right but keeping the Lea Valley Ice centre on your right, take the path parallel with the Lea Bridge Road for a few minutes crossing a small wooden bridge and ahead into the car park which allows you to rejoin Lea Bridge

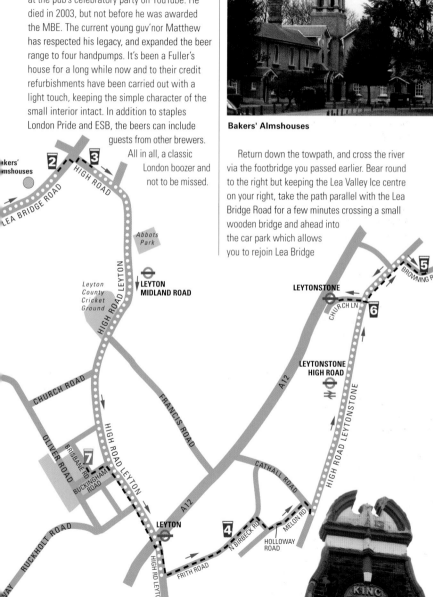

LEFT: **The Drum** RIGHT: **The North Star is in an urban Conservation Area**

Road at the Ice Centre bus stop. Any of the buses (48,55 or 56) will take you to the High Road Leyton/Bakers Arms stop, just a few yards beyond the striking Bakers Arms Almshouses, and a few yards short of the Drum. The almshouses are well worth a brief look as they are really the architectural highlight of the walk. Built from 1857 in the Italianate style by the Master Bakers' Benevolent Institution, the 50-odd dwellings were intended for 'any respectable member of the baking trade fallen into poverty, eligible according to the rules, or to the widow of such'. They survived an attempt to demolish them by the former Greater London Council and were instead listed, and subsequently purchased and refurbished as flats by Waltham Forest Council. Fifty yards further on, the **Drum** 2 is, by J D Wetherspoon standards, an intimate and cosy corner pub which has long been a regular in the *Good Beer Guide*. It was one of the very first acquisitions by the well-known chain, but despite its size it has a good range of guest beers, including frequent appearances of LocAles from East London and Redemption breweries. A pleasant little conservatory-style room at the rear catches the light, and there's a small patio garden beyond. Save some capacity though for the next pub which is a short walk around the corner, and at least as appealing. Cross at the traffic lights and bear right down the Leyton High Road, and on the second left corner, a few yards down, lies the **King William IV** 3. In a fine Victorian building adorned in summer with flowers, newish

London brewer Brodie's have resurrected the brewing tradition here and made their home venue a must-do destination in North-East London. Décor inside is very traditional: dark red benches run right round the large bar room while the red carpet and ceiling complement plenty of dark woodwork on the long bar counter as it snakes around and accommodates one of the largest sets of handpumps you'll see anywhere. They're rarely all in use but nonetheless you'll have a wide choice from Brodie's own extensive portfolio and other guests, all well kept and at keen prices. Food starts about 1pm and continues all day.

Walk a few yards further down to the bus stop (Leyton Green) and take the 69 or 97 down towards Leyton Midland Road station. A few stops further down, the football ground of Leyton Orient FC is hidden in the side streets just west of the road. Now, if it's a Saturday, a midweek match day, or an 'Ale night' (usually a Thursday preceding a home match Saturday) visitors will be made welcome at the excellent **Leyton Orient Supporters Club** 7 bar which has been a past winner of CAMRA's national club of the year award (small admission charge, free to CAMRA members). Expect a couple of Mighty Oak beers supported by several changing guests. Check the opening times and phone number online at www.orientsupporters.org and/or ring ahead before alighting from the bus at Buckingham Road. The club entrance is on Oliver Road to the west of the ground.

Whether or not you take in the club bar, continue by bus (or on foot) down to the Millais Road bus stop by the *King Harold*, one stop beyond Leyton Underground station although we're now technically into Leytonstone. Walk back to the first turning right, Frith Road, and keep going until you come across the distinctive **Birkbeck Tavern** . It's a larger than average traditional two-room back-street local, and also has a well above average reputation for its cask beers, developed over along period. Expect at least three including the house beer, 'Rita's special'. On days when the Orient are at home, this pub will be busy, but it's spacious and well-run, with popular music events in the upstairs function room. Not to be missed in the summer is the lovely garden, one of the best in the area.

Public bar in the Birkbeck

Leaving the Birkbeck, carry on in the same direction along North Birkbeck Road which continues under the same name to the right at the mini roundabout in 250 yards. Then take the first left which is Holloway Road (don't be inhibited by the 'No through road' sign) and head through the bollards and almost straight across into Melon Road. Reaching the end of this street turn right onto Cathall Road and right again to the Harrow Green bus stop on the Leytonstone High Road. The frequent 257 bus should be along in no time to take you the mile or so into Leytonstone town centre. Unless the North Star is yet to open, I recommend staying on the bus two stops beyond Harvey Road where, opposite, you'll see the last pub stop, the Red Lion, and alighting at

the notorious Green Man roundabout, with the eponymous interchange a few yards ahead as you disembark the bus. Head away from it and across the street is narrow Browning Road. Here, little more than a stone's throw from the roundabout and the speeding cars on the A12 below it, is one of London's more unlikely urban Conservation Areas, a quiet and pleasant little oasis of old workers' cottages, and presided over by the charming **North Star** . A traditional two room pub arranged pretty symmetrically (note some surviving etched glass in both doorways), it's a proper community local and resolutely unpretentious. Five changing beers are on offer, with East London's Foundation Bitter and Wye Valley HPA

The King William IV is the home of Brodie's brewery and showcases their beers

Red Lion

among the more regular guests. Whatever's on, you can expect the quality to be good. There's a small but pleasant beer garden, with some tables out the front which catch the sun.

Time now to walk back the short distance to the last pub stop. Return up Browning Road to the High Road, and bearing left to retrace the bus route, it's barely 300 yards back along the road to the **Red Lion** 6. With pubs still closing

in large numbers it's a pleasure to report on the successful refurbishment of a derelict building which had stood empty for some time (although it was briefly an Afro theme bar); now it's helping in the regeneration of Leytonstone. The Antic pub company have carefully restored the striking landmark building and brought it back to its former glory. It opened in 2011 and is currently the easternmost outpost of their growing London estate; in my humble opinion it's one of the best, certainly on the beer front. The internal décor, slightly 'designer shabby', works well for the building, and they've made a good job of the garden too; but it's the beer list, supported by a small but appealing menu, that secures its status. Expect a great range of at least half a dozen ever-changing cask beers with a local emphasis (there are ten handpumps), and some interesting and often higher gravity offerings on the five keg founts. There's an excellent range of bottles in the fridges too. The ambience is relaxed and it looks the sort of place which attracts older locals as well as the upmarket younger clientele.

The central location means it's barely five minutes' walk to Leytonstone Underground station, the quickest way to return to Stratford (for excellent onward transport connections) and Liverpool Street. Just bear right out of the pub onto the High Road and take first left.

PUB INFORMATION

1 **Anchor & Hope**
15 High Hill Ferry, Clapton,
E5 9HG
020 8806 1730
www.anchor-and-hope-clapton.
co.uk
Opening Hours: 1 (12 Fri & Sat)-
11; 12-10.30 Sun

2 **Drum**
557-559 Lea Bridge Road, Leyton,
E10 7EQ
020 8539 9845
Opening Hours: 8-midnight
(1am Fri & Sat)

3 **King William IV**
816 High Road Leyton, Walthamstow, E10 6AE
020 8556 2460
www.williamthefourth.net
Opening Hours: 11-midnight
(1am Fri & Sat); 12-midnight Sun

4 **Birkbeck Tavern**
45 Langthorne Road, Leyton,
E11 4HL
020 8539 2584
Opening Hours: 11-11 (midnight
Fri & Sat); 12-11 Sun

5 **North Star**
24 Browning Road, Leytonstone,
E11 3AR
07961 226197
Opening Hours: 4 (12 Fri & Sat)-
11; 12-10.30 Sun

6 **Red Lion**
640 High Road, Leytonstone,
E11 3AA
020 8988 2929
Opening Hours: 12-11 (midnight
Thu; 2am Fri & Sat)

TRY ALSO:

7 **Leyton Orient
Supporters Club**
Matchroom Stadium, Oliver Road,
Leyton, E10 5NF
020 8988 8288
www.orientsupporters.org
Opening Hours: : match days
from 12.30 Sat; 5.30 weekdays
(not during game)

The Birkbeck Tavern

Regent's Canal I: Islington to Hoxton

WALK INFORMATION

Start: Angel

Finish: Haggerston or Old Street

Distance: 1.9 miles (3km)

Access: Northern Line, or buses (30, 73, 205, 214, 476) from bus stop E at Kings Cross/St Pancras

Key attractions: Islington Museum; Angel Gallery; Regent's Canal

The pubs: Charles Lamb; Prince of Wales; Earl of Essex; Island Queen; Wenlock Arms; Narrow Boat; Baring

The Regent's Canal was built to link the Grand Junction Canal at Paddington with the Thames at Limehouse. The celebrated architect John Nash, one of the canal's movers and shakers, was a chum of the Prince Regent, later King George IV; and it was he who allowed the use of his name for the canal. Beset by various financial and technical problems, it was opened as far as Camden in 1816, and east to Limehouse in 1820. It cost £772,000 to build, which was twice the original estimate. It is this second, eastern half that today has become a very good linear ribbon for good pubs, so much so that this and the next route celebrate some 12 of the best. If there's a drawback to this route, it's that there's not really much walking between pubs at all. The varied range of pubs offer a wide beer range these days but can be on the pricey side, so take plenty of money!

Regent's Canal by the Prince of Wales

The down-to-earth Prince of Wales

Regent's Canal

Start at Angel Underground station on the Northern Line, or bus it eastwards from Kings Cross/St Pancras, and exit onto Islington High Street. The pubs here in the centre of Islington are best left to the crowds; instead walk northwards, keeping to the right hand side on Upper Street. Close to the confusingly named Camden Passage Market, turn right by the *York*

pub into Duncan Street. Head down to the end where ahead through the trees you'll see the Regent's Canal emerging from a tunnel. Islington Tunnel, thee quarters of a mile long and one of three tunnels on the canal, was opened in 1819. A steam-chain tug was introduced in 1826 to reduce bottlenecks caused by boatmen manually 'legging' through it, and this service continued until the 1930s. You can walk down to the towpath here if you want to take a closer look but otherwise turn right into Colebrooke Row and second left at Elia Street to the **Charles Lamb** 🏠 . Feeling far further away from the bustle of Upper Street than it really is, this little backstreet gem has been carefully and traditionally refurbished and is often very busy with appreciative visitors from near and far. You'll get a decent choice of beers here, with Dark Star Hophead the regular, supported by three guests. They take their food seriously here too (best to check the website for times), but not to the extent that drinkers feel sidelined or segregated.

Charles Lamb – a backsteeet gem

It's a simple stroll to the next pub. Further along Elia Street turn left into Sudeley Street and at the far end you'll find the **Prince of Wales 2** . In an area where property values are stratospheric, it's something of a miracle and very welcome, that there's still space for a down-to-earth local which has resisted the tide of gentrification and which doubles as a quieter retreat for discerning locals and visitors alike. It also features on CAMRA's list of London heritage pubs: outside there's some pretty herringbone brickwork, and the often seen set of several former doorways, although today the place has been opened up quite a bit inside. Nonetheless it retains a good deal of its 1930s character, notably in some very good wall panelling. The well-kept beers currently comprise Adnams Bitter and Doom Bar. The steps opposite offer easy access to the canal and a view of the tunnel; otherwise and/ or thereafter, cross the canal and the next stop is already in your sights, just 150 yards or so up Danbury Street. The **Earl of Essex 3** is quite a different beast from the preceding pubs, fresh from a renovation in 2012 which has seen it barge into the reckoning as a beer destination in an area not short of

competition. With its central island bar counter and more varied and intimate seating, the Earl feels more inviting than some other modern refurbishments, and they've retained quite a number of features which provide links with the past. Look out for the handsome old bar back complete with gilded lettering and a couple of old Watney red barrels (diminutive and empty I'm pleased to say!); and some surviving etched glass, as well as the external glazed tiles.

Inside the Earl of Essex

LEFT: **The Island Queen – a restored Victorian gem** RIGHT: **The canalside Narrow Boat**

The star turn here though is the extensive beer list: five cask ales (and a cider) on tap, are complemented by a very wide range of craft-keg beers on tap, and an excellent bottled beer list. Moreover, by the time you read this, the planned on-site Earls microbrewery will probably be open. To help you decide, the beer menus provide tasting notes. Additionally, in an area where beer prices are on the uppish side, it's well worth knowing that the Earl offers 10% off all draught beers to card carrying CAMRA members! Unusually for the area there's a pleasant secluded garden at the rear.

Unless you want to visit the organic *Duke of Cambridge* at the top of Danbury Street (more of a foodie joint these days but offering organic beers from Pitfield and Freedom breweries), retrace your steps as far as Noel Road, just before the canal bridge, and turn left down this tree-lined street to reach the **Island Queen 4** in no distance at all. This is a restored Victorian gem, named after the monarch and her fondness for the Isle of Wight. Despite losing some of its original screenwork and having been modernised, it nonetheless retains a distinctive and attractive identity. The frontage still has three doorways and some impressive curved windows although sadly the glass is now all clear. Inside the impression is one of height, space and grandeur around the central island bar area with its elegant stillion. To the left you can see how originally a porch would

have led in from the door entrance: to the right note the mosaic floor. A separate room survives, divided by a nice screen but minus its door, and there is a corridor to the upstairs rooms. Etched glasswork by Morris of Kennington, who were responsible for the wonderful glass in the *Princess Louise*, High Holborn (see Walk 9), survives here and the lincrusta (heavily embossed paper) ceiling is another feature. There are now four beers available, with Taylor Landlord (very popular with the regulars) and Doom Bar on as fixtures, supported by two changing guests and always featuring a 'LocAle'. The pub offers a pleasant ambience for eating as well as drinking – see the website for all the menus. Playwright Joe Orton lived in 25 Noel Road with his lover Kenneth Halliwell for the last few years of their lives, and was a regular in the Island Queen; it's ironic that the council has erected a blue plaque on his former abode. This was the same council which pressed for severe prison sentences against the two men, when they were found guilty of defacing local library books in 1962!

At the far end of Noel Road, right by the bridge crossing the canal, stands the **Narrow Boat 5**. In many ways this über-smart gastropub is the very epitome of the gentrification of the area, but in this case it's all about location, for the pub makes the most of its site alongside the canal. Wide sliding doors afford a view out across the water, and in good weather the pair of balconies offer the best seats in the house, right above the canal towpath. Downstairs, there's access to canalside seats. Since Young's acquired the Narrow Boat they have widened the beer choice, three of their own beers being complemented by three rotating guests with a clear local flavour – the likes of London Fields and East London are among the most frequently seen. Food? Well, you'll not go hungry here, with everything from snacks and sandwiches upwards; the problem might be bagging a table to eat at.

To continue the walk, rejoin the towpath and continue eastwards as far as the next footbridge in about 200 yards. Cross the canal onto Shepherdess Walk, and right into Sturt Street. In an area of change with council blocks standing cheek-by-jowl with new apartments, the **Wenlock Arms** **6** at the far end of the street looks increasingly incongrouous, a Victorian remnant somehow clinging on against a sweeping tide of modernity. In fact many cask ale drinkers will be familiar with this pub as it has a long and proud record as an award-wining alehouse; but more recently it's also faced a very uncertain future with attempts to sell the site for redevelopment having been thrown out by Hackney Council. The very latest at the time of

writing is that the future of the pub should be secured with a more modest development in the upstairs part of the building. Let's hope so for the Wenlock is a great contrast to the gentrification of many other local pubs – an unpretentious street corner boozer which concentrates on serving a wide range of interesting and well-kept ales from all parts, alongside a range of imported beer and real cider. The shabby benches and tatty décor all add to the charm of this great pub, unspoilt by progress. Besides its solid support for the cause of good cask beer, it is also well known for its blues and jazz, usually on Friday and Saturday evenings.

Return to the canal and continue along the towpath to the next bridge, which carries New North Road across the canal. Leave the canal again here and take Baring Street which runs parallel to the canal on the north side. A loop of the road forks off to the left but you'll probably spot the **Baring** **7** before you reach the fork. Occupying a curving five bay frontage in a Victorian building, this is yet another pub which has been gentrified to an extent, but it still retains a more traditional, community feel than some other makeovers. The long bar that wraps round at the right-hand end gives access to a garden

Along the Regent's Canal

Interesting ales on the bar at the Wenlock Arms

area at the rear. There are four cask ales on the bar, Shepherd Neame Spitfire and Taylor Landlord being the regulars supported by two changing guests, one of them usually a LocAle. In addition there's a wide range of keg beers, and an extensive menu if you want to finish off the walk with a meal. Sometimes the TV can intrude as major sporting events are advertised and shown.

From the Baring, the best homeward transport options are buses 21, 76 and 141 from Baring Street down to Old Street on the Northern

Line for Underground services, or return to the canal and make for Haggerston station on the Overground, about half a mile.

LINK Return to the canal and continue east to pick up Walk 19 between *Howl at the Moon* and the *Fox*, or leave the canal at the De Beauvoir Road bridge and take the next left for the *Stag's Head* on Walk 16.

PUB INFORMATION

1 Charles Lamb
16 Elia Street, N1 8DE
020 7837 5040
www.thecharleslambpub.com
Opening Hours: 12 (4 Mon & Tue)-11; 12-10.30 Sun

2 Prince of Wales
1a Sudeley Street, N1 8HP
020 7837 6173
Opening Hours: 11-11; 12-22.30 Sun

3 Earl of Essex
25 Danbury Street, N1 8LE
020 7424 5828
www.earlofessex.net
Opening Hours: 12 (3 Mon)-11.30 (12.30 Fri & Sat)

4 Island Queen
87 Noel Road, N1 8BD
020 7704 7631
www.theislandqueenislington.co.uk
Opening Hours: 12-11.30 (midnight Fri & Sat)

5 Narrow Boat
119 St Peters Street, N1 8PZ
020 7288 0572
thenarrowboatpub.com
Opening Hours: 11 (12 Sun)-midnight

6 Wenlock Arms
26 Wenlock Road, N1 7TA
020 7608 3406
www.thewenlockarms.com
Opening Hours: 12-midnight (1am Thu-Sat)

7 Baring
55 Baring Street, N1 3DS
020 7359 5785
thebaringpub.com
Opening Hours: 12-11 (10.30 Sun)

Earl of Essex

Regent's Canal II: Hoxton to Mile End

WALK INFORMATION

Start: 🚇 Hoxton

Finish: Mile End Road, for 🚇 Mile End

Access: London Overground; bus 243 from Waterloo/Farringdon/Old Street

Distance: 4.7 miles (7.5km)

Key attractions: Hoxton Street Market (hoxtonstreetmarket.co.uk) Victoria Park; Broadway Market; Geffrye Museum (www.geffryemuseum.org.uk)

The pubs: Howl at the Moon; Fox; Dove; Eleanor Arms; Palm Tree

The second part of the Regent's Canal epic involves quite a bit more walking than the first, especially between the Dove and the Eleanor Arms (about a mile and a half). As such, it's an attractive option to do this route on a bicycle, which is permitted (although pedestrians have priority) on the canal towpath. As a walk it's just as rewarding as the first, more so in some respects for the variety of canal-side land use and the traverse of a changing area of London. The pubs, a mixture of the resolutely traditional and the very new, reflect the social changes which are occurring in the area. There's an opportunity to cut across Victoria Park, surely the most notable of the open spaces of East London. The Geffrye Museum, specialising in the history of the English domestic interior, is right by Hoxton station and as it opens at 10am most days (noon on Sunday; closed Mondays), offers a good cultural opportunity at the outset.

The canal at Hackney

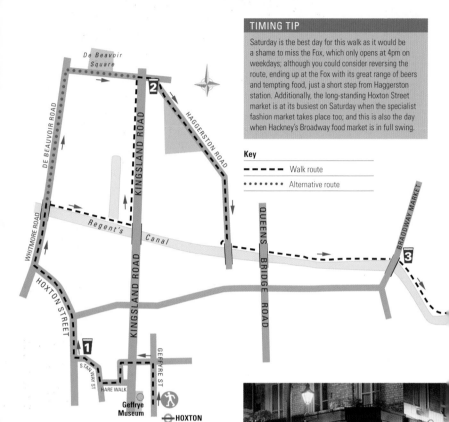

TIMING TIP

Saturday is the best day for this walk as it would be
a shame to miss the Fox, which only opens at 4pm on
weekdays; although you could consider reversing the
route, ending up at the Fox with its great range of beers
and tempting food, just a short step from Haggerston
station. Additionally, the long-standing Hoxton Street
market is at its busiest on Saturday when the specialist
fashion market takes place too; and this is also the day
when Hackney's Broadway food market is in full swing.

Key

– – – – – Walk route

• • • • • • • Alternative route

Start at Hoxton station on the London
Overground, and emerge from the station
on the west side of the railway, with the rear
garden of the Geffrye Museum directly ahead.
Walk to the right (northwards) and bear left at
the first junction to reach the Kingsland Road
in 100 yards. Left again here, and unless you're
visiting the museum (entrance along on the left),
cross the road and take the narrow lane, Hare
Walk, between the modern flats just a few yards
along on the right. At the end, turn right again
and follow this road round to the junction with
Hoxton Street where you'll come across the
market and the first pub of the day, **Howl at
the Moon** 1. It's another story of a successful
conversion of a disused pub in a once run-down
but now revitalised area. A single spacious room
looks out onto the street, and with the market
taking place right outside there's often plenty

Howl at the Moon

to look at. Punters can choose from a variety of
seating styles and enjoy a range of five real ales
and a traditional real cider. Expect Dark Star
and Brodie's on tap, with mainly local guests,
from the likes of London Fields or Redemption.
The beers are complemented by English food at
reasonable prices.

The Fox has a tempting range of beer and food

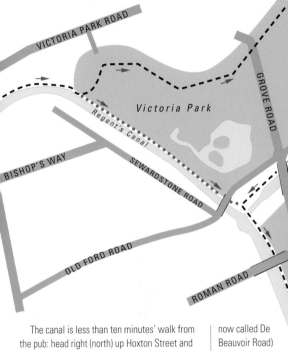

The canal is less than ten minutes' walk from the pub: head right (north) up Hoxton Street and follow it as it curves round to the left, before bearing right at the road junction into Whitmore Road. You'll come to the canal bridge shortly, and access to the waterside is to the left once across. Pick up the canal towpath under the bridge, and head east to the next bridge where leave the canal onto busy Kingsland Road. Although the ten minute walk up the road to the north is hardly pleasant, the pub at the end of it is ample reward.

A pleasanter alternative route to the Fox is to continue north at the canal bridge (the road is now called De Beauvoir Road) for a few more minutes until at St Peter's church bear right which leads onto De Beauvoir Square, the centrepiece of Richard Benyon de Beauvoir's very early Victorian 'new town' development. The houses around the square are very attractive

Canalside scene near Victoria Park

with interesting features, such as shaped gables, sculptured chimneys and windows with lozenge-patterned leaded lights. Keep directly east onto St Peter's Way which brings you out on the Kingsland Road directly opposite the Fox!

The **Fox** 2 continues the theme of intelligent renewal which has become a feature of the best pubs in this area of inner London. This large Victorian pub, despite being geographically challenged insofar as it's midway between Shoreditch and Dalston, has put itself firmly on the map since its re-opening in 2012, with a tempting range of beer and food. Bar staff seem well-informed about their beer, which includes an interesting range in cask on eight handpumps, with a strong emphasis upon local suppliers, so expect the likes of Hackney, London Fields and Brodie's to be much in evidence. The same can be said for the keg beers (Thornbridge Jaipur is a favourite but supported by some other strong contenders from home and abroad) whilst in the fridge there's an extensive range of bottles from around the world; so you'll not want for choice here no matter how long you might stay. The food (all sorts including sharing plates and Sunday roasts) is taken very seriously too, and as such it's a very strong contender if you intend to eat whilst undertaking this route. The main bar room is spacious and open, and in summer a very appealing alternative is to head upstairs to the roof terrace which offers sheltered tables amongst leafy planters. *Time Out* rightly concluded that 'This is how to reopen a pub and appeal to the progressives and traditionalists alike'.

It would be tempting to settle in here, and forget that you have a few miles to cover, but there's a walk now of the best part of a mile to fill the lungs and work off at least some of the calories. Bear right out the pub and sharp right again (Haggerston Road) and follow the lane down past some lovely old Victorian cottages facing a green, and then past the church and an area of more modern housing until you reach the canal again, access to which is via steps on the right before the bridge. Again turn left under the bridge to continue eastwards. The canal-side path traverses an area of post-war flats before you come upon a rare lock – just beyond this, leave the canal temporarily once again at the southern end of Hackney's Broadway Market. Since 2004 a new Saturday food market has been the catalyst for the gentrification of the former run-down area although Hackney Council have ruffled a few feathers in the process.

Turn left and walk up Broadway Market for no more than 100 yards to arrive at the **Dove** 3 with its distinctive and attractive tiled exterior. Renamed, and made over some time earlier than the street, this bustling freehouse chimes perfectly with the new vibe in the area, and although the rambling interior is far larger than it looks from outside you'll be lucky to get a seat at the weekend as it attracts a mixed crowd. There are six cask ales, including three guests, with East London Pale and Crouch Vale Brewer's Gold currently among the fixtures; but despite this it's as a destination for Belgian beers, both on draught and in bottle, that the Dove is best known. Reports of service and welcome are very mixed, it has to be said, and prices for some of the beers are very high. The unisex toilets are an unusual feature.

It's a longer walk to the next pub, so return to the canal and continue eastwards (if you're on a bike, Andrews Road runs parallel with the canal as far as Mare Street, the next road junction and may be easier). A few minutes beyond the Mare Street bridge you'll reach the western gate into Victoria Park, and unless you're pushed for time and wish to skip the slightly off-piste Eleanor Arms, (in which case continue on the towpath), leave the canal and take the path following the northern perimeter of the park. At over 200 acres Victoria Park is the largest in the East End. Laid out in the early years of the monarch's reign, it later became a key amenity for the working classes of the East End. As well as an essential green space the 'People's Park' became a centre for political meetings and rallies with its own Speaker's Corner to rival that at Hyde Park; here, the largest crowds were to hear socialist speakers such as William Morris. Cross the Grove Road via the gates by the *Royal Inn On The Park*, and in less than 200 yards beyond, bear right on the path that passes the striking Grade II* Burdett-Coutts Memorial Drinking Fountain, gift of the wealthy philanthropist and erected in 1862 allegedly at a cost of £6,000, a small fortune in those days. Head on the same bearing to leave the park by the Gunmakers Gate, crossing the canal as you leave the park, and walk the short distance up to the Old Ford Road. A short step to the left brings you to the **Eleanor Arms** 4. This East End local won't win many prizes for its

The Eleanor Arms

architecture but you can rely on a friendly welcome and a well-kept pint here, as its frequent appearance in the *Good Beer Guide* testifies. The single room wraps round the bar and the rear area has the pool table and the TV; but there's also a beer garden. Beers are from Shepherd Neame, including seasonals, whilst if the tank is low after the walk across from Hackney, food consists chiefly of filled baguettes. If you're here on a Sunday you may be lucky enough to catch the regular jazz jam session.

The Dove sits in the midst of busy Broadway Market

The Palm Tree is adorned with Truman's distinctive eagle

Return to the canal bridge you just crossed and drop down to the towpath; this waterway is actually the Hertford Union, London's shortest canal, which connects the Regent's Canal with the Lee Navigation, a little over a mile to the east. To return to the former, head west (left when reaching the bridge) and walk for about 7-8 minutes. Once back at the junction, head south (left on the Regent's Canal) once again towards Globe Town and Mile End, but not for long, for once under the road bridge and just beyond a small wetland area to the left hand side of the towpath the last pub of the day stands on its own, in the midst of open space which was once housing. The **Palm Tree** ⑤ is distinctive on account of its unspoilt exterior, branded in the signage and style of the former Truman's brewery which of course once owned so many pubs in the East End. Truman's distinctive eagle adorns the corner elevation, whilst the company's ceramic work

survives right the way round at ground floor level. Inside there are still two quite separate bar rooms, the main one retaining its curving bar counter and old tiled chequerwork at its foot. Note too the dinky little island stallion holding the bottles and optics. The smaller 'posh room' round the back has similar if slightly better quality fittings, and both rooms have some old tables. Note the framed piece of old etched glasswork in the rear room: the now long-serving landlady apparently saved this piece from workmen from the brewery who were smashing the Victorian screens when they moved in. The two beers on tap here are changing and often unusual ales from all over.

Leaving the Palm Tree, it's about a ten minute walk along the canal to reach the Mile End Road, and if you're not taking a bus from here, the Underground station is about a further five minutes east, to your left.

PUB INFORMATION

① **Howl at the Moon**
178 Hoxton Street, N1 5LH
020 3341 2525
www.hoxtonhowl.com
Opening Hours: 12-11 (1am
Fri & Sat)

② **Fox**
372 Kingsland Road, E8 4DA
07807 217734
www.thefoxe8.com
Opening Hours: 4 (12 Sat)-
midnight; 12-11.30 Sun

③ **Dove**
24-28 Broadway Market, E8 4QJ
020 7275 7617
dovepubs.com
Opening Hours: 12-11 (midnight
Fri & Sat)

④ **Eleanor Arms**
60 Old Ford Road, E3 5JP
020 8980 6992
www.eleanorarms.co.uk
Opening Hours: 12 (4 Mon)-11;
12-10.30 Sun

⑤ **Palm Tree**
127 Grove Road, E3 5RP
020 8980 2918
Opening Hours: 12.30-midnight
(2am Sat); 12-midnight Sun

The Dove

A beer circuit of Wandsworth Common

WALK INFORMATION

Start and Finish: Clapham Junction

Distance: 3 miles (4.8km)

Access: Waterloo, Victoria and East Croydon; or London Overground

Key attractions: Wandsworth Common; Wandsworth Nature Study Centre; Royal Victoria Patriotic Building (www.rvpb.com)

The pubs: Beehive; Powder Keg Diplomacy; Roundhouse; Le Gothique; County Arms; Eagle Ale House; Draft House Northcote; Falcon

If I had to pick my Desert Island London pub walk, this excellent saunter around Wandsworth Common would have to be a serious contender. Apart from the pleasant if rather fragmented Common itself, there's plenty of appeal in the built environment, from the amazing Royal Victoria Patriotic Building to the bohemian atmosphere of the Northcote Road. Add to this some great pubs and bars scattered liberally at frequent intervals along the way, and it would be a difficult route not to like. Moreover the last pub is just a step from the station so there should be no worries about finding your way home. There are eight pubs on this circuit so, depending upon time and capacity, you might wish to be selective.

Victorian grandeur at the Falcon

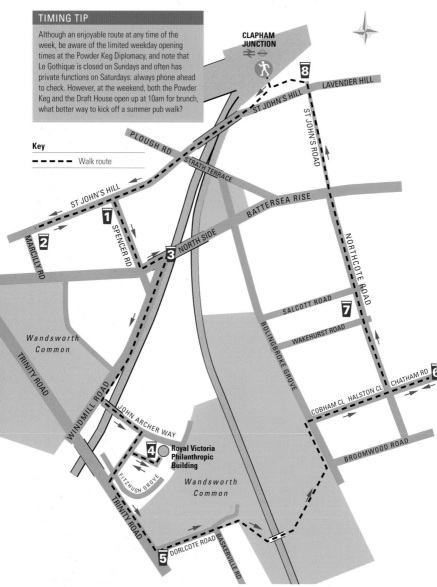

TIMING TIP

Although an enjoyable route at any time of the week, be aware of the limited weekday opening times at the Powder Keg Diplomacy, and note that Le Gothique is closed on Sundays and often has private functions on Saturdays: always phone ahead to check. However, at the weekend, both the Powder Keg and the Draft House open up at 10am for brunch, what better way to kick off a summer pub walk?

Key

- - - - Walk route

Start at Clapham Junction, which isn't billed as Britain's busiest railway station for nothing, and head for the new exit at the southern end of the long footbridge which disgorges you onto St John's Hill by the rail bridge. It's not the most inspiring of urban environments but it will improve! Cross the rail bridge and continue ahead at the traffic lights, beyond which

it's a good 5 minute walk into a more bohemian area with some trendy shops and eateries before, just beyond Spencer Road on your left, you'll come across a newish bar which reflects the surroundings. The oddly-named **Powder Keg Diplomacy** 1 is a skilful conversion of a former curry house into an appealing modern style bar and eatery. The bar area is beset with

The Powder Keg Diplomacy

collaborative brews between the staff and Peter Haydon's Head in a Hat Brewery at the *Florence*, Herne Hill. All in all, a welcome addition to the already very good portfolio of drinking holes on this excellent and well-tested circuit.

By way of almost complete contrast, and just a couple of minutes further along the road on foot, the tiny **Beehive 2** remains a traditional no-nonsense one bar pub attracting a mainly local clientele. It's smart and clean, but still retains a public bar atmosphere which in my book is a definite plus. It's even got a jukebox! A seasonal from the Fuller's portfolio and a rotating guest complement London Pride and ESB on the four handpumps. It's primarily a drinker's pub although bar food is available.

the usual sofas and tables, whilst at the rear there's a classy conservatory for the diners. The website recommends the cocktails, but this is a bar which has definitely set out to make an effort with its beers as well. On handpump, there are three rotating beers with Windsor & Eton and Oakham among the favoured breweries. Complementing these are half a dozen keg taps which offer some interesting choices from home and abroad; and in addition there are around fifty bottled beers, with a strong UK emphasis. There are monthly 'meet the brewer' events, and occasional

Retrace your steps to Spencer Road, just beyond the Powder Keg Diplomacy, and turn right. At the end of the street you'll catch your first glimpse of Wandsworth Common ahead, although this is a small outlier cut off by the railway line nearby which sliced through the Common in 1837. Bear left and on the next corner is the **Roundhouse 3**. The noteworthy mosaic at the entrance suggests that the original name was the Freemasons, and indeed it sems to have switched back and forth between the names

The traditional no-nonsense Beehive

THE COMMONS OF SOUTH LONDON

It's appropriate to dedicate this walk around Wandsworth Common to those of our forebears who fought to stop greedy landowners and gentry from enclosing common lands across South London, in particular in the eighteenth and nineteenth centuries, enabling us to enjoy the admittedly fragmented and truncated remains of them today. In Wandsworth's case, the main culprit was Earl Spencer (the same family that later gave us Lady Di) who along with others had already done great damage by the time he gave in to popular pressure and agreed to transfer much of what remained to what later became the Wandsworth Common Preservation Society. Read much more about all this and other South London Commons at www.alphabetthreat.co.uk/pasttense/pdf/fences.pdf

The curving façade of the Roundhouse

you're now facing one of South London's architectural treasures and, for its size, a pretty well-hidden one. The Royal Victoria Patriotic Building, constructed between 1857 and 1859 (another enclosure from the Common, it has to be said), was originally built as an orphanage and later became a school and hospital, along with a wartime home to MI5 and MI6; Rudolf Hess was apparently detained in the cellar dungeon. Having fallen into dereliction after the war, plans were made to demolish it, but after pressure from the Victorian Society and the Wandsworth Society, the building was listed, saving it from destruction. In 1980 it was acquired for £1 subject to the performance of a schedule of repair and restoration works. The magnificent hall with painted ceiling, totally destroyed by arson, was carefully reconstructed, and deservedly won a Civic Trust Award as well as the prized Europa Nostra Order of Merit. Now the building houses a Dance and Drama school, flats and studios, workshops, and **Le Gothique** ▢, a restaurant and bar extraordinary, and one of London's first gastropubs. Signs should help you find the bar, sequestered around the rear of this remarkable building: easiest is to bear right around the front elevation, and then left (noting the exit (ahead) you'll take to continue the route) and keep left. Closed on Sundays and usually closed for private parties on Saturdays (it's well worth ringing ahead to check), the attractive bar offers a changing range of ales but in a typical week features beers from Shepherd Neame, Downton and Sambrook's. The twice-yearly beer festivals (held on the last weekends of March and October) are massive events with 150 beers and 30 ciders overflowing into the cloistered garden and restaurant. If you are doing the trail during the week, this would make a good lunch stop – the garden eatery in the Victorian cloisters is highly rated.

over time but the elegant curving corner façade in fine yellow brickwork, and classy Victorian sash windows justifies the current choice. Inside it's a smart gastropub in line with the location: high and airy, with large windows, and there is an array of comfy seating around the bay frontage. You can sit outside too, although it's rather noisy given its location. The place has built a solid reputation for its beers, with a LocAle emphasis: Sambrook's supply Wandle as the house cask regular, supported by two other rotating guests, one often from Hogs Back; and in addition there are several keg taps with one or two interesting offerings, and a bottle list of around 20.

Now leave the pub and cross the main road outside, taking the road opposite (Spencer Park) running alongside the railway on one side and the Common on the other. You'll pass the memorial to the Claphmam Junction rail disaster of December 1988 which killed 35 people when three rush hour trains collided in the cutting below. A little further beyond that is the forlorn remains of a smock windmill, all that remains of a project by the then London and South Western Railway to pump water from this railway cutting. (If Le Gothique is closed and you don't want to detour through the grounds, simply continue straight ahead past the windmill and turn left into Trinity Road).

Just beyond the mill, turn left over the railway into a modern housing development (John Archer Way, which is named after the founding member of the Fourth International and a veteran of the Trotskyist movement who died in December 2000; right here in ultra-Tory Wandsworth). That aside,

OK, follow that! Exit the grounds by retracing the route halfway, to the corner of the front wall of the building, and then left, and follow Fitzhugh Way as it twists left and right before disgorging you onto the busy dual carriageway of Trinity Road; ask at the bar if you are unsure. Turn left to keep the (fenced in) Common on your left, but already our next pub can be seen not too far off on the other side of the road. The **County Arms** 5 is an imposing Victorian building which is difficult to miss. Young's gave this grand old pub a heavy makeover about ten years ago, bringing it in line with the well-heeled local clientele, although a few vestiges of the old building remain – a very nice entrance mosaic, screenwork (with some good etched glass), splendid fireplaces and decent woodwork. This is joined today by modern seats, chunky tables and an upmarket eating area towards the rear. Beyond this there's a large and secluded garden area which makes a pleasant summer retreat. There are four handpumps, one of which offers a guest which may come from beyond the Wells & Young's portfolio.

Right outside there's a handy controlled crossing and, using this, walk down Dorlcote Road with the Common on your left and then take the track running at about 45 degrees to your right at a junction of paths, and this will quickly lead

to the footbridge over another railway line. Now head half left on a clear path which runs across the Common to meet the B229 road, Bolingbroke Grove. Cross this carefully and about 100 yards further up the road to the north, look for Cobham Close on the right, just before the modern block of flats. Keep straight ahead when this becomes a footpath, and cross the Northcote Road directly into Chatham Road. Halfway up here, on the right, you'll find the **Eagle Ale House** 6. In a distinctive and characterful building, this independent establishment offers a relaxing ambience with comfortable seating arranged informally around the L-shaped bar counter. Bookshelves add to the appeal. There are basic bar snacks but this is a quality beer house first and foremost, which has carried off the coveted local Pub of the Year award for 2013. Expect between four and eight beers to be available in this LocAle-accredited house, depending upon the time of week: Surrey Hills and Pilgrim are among the favoured brewers in an interesting and changing selection. There is a heated marquee in the rear courtyard garden for special occasions, including beer festivals.

The Royal Victoria Patriotic Buillding – home to Le Gothique

Return to the Northcote Road and turn right. The longish walk down this road into Clapham Junction is punctuated by interesting shops, many of which have a bohemian flavour. Since the last edition of this guide, another attraction appears a few minutes down on the left: at the junction with Salcott Road stands one of the Draft House chain, which numbers five outlets across London. The **Draft House Northcote** 7, in keeping with the others in the chain has a very modern internal style, although housed in an attractive old end-terrace Victorian building. Run by avowed beer enthusiasts, the place offers a wide and interesting selection which adds to the already extensive range sampled on this walk: Sambrook's Wandle is the regular, and the two rotating guests have a local emphasis. On keg, look out for Camden Brewery beers and Budvar Dark, while in the fridge there's a good variety of around fifty bottled beers. Food is available all day from noon, and just in case you're tackling the route in reverse, they're open from 10am at weekends.

For the final stop on this marathon of a pub walk, continue down Northcote Road (or if you prefer, take bus 319 or G1 from the Salcott

Road stop, alighting at Clapham Junction: two stops) crossing straight ahead at the traffic lights into St John's Road and, at the far end, on the opposite corner of the crossroads stands the imposing **Falcon** 8. Aptly described by CAMRA's Heritage Pubs group as 'mightily impressive', inside this late Victorian pub, possibly the longest continuous bar counter in the country curves around a spacious servery. A real impression of height prevails in the bar back and the windows; and some fine screen work survives, as does a stained glass window depicting the eponymous bird of prey. Don't expect to have the place to yourself: it may be very busy and bustling, especially in the evenings; but it's unmissable, not only on account of the architectural features but, these days, also because of the excellent range of beers on tap. It has become a permanent beer festival under the enthusiastic young management, with about twenty ales available; and when a beer festival is happening this can double. There's a spacious rear area set aside primarily for diners, which makes a good place to relax and enjoy some food with your ales, before the short walk to your right on leaving the pub to catch your train at the station.

PUB INFORMATION

1 Powder Keg Diplomacy
147 St John's Hill, SW11 1TQ
020 7450 6457
www.powderkegdiplomacy.co.uk
Opening Hours: 4 (5 Mon, 10- Sat)-11 (midnight Fri & Sat); 10-11 Sun

2 Beehive
197 St John's Hill, SW11 1TH
020 7450 1756
www.beehivewandsworth.co.uk
Opening Hours: 12-midnight

3 Roundhouse
2 North Side, Wandsworth Common, SW18 2SS
020 7223 6186
www.theroundhousewandsworth.com
Opening Hours: 12-11 (1am Fri & Sat, 10.30 Sun)

4 Le Gothique
Royal Victoria Patriotic Building, John Archer Way, off Windmill Road, Wandsworth Common, SW18 3SX
020 8870 6567
www.legothique.co.uk
Opening Hours: 12-midnight; may be closed for functions Sat & Sun

5 County Arms
345 Trinity Road, SW18 3SH
020 8874 8532
www.countyarms.co.uk
Opening Hours: 12-11 (midnight Fri & Sat, 10 Sun)

6 Eagle Ale House
104 Chatham Road, SW11 6HG
020 7228 2328
www.eaglealehouse.co.uk
Opening Hours: 2 (12 Sat)-11; 12-10.30 Sun

7 Draft House Northcote
94 Northcote Road, SW11 6QW
020 7924 1814
www.drafthouse.co.uk
Opening Hours: 12 (10 Sat & Sun)-11 (midnight Thu-Sat)

8 Falcon
2 St John's Hill, SW11 1RU
020 7228 2076
www.nicholsonspubs.co.uk/thefalconclaphamjunctionlondon
Opening Hours: 10-11.30 (midnight Thu-Sat; 11 Sun)

Croydon – London's edge city

WALK INFORMATION

Start and Finish: Whitgift Hospital almshouses, junction of George Street and North End

Distance: 1 mile (1.6km)

Access: ⮂ ⇄ East Croydon (500 yards) or ⮂ ⇄ West Croydon (400 yards). ⮂ George St (50 yards)

Key attractions: Whitgift Hospital; Croydon Old Palace (www.friendsofoldpalace. org); Surrey Street market; London's only on-street trams

The pubs: Dog & Bull; Green Dragon; Spread Eagle; Royal Standard; Bull's Head; Half & Half; Skylark. Try also: George

With a population well in excess of Southampton or Brighton, Croydon functions in all but name as London's 'edge city', hence my licence with the title of this walk. Croydon retains a strong identity of its own, and despite the sixties demolitions, the 'concrete jungle' image, and its recent troubles many of its inhabitants are fiercely loyal to the place; if you've never ventured this way, this walk is a great opportunity to find out why. Its once numerous traditional pubs have suffered tremendous loss and damage but, true to form, it has bounced back and today the centre of this vibrant town is a great place for a pub walk. Perhaps it's in keeping with the rest of the place that the majority of the destinations on this tour are modern conversions rather than traditional old pubs, but all in all this is a top-notch pub walk which can hold its own with any in Central London.

Surrey Street market

Whitgift Almshouses in the centre of town

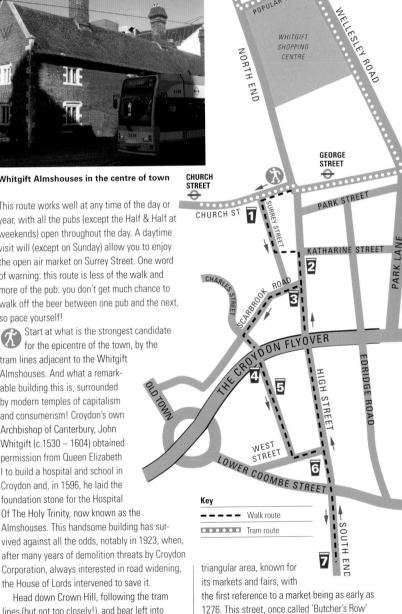

This route works well at any time of the day or year, with all the pubs (except the Half & Half at weekends) open throughout the day. A daytime visit will (except on Sunday) allow you to enjoy the open air market on Surrey Street. One word of warning: this route is less of the walk and more of the pub: you don't get much chance to walk off the beer between one pub and the next, so pace yourself!

Start at what is the strongest candidate for the epicentre of the town, by the tram lines adjacent to the Whitgift Almshouses. And what a remarkable building this is, surrounded by modern temples of capitalism and consumerism! Croydon's own Archbishop of Canterbury, John Whitgift (c.1530 – 1604) obtained permission from Queen Elizabeth I to build a hospital and school in Croydon and, in 1596, he laid the foundation stone for the Hospital Of The Holy Trinity, now known as the Almshouses. This handsome building has survived against all the odds, notably in 1923, when, after many years of demolition threats by Croydon Corporation, always interested in road widening, the House of Lords intervened to save it.

Head down Crown Hill, following the tram lines (but not too closely!), and bear left into Surrey Street in 100 yards. Along with the High Street and Crown Hill, Surrey Street formed a triangular area, known for its markets and fairs, with the first reference to a market being as early as 1276. This street, once called 'Butcher's Row' still sports a surviving remnant of the butchers' shambles complete with iron and timber columns supporting galleried upper floors above the shops. The alley on the left was the original home to the late lamented Beano's Records, the self styled 'largest secondhand record shop in the world', in which your scribe spent many an hour and too much money in his youth. Across the street, sporting a handsome brick frontage, is the first stop on the tour, the **Dog & Bull 1**. This Young's house (with beers from the Wells & Young's stable) is almost certainly the oldest pub in town today; it has a Georgian frontage, of very attractive dark brickwork, complemented by a pleasing pendant lantern and a hanging pub sign. It's easy to see where an adjacent shop has been absorbed into the pub; this took place about 25 years ago. It's always been a market pub, and when the market was bigger and livelier than today the pub was an urban classic, bustling with traders and customers, resolutely working-class in character with plain and simple fittings, but clean and well-kept. Today it's lost a lot of that character; it's still likelier to be busier during the day than in the evenings, although the conversion of the old yard into an attractive garden has drawn in a new crowd, and there has been a certain smartening-up inside. I think this has gone quite far enough and I hope Young's refrain from

EAST CROYDON GEORGE STREET

further 'improvements' and respect the location and history of this old pub. The interior retains its island bar, with a separate rear room and the area off to the right in the former shop already referred to. Incidentally, this is the pub which HRH Prince Charles, Prince of Wales, visited in 1994 and was photographed pulling a pint of bitter in the same way that his grandmother had done in an earlier well-known picture which also used to hang in many pubs in Young's estate.

Returning to the street, walk further along, passing an area where modern building on both sides (most recently a pretty grim wall of apartments, thrown up in what's meant to be a conservation area) has spoilt the character of the street; but down to the right on Matthew's Yard good conservation has taken place. Whilst the Victorian gasworks and flour mill have been lost, the old 1880 granary of the former Page & Overton brewery, with its original Victorian hoists, pulleys and loading bays has been restored and part of it is now a nightclub. The impressive and striking castellated building on nearby Overton's Yard is part of Croydon's first waterworks which supplied a million gallons of water a day from 1851. It took advantage, like the brewery, of strong springs which rose immediately west of Surrey Street and fed the headwaters of the River Wandle, into whose valley you walked downhill at the start of the walk. The river itself has sadly been buried in central Croydon today.

Take the steps opposite and climb back out of the valley to re-enter the High Street in the centre of what is very much the 'yoof strip' of town at night, and turn right. Just a short step opposite, and on the corner of Katharine Street by Croydon's impressive Victorian town hall, is the **Spread Eagle 2**. This fine building, a former bank, has been the subject of a very good conversion by Fuller's. The ambience is relaxed, the fittings do justice to the gravitas of the

The Spread Eagle, in the shadow of Croydon Clocktower

The bustling centre of Croydon

There's often live music upstairs, including good jazz on Sunday afternoons. At the time of writing a window adorned with messages on sticky notes on a 'we love Croydon' theme offers an uplifting post-riots vote of confidence in Croydon and is threatening to become a permanent fixture!

Leave the Dragon and drop back down the surprisingly steep hill (on Scarbrook Road alongside the pub's side wall) onto the old floodplain of the River Wandle. Once the site of the Scarbrook Pond, the foot of the road now plays host to a couple of ugly car parks and some modern blocks of apartments. You'll also catch a good view of Croydon's well-known flyover, built in the late 1960's as part of its Brave New World of skyscrapers and urban freeways. In connecting the town centre across the Wandle Valley to Duppas Hill and the west, wholesale demolition of narrow terraced streets took place, and a large number of old pubs were lost. Our next call is one of the survivors, but only just! Turn left and walk under the flyover; and on the corner, opposite the grim multi-storey car park and with its garden pretty well under the flyover itself, lies the **Royal Standard 4** . Despite the compromised location (but to be fair the street beyond the pub remains an area relatively untouched by the march of modern Croydon), the pub is a classic street-corner local, a real gem, the likes of which are becoming rarer all the time. With no fewer than four old doorways pointing to its former compartmentalised interior, it's now all interconnected although with some interesting nooks and corners. The area around to the rear, with its own serving hatch, is the result of a 1980s extension to the public space which improved the pub immensely. A good range of Fuller's beers is available, including Chiswick Bitter, my personal Fuller's favourite; and beer quality here is always reliable, evidenced by a 25-year unbroken run in the *Good Beer Guide*. It doesn't get as busy as once it did, but the Standard is still a great traditional Croydon boozer.

building, and the décor is smart but traditional. There's even a small terrace outside under the adjacent Clocktower. A wide range of Fuller's beers are available, and they offer a generous 50p per pint discount on production of a current CAMRA membership card. There's a full food menu if you're feeling peckish.

On leaving the Spread Eagle, it's only a short stroll south along the High Street, past the old *Ship Inn*, and you'll spot the next port of call, across the street where the top end of Surrey Street rejoins the High Street. The **Green Dragon 3** is another bank conversion, this one currently in the estate of the Stonegate pub company. Under the experienced stewardship of Esther, the licensee, this successful and vibrant urban pub offers a welcome to a remarkably diverse clientele, and has been a winner of the local CAMRA Pub of the Year award. Service from the young staff is attentive and efficient, and from the six handpumps and two gravity dispenses there's a good range of beers to choose from, with Dark Star, Hog's Back and Westerham among the regularly represented breweries.

The Green Dragon's 'Love Croydon' window

Continue along the street, and you've hardly time to draw breath before encountering the **Bull's Head** 5 on the next corner. As far as the real ale drinker is concerned this little local has lived in the shadow of the Royal Standard for many years but has improved steadily in the range and quality of ales, so that today it's well worth including on a quality tour of Croydon's pubs. The interior is now simplicity itself – an L-shaped bar arranged around a similar shaped

servery. Fittings are plain but comfortable, and there's a dartboard at one end. Beer-wise, expect Courage Best and Doom Bar as regulars, with a couple of selections from the Enterprise list and one guest, with the guv'nor favouring the new Croydon brewery Cronx at the time of writing. He also lays on three beer festivals a year: check the pages of 'London Drinker' for these.

Head up back to the main High Street, noting the handsome listed Wrencote House opposite, reputedly designed by a pupil of Sir Christopher Wren and built around 1720. Bear right and walk down the main road for few minutes, before, on the corner of West Street, coming upon pub number six, the **Half & Half** 6 . A shop conversion on a rather more modest scale than earlier examples, this in its previous incarnation was the mildly famous *Beer Circus* which in the early 'noughties' dispensed the widest range of bottled foreign beers in Greater London, and although the place was rather tatty it was frequently packed. The new owners have smartened the place up nicely, not least the toilets, but have retained two handpumps, dispensing Dark Star Hophead and a rotating, often locally brewed, guest. They have a more modest but nonetheless still worthwhile range of American, Czech, Belgian and German bottled beers on offer too.

The Royal Standard – a classic street-corner boozer, dwarfed by the bulk of the Croydon flyover

LEFT: **The Bull's Head has improved steadily** RIGHT: **The Skylark is a *Good Beer Guide* regular**

If you're still on your feet, it's a five minute stroll, a marathon by the standards of this route, to the final official stop. Continue south to the traffic lights and carry straight on, the road is now called South End. Pass the cycle shop on the opposite side of the road. On 'our' side of the street a little further is the **Skylark 7**. Like the *George* (see Walk 29) this former gymnasium hosts another well above average JD Wetherspoon in an attractive Art Deco building. Although the interior follows the well-established JDW pattern, the spacious drinking area is arranged on two levels and the ambience is very relaxed. Beer range is nearly always good, and often includes locally-sourced microbrewery offerings; quality is good, and the pub is another *Good Beer Guide* regular.

By now, you will either be ready for a walking workout – in which case you may appreciate the opportunity to walk back into town along the main road, which will take about ten minutes; or you'll be dead on your feet, and in that event I would recommend the bus – any bus heading north will take you back into the centre. If you're a real heavyweight and still have space for more, the George, on George Street, has the best beer range in Croydon, served in excellent condition, as evidenced by its local CAMRA Pub of the Year award in 2011. For a full description, see the entry on the Tramlink tour, Walk 29, page 178.

PUB INFORMATION

1 Dog & Bull
24 Surrey Street, Croydon,
CRO 1RG
020 8667 9718
Opening Hours: 11-11 (11.30 Fri
& summer Sat); 12-10.30 Sun

2 Spread Eagle
39-41 Katharine Street, Croydon,
CRO 1NX
020 8781 1134
Opening Hours: 11-11 (midnight
Thu-Sat); 12-10.30 Sun

3 Green Dragon
58-60 High Street, Croydon,
CRO 1NA
020 8667 0684
www.greendragoncroydon.co.uk
Opening Hours: 10-midnight
(1am Fri & Sat); 12-10.30 Sun

4 Royal Standard
1 Sheldon Street, Croydon,
CRO 1SS
020 8688 9749
www.royalstandard-croydon.
co.uk
Opening Hours: 12-midnight
(11 Sun)

5 Bull's Head
39 Laud Street, Croydon, CRO 1SX
020 8760 0150
Opening Hours: 11.30-11
(midnight Fri & Sat)

6 Half & Half
282 High Street, Croydon,
CRO 1NG
020 8726 0080
www.halfandhalf.uk.com
Opening Hours: 12 (3 Sat)-
midnight; 3-11 Sun

7 Skylark
34-36 South End, Croydon,
CRO 1DP
020 8649 9909
Opening Hours: 9am-midnight
(1am Fri & Sat)

The Half & Half has an interesting range of bottled beers

Carshalton & the Wandle Trail

WALK INFORMATION

Start and Finish: ⇌ Carshalton (NB NOT Carshalton Beeches); or ⊖ Morden and walk via Wandle Trail

Distance: 2 miles (3.2km)

Access: Trains from ⇌ Victoria (30 mins) or via Thameslink services from ⇌ Blackfriars (30 mins)

Key attractions: Wilderness Island Local Nature Reserve; River Wandle Trail; Grove Park; Honeywood Museum; Carshalton House Water Tower

The pubs: Railway Tavern; Lord Palmerston; Sun; Windsor Castle; Racehorse; Hope. Try also: Greyhound

The Railway Tavern

Despite being overwhelmed by suburban development nearly a century ago, locals still talk about 'the village', and the centre of Carshalton stills retains a distinctive identity. Several parks and open spaces, some quite small, straddle Carshalton's river, the Wandle, and there are a number of attractive buildings, especially those assembled around Carshalton Ponds. The Wandle Trail offers a pleasant stroll along an almost continuous ribbon of open spaces from Morden, three miles north; and for the more energetic, I would strongly recommend this well-signed walk to build up a thirst – it's full of interest all the way. Start at Morden Hall Park, just minutes from the Underground station.

The walk described here is rather more compact, and picks up the Wandle Trail much closer to the village at Wilderness Island, one of the best spots on the river, before a short walk up into the village centre.

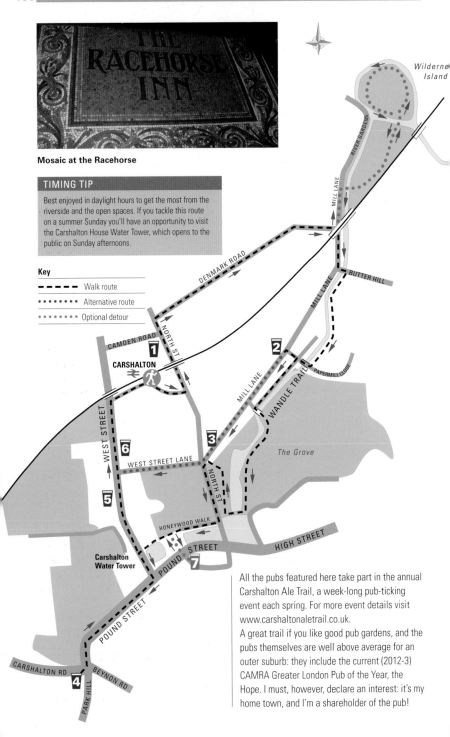

Mosaic at the Racehorse

TIMING TIP

Best enjoyed in daylight hours to get the most from the riverside and the open spaces. If you tackle this route on a summer Sunday you'll have an opportunity to visit the Carshalton House Water Tower, which opens to the public on Sunday afternoons.

Key

- - - - Walk route

• • • • • • Alternative route

• • • • • • Optional detour

All the pubs featured here take part in the annual Carshalton Ale Trail, a week-long pub-ticking event each spring. For more event details visit www.carshaltonaletrail.co.uk.

A great trail if you like good pub gardens, and the pubs themselves are well above average for an outer suburb: they include the current (2012-3) CAMRA Greater London Pub of the Year, the Hope. I must, however, declare an interest: it's my home town, and I'm a shareholder of the pub!

There's always a mouth-watering choice on the Hope's guest taps

Head left out of the station and walk down to North Street at the foot of the hill. Turn left again, under the bridge, and you've already arrived at the first stop of the day. The **Railway Tavern** [1] now opens at 10am but I'd phone ahead to check if you're planning an early start. Like a number of Carshalton pubs it was a former Charrington's house until about 1980 when it was acquired by Fuller's. An unassuming but attractive Victorian corner pub, it now has a single drinking area around the horseshoe bar. At the time of writing it's Hobson's choice with the beer: London Pride. The previous guv'nor developed the attractive garden at the side of the pub, which is a very pleasant retreat for an early pint. If you've opted for the walk from Morden, you'll miss this pub at the start but in consultation with your map you can include it later in the round.

From here, cross North Street and head down Denmark Road, almost opposite. Five minutes of mundane suburbia will bring you down to the River Wandle at the far end of the street. Cross to the riverside and turn downstream, away from the striking Three Arch Bridge, for just a few yards the entrance to Wilderness Island, over the river bridge. A detour to take in this small but well-wooded local nature reserve is recommended: it's an area with quite a history. There are no pubs here, and it's very much an optional extra to walk around the small but well-wooded site, but it's an

area with quite a history. At the far end of the site, over the further bridge, is the confluence of the two branches of the river, from Croydon and Carshalton. It was a very important mill site, and the terminus of a branch of the old Surrey Iron Railway, the world's first public railway. For those with an interest in this small river with a big history, I might humbly recommend my book *A River Wandle Companion* (www.wandlebook.co.uk). Back at the entrance to the reserve, walk back upstream now, under the bridge, and reach the road junction of Mill Lane and Butter Hill. Here the corner building is the much disguised remains of an old snuff mill, but maybe of more interest is the fish pass running up the former wheel pit, installed by the Wandle Trust to assist trout in reaching the upper reaches of the river, and visible from the bridge. Cross the bridge and turn sharp right along the riverside, along a restored stretch which until twenty years ago was factory land with no public access. Now it's a link in the Wandle Trail, which hugs the riverside almost continuously from the source to its confluence with the Thames at Wandsworth. Pass the wooden footbridge and meet a road shortly beyond. Unlikely as it may now seem, here once stood one of the most celebrated paper mills in England. Only the name of the road is left to offer a link to the past. Turn right here to rejoin Mill Lane right by the

The Sun stands on a prominent corner site

Lord Palmerston 2. The only survivor of several workingmens' pubs which once stood on this street, the 'Palm' still sports its old Courage red cockrel outside, and retains its traditional, two room layout: public bar and lounge. You may be able to spot the old pewter sinks which have survived here! There are as a rule three beers to select from, and although there is sometimes an alternative, it's usually Sharp's Doom Bar, Courage Best and Wells Bombardier.

Return to the Wandle Trail which now runs on the right hand bank of the river (walking upstream). In just 100 yards turn left and cross the river again, and follow the path into The Grove, an attractive riverside park which allows you to follow the river right up to Carshalton Ponds, the present-day source of the Wandle, in the village centre. Following the riverbank, pass the cascade and the large house, also known as The Grove on your left. The park was once the grounds of this once private mansion, bought by the local council for the town in 1924. At the graceful and slender

Leoni Bridge pause to admire the view across the pond to the substantial parish church, before crossing the bridge and following the main path, away from the river a little, round and down to exit onto North Street. If it's after sunset the gates into the park will be closed and you'll need to continue along Mill Lane. A few yards further on, unmissable and very distinctive on a prominent corner site, stands the **Sun** 3. As one might expect from the size and decoration of the building, this was in the past a far more important and imposing hostelry than the others we have visited so far. Built in 1870 just after the coming of the railway it was a hotel aimed at the new trade and traffic the railway would bring. The name is said to derive from the fact that the windows in the hotel rooms could expect sunlight nearly all day in view of the orientation of the building.

After a period of ups and downs the Sun has been given a completely new lease of life under its new owners. I have to admit that the total redesign of the interior with some very good quality fittings has more than compensated for the otherwise regrettable loss of the separate public bar. The smart but tasteful refurbishment is complemented by a total transformation of the back yard into a charming pub garden which is a very popular hangout in almost all weathers. Although the pub majors on good quality food, it has also installed a set of five handpumps offering a changing and interesting range of beers, often from small independent breweries.

It's possible at this point to shorten the route by heading up West Street Lane across the road from the Sun to rejoin the trail at the Racehorse (see map); but the official route heads back up North Street, between the walls, and into Honeywood Walk, on your right, alongside the western of the town's twin ponds. There's a great view of the parish church, the Greyhound (see below) and to the right, Honeywood, an Edwardian mansion which now functions as a museum and tea room. If you wish to take in the **Greyhound** 7 this is the time to do so: it's been a Young's house for well over a century but like many other locals I am very sore about the internal alterations carried out by the company which in my opinion has all but destroyed the character of the place, and there are rumours that another round of 'improvements' will shortly target the Swan Bar, currently the only room I would recommend, if you can find it open. Beers are from Wells & Young's, with guests. If you do visit, look for the lovely old greyhound floor mosaic at the Swan Bar entrance, assuming it hasn't been buried under a carpet!

Return, if need be, to the route at the corner of the pond, by the little gatehouse to The Lodge and at the entrance to Festival Walk, a pleasant footpath which leads past a venerable old London plane tree, the capital's largest specimen, and the entrance to the grounds of the Ecology Centre, with views of the unusual water tower ahead. The unique Grade II-listed building contained a water-powered pump, which supplied water to Carshalton House (still standing behind the high wall, and now a school) and the fountains in its garden. However, the building was and is much more than this as it contains a suite of rooms, the highlights being an orangery and a remarkable early 18th century bathroom with a plunge bath lined with Delft blue tiles. It's only open to the public on summer Sundays, check the website (www.carshaltonwatertower.co.uk).

Follow the wall south alongside West Street to the junction fifty yards away and follow the road round to the right up to the traffic lights in 300 yards (you might prefer to cross to the other side where the footway is wider). At the lights, occupying a prominent position, is another well-known drinking landmark, the **Windsor Castle** 4. This *Good Beer Guide* regular is a spacious one-room pub with a pleasant garden which you may need help in finding. Once a *de facto* free house and an erstwhile winner of CAMRA's London Pub of the Year award, the Windsor is now in the hands of Shepherd Neame, offering a rare local opportunity to sample a range of three of their beers. However the tradition of offering guest beers here continues, and a further three handpumps dispense two rotating guests and Long Man Best Bitter from the eponymous Sussex micro. Food, from simple bar snacks and light bites to a restaurant menu, is available at most times, with a Sunday carvery. Check the website for the menus.

Retrace your steps down to the Water Tower but this time continue along West Street, passing some attractive old weatherboarded houses on the right. The buildings on either side of the entrance to Old Swan Yard on the left are both interesting. That on the near corner is the former *Swan* itself (now a private house), from where the daily coach to London once departed; the larger one on the opposite corner is the former National Schools building. A short step beyond and a rather poor new pub sign announces the **Racehorse** 5. This substantial looking pub is

The Wandle runs through The Grove

the second on this trail to boast a separate public bar, and the second to have a rather fine floor mosaic in the entrance lobby. The room on the right is the plain public bar; that on the left the larger saloon, where you'll want to head if you plan to eat. The pub, in the Enterprise Inns estate, has had more than one change of management of late but the new licensees are promoting their menu and an expanding bill of live music, as well as their real ales. Currently there are two regulars, Young's Bitter and Doom Bar, and a couple of changing guests. Food is available pretty much all day apart from Mondays.

The final port of call is visible by its sign another hundred yards down the road when you leave the Racehorse. For London beer scene aficionados it may need no introduction, for the **Hope** 6 is the 2012 CAMRA Greater London Pub of the Year, a remarkable rags-to-riches story for a pub that came close to calling time forever just a few years ago. A group of local people got together and negotiated a long free-of-tie lease from Punch Taverns, and are now hoping to buy the freehold outright. Starting with a couple of cask ales the beer range has expanded steadily under the careful and knowledgeable stewardship of the

young cellar manager and his team so that it is now among the most ambitious outside of Central London, and quality is second to none. On handpump, expect two regular beers (one traditional bitter and a lighter hoppy companion) plus five rapidly rotating guests from some of Britain's best micros, among them Arbor, Magic Rock, Brodie's and Redemption. Additionally there are some exciting and rarely seen (even in London) craft keg offerings, often at industrial grade gravities; and a small but serious list of bottled beers. All draught beers are available in multiples of one third of a pint, a useful option if you're going up-gravity.

The pub is a real community hub and you can expect a friendly welcome. Local events are advertised here and there are frequently impromptu music sessions and other happenings. Check the website for details of upcoming beer festivals, usually themed, and taking place with remarkable frequency in the spacious garden.

If you miss the last train home (and it's a hard pub to leave) ask at the bar for directions to bus stops: the 157 in particular runs late and will take you to the Underground railhead at Morden, or into Croydon for all-night trains.

PUB INFORMATION

1 Railway Tavern
47 North Street, Carshalton,
SM5 2HG
020 8669 8016
www.railwaytaverncarshalton.
co.uk
Opening Hours: 10-11 (10.30 Sun)

2 Lord Palmerston
31 Mill Lane, Carshalton,
SM5 2JY
020 8647 1222
Opening Hours: 11-11;
12-10.30 Sun

3 Sun
North Street, Carshalton,
SM5 2HU
020 8773 4549
www.thesuncarshalton.com
Opening Hours: 12 (5 Mon)-11
(midnight Fri & Sat); 12-10.30

4 Windsor Castle
378 Carshalton Road, Carshalton,
SM5 3PT
020 8669 1191
www.windsorcastlepub.com
Opening Hours: 11-11 (11.30 Fri
& Sat); 12-10.30 Sun

5 Racehorse
17 West Street, Carshalton,
SM5 2PT
020 8647 6818
www.racehorseinns.co.uk
Opening Hours: 11-11;
12-10.30 Sun

6 Hope
48 West Street, Carshalton,
SM5 2PR
020 8240 1255
www.hopecarshalton.co.uk
Opening Hours: 12-11 (10.30 Sun)

TRY ALSO:

7 Greyhound Hotel
2 High Street, Carshalton,
SM5 3PE
020 8647 1511
www.greyhoundhotel.net
Opening Hours: 11 (12
Sun)-midnight

Kingston & Teddington via Bushy Park and the Thames Path

WALK INFORMATION

Start: Kingston (or Fulwell for linear walk omitting Bushy Park).

Finish: Kingston

Distance: 6.6 miles (10.7km) for the circuit from Kingston

Access: From Waterloo/Clapham Junction; or by X26 express bus: Croydon-Carshalton-Kingston-Heathrow

Key attractions: Bushy Park; Thames Path

The pubs: Roebuck; Masons Arms; Clock House; Boaters Inn

Bushy Park in autumn

Nowhere near as well-known as Richmond Park, Bushy Park is also a Royal Park, originally laid out for hunting but these days the stags have an easier time of it. At just half the size of Richmond that still makes it pretty large: 450 hectares. It's big enough to enable you to feel that London is a long way off; the perfect place for a longer walk before enjoying the first pint of the day. There are options to lengthen the Bushy Park section by taking in the woodland gardens riverside walks along the Longford River. The pubs selected here offer between them a wide choice of beers, and if the sun is out when you arrive at the Boaters, you may well wish to linger by the riverside with the option of an all-day food menu.

Be aware that's about three miles to the Roebuck from Kingston station. If you get cold feet (or it starts raining) catch a 285 (towards Heathrow) from Wood Street in Kingston to the Roebuck instead!

Arriving by train at Kingston (the X26 stops in Wood Street which is much closer to Kingston Bridge) you don't see the town at its best, so pick your feet up and head along the foot/ cycle way sharp right out the station and follow it for about 250 yards before it leads you to the right under the railway (still on the cycle route) and then sharp left to the riverside, where head left along the Thames and under Kingston Bridge, turning up the slope on the north side to join the road on the bridge. Things improve quickly from here. Once across the bridge swing round left and cross the road by the *Old King's Head* into Church Grove. Look for then gateway in about 100 yards with the London Loop sign and head onto the gravel path lined with chestnuts, past the skatepark. This brings you into Bushy Park proper in a few moments. The deer park stretches away from you

towards the horizon, without any sign of the first pub! There are around 300 red and fallow deer still roaming freely throughout the park, just as they would have done when Henry VIII hunted here.

There are good maps at each of the entrances so you can plot your own way across the park. To follow the route here, head across the grass track leaving at about 45 degrees right beyond the cricket square, reaching the left hand edge of the plantation of deciduous trees ahead (the Oval Plantation). Keep close to the edge of the trees as the tracks bifurcate, bringing you quickly to the Heron Pond, a pleasant spot to stop for your flask if you have one with you. From here track around the pond to the south (left) and cross the first rustic wooden bridge at the far end, as the car park looms into view. Now bear half left away from the pond and head obliquely towards the road across the park, the Chestnut Avenue, crossing this close to the palisaded compound which is part of the woodland gardens. Keep these on your immediate left as you follow parallel to the road on a good path. Bear left to follow another road and pass

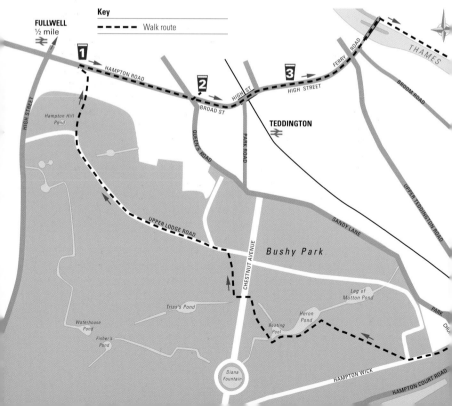

The difficult-to-miss Roebuck

the two gatehouses to Bushy House, as you take the right fork at the sign to 'Water Gardens [and] Hampton Hill'. It's another mile or so via this untrafficked road, and then a short path section where it bears left to the water garden, before you reach the Laurel Road gate. Once you get there, it's straight up the road ahead to the junction with Hampton Road and left, when you'll see the first stop of the day on the next corner. The **Roebuck 1** stands out a little too much with its gaudy red paint job, but once inside it's a different story. Homely and intimate with numerous nooks and corners in its opened out layout, every surface is covered with a remarkable collection of ephemera, and each time you visit you'll doubtless see something new. In one corner there's a display of the various awards the pub has picked up for its beer and its flower displays. This local is well-patronised, and no wonder, for apart from the inviting atmosphere there's a tempting range of beers: regulars Young's Bitter, St Austell Tribute and Sambrook's Junction are joined by two constantly changing guests; expect them to be in very good condition. To complement

this on weekday lunchtimes (until 2pm) there's a tempting array of food from sandwiches to full meals. You may not fall victim to them, but traffic lights in the bar and garden turn amber, then red as 'time' looms.

The next leg involves a traverse of about half a mile down the Hampton Road to Teddington, with not much to recommend it, so I would favour catching a bus (both the 285 and R68 will do) three stops down to Teddington Memorial Hospital at the junction with Stanley Road. Cross Stanley Road and between the two modern blocks at the junction you'll see the **Masons Arms 2** down the pedestrian alley. The part-tiled exterior goes back to a mid twentieth century rebuild, and the most interesting thing about it is arguably that there are no less than five separate doorways, most now blocked off, of course. For a suburban pub it's very rare to see quite this many. The entrance on the corner has only recently been brought back into use, and it's been done to blend in well. In the capable hands of licensee Rachel (Rae to the regulars) who has 20 years' experience in the place, the Masons, not long free of tie, has now become a must for discerning beer drinkers in Teddington. A comfortable carpeted drinking area, with stove at one end, wraps around the spacious servery; choose from four ales, regulars Downton Quadhop and Sambrook's Junction joined by two changing guests. Some interesting old prints on the wall show the changing appearance of the pub over the years, but pride of place (in what was once a Watney's house) must surely go to the 'Party Seven' can of Red Barrel behind the bar.

Continue along Teddington's main street (or take the bus, 285 or R68) two more stops over the railway bridge and into the High Street, where opposite Field Lane you won't miss the **Clock House 3** in a prominent location despite advertising itself as Teddington's 'hidden gem'!? Maybe to a blind man... Like the Masons, this was once in the estate of the old Isleworth brewery, but a major makeover about five years back has pretty well obliterated anything of the past. The interior is intensely modern: high seats, floorboards, straight lines, around a horseshoe bar with an outside paved area and a rear dining room. The result is not to

Listed suspension bridge at Teddington Lock

my taste but it may be to yours. Something you can rely on is the beer quality which has earned the pub a place in the *Good Beer Guide*. Expect Fuller's London Pride and Sharp's Cornish Coaster as regulars with a couple of changing guests, often favouring reliable local micro Twickenham. Food on weekday lunchtimes is available until 3pm, if you're planning ahead.

The walk continues by following the length of Teddington High Street (pleasanter than most) to the junction with the A310 Kingston Road, where cross ahead into Ferry Road for the short walk down to the Thames. You'll pass two further pubs at this point, the *Tide End Cottage* (Greene King) and the *Anglers* (Fuller's), quite satisfactory as additional stops although not, I would suggest, at the expense of the next official call on the walk. To get there, cross the river and the navigation by Teddington Lock here, the former on a pretty suspension bridge, which dates

back to 1888, and was listed in 2005. The lock itself, at the highest point of the tidal Thames, was constructed in 1811-12. Once on the Surrey side it's simply a matter of following the river closely on the path (the cycle path is a few yards 'inland') along a pleasant mile or so, lined with boats, until approaching Kingston once more, you reach the narrow riverside park of Canbury Gardens, and, adjacent a boathouse which gives the pub its name, the **Boaters 4** . The building would win no awards but the location is its trump card, right on the river and with an outside terrace to complement the room-with-a-view within. The other draw of course is the beer menu, which has seemingly got better with every change of licensee. Expect five changing guests alongside the house beer, with an emphasis upon the local – Dark Star, Sambrook's and Surrey Hills often to be seen, whilst two offerings from Meantime on the keg founts are also available. There are plans to expand the bottled beer range, which already contains several from North London micro Camden Town. With this the last stop on the route it's useful to know that a full food menu is available pretty much throughout, with a short afternoon interregnum during winter; phone ahead if it's critical.

A short walk further along the riverside will return you to the path you reached the Thames on earlier in the day if you started here, just before the rail bridge, where head inland and keep to the cycle route back to the station in about five minutes. If you're of a mind to linger in Kingston for more refreshments, and you could do worse, consult your *Good Beer Guide* along with your street map.

PUB INFORMATION

1 Roebuck
72 Hampton Road, TW12 1JN
020 8255 8133
Opening Hours: 11-11 (11.30 Fri & Sat); 12-4, 7-10.30 Sun

2 Masons Arms
41 Walpole Road, TW11 8PJ
020 8977 6521
Opening Hours: 12-11 (11.30 Fri & Sat); 12-10.30

3 Clock House
69 High Street, TW11 8HA
020 8977 3909
www.theclockhousepub.com
Opening Hours: 11-11.30 (midnight Fri & Sat; 11 Sun)

4 Boaters
Canbury Gardens, Lower Ham Road, KT2 5AU
020 8541 4672
www.boaterskingston.com
Opening Hours: 11 (12 Sun)-11

STARTING AT FULWELL STATION

It's only about five minutes down to the Roebuck from Fulwell station: exit onto the A311 Wellington Road, and turn left (south) heading down to the traffic lights. Here, turn left again, and the Roebuck is the unmissable building on the next corner.

Richmond & Twickenham via the Thames Path

WALK INFORMATION

Start: ≥ ⇔ ⊖ Richmond

Finish: ≥ Strawberry Hill

Distance: 4.5 miles (7.2km)

Access: From ≥ Waterloo/ Clapham Junction

Key attractions: Richmond; Ham House; Marble Hill House and park; Orleans House Gallery; Eel Pie Island; Thames Path

The pubs: Waterman's Arms; White Cross; Victoria; Roebuck; White Swan; Sussex Arms; Rifleman; Prince of Wales

Richmond is one of London's most elegant suburbs and occupies an enviable position on one of the loveliest reaches of the Thames. Once a favoured royal residence, Richmond Palace was rebuilt under Henry VII and renamed after his earldom in Yorkshire. Oliver Cromwell destroyed most of it after 1649. This walk takes in several pubs in the town before leading off upstream into Twickenham, with another handful of very good drinking options. Provided the ferry is operating (see below), the riverside walk is best down on the Surrey side before crossing into Middlesex and continuing into Twickenham. *En route* there are also cultural opportunities, notably at Ham House. For those who prefer to leave the bulk of the drinking until the walking is done, consider leaving some or all of the Richmond stops until the end, returning by train or bus to Richmond from Strawberry Hill. The best pubs for beer range are the Roebuck and the Sussex Arms.

The stone arches of Richmond Bridge

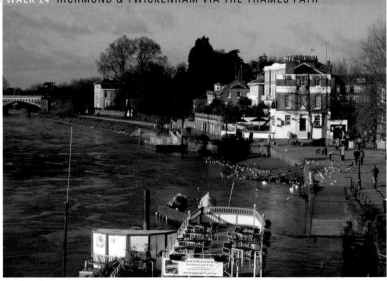

Richmond riverside and the White Cross

Start at Richmond station with its frequent and fast trains from Central London. Upon exit cross the road at the pelican crossing and head through the covered passageway directly ahead (Capital Ring path sign) meeting a quieter road (Little Green) in fifty yards where bear left. Cross the railway bridge and pass Richmond Theatre to arrive at the corner of Richmond

Green. This open space was originally a common where villagers pastured their sheep, but later on it became a medieval jousting ground alongside Richmond Palace. It's now a haven of tranquillity very close to the centre of town and bordered by attractive, mostly Georgian houses. The terrace on the far side next to the old Palace is called Maids of Honour Row, so-named as this was where the unmarried daughters of monarchs once lived. Stay on pretty much the same bearing, on the path, keeping

TIMING TIP

If planning to use Hammerton's Ferry it's strongly recommended you establish that the service is definitely operating by phoning them (020 8892 9620). There's no service in November and a limited one in winter. Given the attractive riverside views this is a walk best enjoyed on a long sunny day. At very high water levels, be warned that both riverside paths are liable to flooding.

Key

– – – – Walk route

• • • • • • • Alternative route

to the left hand side of the Green as you look at it. At the far side, swing left and exit into the town centre via King Street. There are maps on the Green if you need help!

Turn down Water Lane by the *Old Ship*. This narrow and atmospheric street runs down to the river, and the **Waterman's Arms** 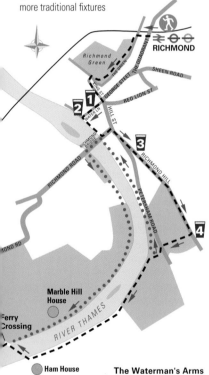 still looks like it might be hiding some smugglers or at least lightermen from the days of river trade. It started life as a simple beerhouse, originally named the *King's Head*. Inside it's still quite intimate and retains some more traditional fixtures

and fittings. It offers Young's staple beers and seasonals, and Twickenham's Naked Ladies is a fixture here too. For a small pub the menu is extensive (available all day), and features Thai and Chinese dishes alongside more traditional fare.

Just yards down the lane you'll reach the river, and the elegant Richmond Bridge. Constructed in 1777, this is the oldest Thames bridge still in use and arguably one of the most handsome. To your right is the **White Cross** 2 , a Richmond institution. The name stems from a convent built by Henry VII in 1499, with a white cross being the friars' insignia. There has been a pub here at least since 1780 although the present building dates from 1835. It's a very spacious but popular pub and at certain times you might find it difficult to get a seat. For this iconic pub it's all about location, with great views over the water from the window seats; in fact the pub is so close to the river that the tide regularly inundates the shore here and entry to the pub is only via the side steps. The interior is smart but not vulgar, and I'm pleased that they have retained a floorboard covering around the bar. Beers are of course from Young's with seasonals which can feature other breweries; and there are beer festivals at least twice annually – check the website. It's a pleasant place when it's quiet earlier in the day; if it's overrun by the hordes in high summer it's perhaps best to leave this one and move on.

Walk to the bridge, and gain the roadway either via the slope or the steps. Turn left up to the road junction (note the 1930s Art Deco Odeon cinema with Egyptian-style decoration on the exterior). Turn right onto Hill Street and, crossing the road, fork to the left onto Hill Rise keeping the little green on your right. Here sits Richmond's smallest pub, the **Victoria** 3 . There's only a single room although clearly there were once at least two. On the comfortable seats overlooking the green you can enjoy a choice of three ales, Doom Bar, Young's Bitter and a guest. An alternative place to sit is the rear courtyard. Appropriately for such a small pub, food is confined to simple snacks.

For the last official stop in town, and the widest beer choice in Richmond, continue up Hill Rise for the best part of half a mile – the distance will go quickly though for as you climb higher onto Richmond Hill you'll be able to cut

The Waterman's Arms

LEFT: **The single-room Victoria** RIGHT: **One of Europe's greatest 17th-century houses: Ham House**

into the Terrace Gardens on the right hand side of the road, with an increasingly wide panorama across the river and the country beyond. It's one of London's iconic views, which has long inspired writers and artists, and along the terrace here you'll find the **Roebuck** 4 . It would be worth coming here for the view alone but these days the pub is also a destination in its own right, for its great choice of well-kept ales. Expect no less than seven changing beers from near and far (London Pride, the eighth, is a regular). There's also an extensive food menu available at most times. Looking out, you should be able to pick out several landmarks, from the roof of Ham House close to the river below you, to the rugby stadium at Twickenham across the river further right.

There's a set of steps, a few yards right of the pub, from the terrace down towards the riverside. Take these, and at Petersham Road, look for the entry to the riverside path a few yards to the right again. Now it's decision time. If you're confident of your ferry connection, bear left along the riverside past Petersham Meadows, and it's a few more minutes of pleasant riverside path before you arrive by Ham House, and the ferry pontoon. Ham House is a very worthwhile detour if you've built it into your itinerary; The National trust describe it as 'unique in Europe as the most complete survival of 17th century fashion and power'. Once across the ferry, at a point close to Marble Hill Park, pick up the route at * below.

The alternative route at the riverside is to head back downstream to Richmond Bridge, and cross to the Twickenham (north) side, and pick up the Thames Path heading upstream. It's a very nice walk along the banks of the river passing Marble Hill House, a fashionable Georgian villa in the Palladian style, built for Henrietta Howard, mistress of King George II when he was Prince of Wales. The grounds are also open to the public. Pass the ferry pontoon (*where readers taking the ferry join us) and continue a little further to where the Thames Path leaves the riverside by Orleans House. Originally built as country retreat, it features the distinctive Octagon Room, built around 1720, and is now a gallery in the hands of the local authority. See www.richmond.gov.uk/orleans_house_gallery for opening hours and admission details.

The pleasant little lane, called Riverside, winds beyond the gallery and in this old part of Twickenham is the next pub stop, the **White Swan** 5 . Sited a safe distance from the water's edge (although the basement is reserved for the facilities and you need to climb up to enter the pub), this is an attractive old building which has been tastefully brought up to date inside, with stripped floors and a classy paint job on the interior timber. There's plenty of seating inside, including a nice window bench; if you're lucky, you might be able to bag the outside veranda seats with river views. The Swan is now a free house, and the five beers are sourced from all over but with a local emphasis: Twickenham and Sambrook's are favoured micros alongside regular Sharp's Doom Bar. As you might expect, there's a wide menu available all day weekends, with an afternoon break during the week.

Carry on down the lane, passing some pretty houses, until you emerge by the *Barmy Arms* and, the footbridge onto famous Eel Pie Island. This little ait in the Thames has had a remarkable history, perhaps most notably as a venue for all sorts of famous rock and blues artists who performed at the legendary Eel Pie Hotel on the island, particularly during the 1960s. The hotel was destroyed by fire in 1971, but not before it had been occupied by an anarchist/hippy commune including illustrator Clifford Harper. The Who frontman Pete Townshend had his studios here, but these days it's most well-known as an artists' retreat. You can cross onto the island via the footbridge and walk around.

Head directly away from the river here into King Street in Twickenham town centre. The walk to the next pub has little to recommend it, so jump on a bus (this side of the road, westbound). Take route 110, 490 or H22, for four stops, just past Twickenham Green, to First Cross Road. If you do decide to walk it, fork right at the junction just up to the left, and walk along the northern side of Twickenham Green. The bus will deposit you almost outside the **Sussex Arms** ⑥. It presents a handsome frontage to the street, and inside this prewar local there are still some period features such as wood panelling and brickwork,

but the real draw is the remarkable range of beer and cider taps, which currently stands at eighteen. This follows a recent makeover as an ale and cider house. Expect rapidly rotating and interesting stuff from all over the place, supporting independent breweries. The informed service and well-kept beer, supported by well-regarded food, has made the Sussex a firm favourite with just about all its visitors, and there can be few if any suburban pubs which offer such a range of ales. The interior ambience is pleasant enough, but there's also a large garden which features a boules pitch.

Continue along the Staines Road for five minutes or so until you reach Fourth Cross Road, and head down the street of pleasant late-Victorian villas. Right near the bottom of the road is a traditional old street corner local which offers a nice contrast to the Sussex. The **Rifleman** ⑦ now sports a new pub sign, dedicating the pub to local Rifleman Frank Edwards, the 'Footballer of Loos'. Ask about the story inside. The Rifleman retains a traditional feel with seating arranged on the wooden floor around the horseshoe bar; and despite the presence outside of the Courage cockrels, these days the beers are more diverse, with a choice of up to five including one or two from locals Twickenham, with Butcombe Bitter and Young's Bitter among the other regulars.

It's only the shortest of steps to the last pub: simply head down to the bottom of the road and you'll see it there on the corner. The **Prince of Wales** ⑧ is a substantial double-fronted

The Sussex Arms offers eighteen beer and cider taps

The traditional interior of the Rifleman

Victorian house with some period detail remaining, among those a badge from former owners the little lamented Watneys atop the pub sign. Inside, the central bar dominates the smart and rather formal rooms, with a variety of seating including leathery sofas. The beer range and quality, as testified by a 2011 local CAMRA Pub of the Year award, is light years ahead of its former Watneys days. Expect seven, with one from the local Twickenham micro among the fixtures. There's food available each day except Monday, and it ranges from snacks to a serious menu. In good weather, check out the spacious garden, but be prepared to share it with dogs and free-range children.

To get home, or to return to Richmond, it's a ten minute walk to Strawberry Hill station: cross the Hampton Road, bear right and take Wellesley Road, the first left. If you don't fancy the walk, step up to the bus stop, on the same side of Hampton Road, and take bus 267 or 281 to Twickenham station, for trains back to either Richmond, or Clapham and Central London. The frequent R70 bus leaves from the same stop and goes all the way to Richmond.

PUB INFORMATION

1 Waterman's Arms
10-12 Water Lane, Richmond, TW9 1TJ
020 8940 2893
Opening Hours: 11 (12 Sun)-11

2 White Cross
Riverside, off Water Lane, Richmond, TW9 1TH
020 8940 6844
www.thewhitecrossrichmond.com
Opening Hours: 10-11 (10.30 Sun)

3 Victoria
78 Hill Rise, Richmond, TW10 6UB
020 8940 2531
Opening Hours: 11 (10 Fri & Sat)-11 (midnight Thu-Sat); 12-10.30 Sun

4 Roebuck
130 Richmond Hill, Richmond, TW10 6RN
020 8948 2329
Opening Hours: 12-11; 11-midnight Fri & Sat; 12-10.30 Sun

5 White Swan
Riverside, Twickenham, TW1 3DN
020 8744 2951
whiteswantwickenham.com
Opening Hours: 12-11 (10.30 Sun)

6 Sussex Arms
15 Staines Road, Twickenham, TW2 5BG
020 8894 7468
www.thesussexarmstwickenham.co.uk
Opening Hours: 12-11 (10.30 Sun)12-10.30 Sun

7 Rifleman
Fourth Cross Road, Twickenham, TW2 5EL
020 8893 3836
www.theriflemanpub.co.uk
Opening Hours: 2 (12 Fri-Sun)-11(10.30 Sun)

8 Prince of Wales
136 Hampton Road, Twickenham, TW2 5QR
020 8894 5054
www.princeofwalestwickenham.co.uk
Opening Hours: 12 (4 Mon)-11 (midnight Thu-Sat); 12-10.30 Sun

Isleworth to Kew along the Thames via Syon Park

WALK INFORMATION

Start: Isleworth

Finish: Kew Green, for Kew Bridge or Kew Gardens

Distance: 3.6 miles (5.8km)

Access: From London Waterloo & Clapham Junction

Key attractions: Kew Botanic Gardens; Kew Steam Museum; Osterley Park; Syon Park House and gardens

The pubs: Red Lion; London Apprentice; Magpie & Crown; Brewery Tap; Watermans Arms; Express Tavern; Botanist

This is a varied walk of about three miles, full of interest, and strongly recommended for a sunny weekend. It takes us through Old Isleworth on the bank of the Thames, into Syon Park and on to Brentford, where we rejoin the river before crossing Kew Bridge and finishing at the Botanist brewpub, close to Kew Green. Throw in several top-notch pubs, offering, between them, among the widest variety of beers from independent breweries in South West London and it's easy to see why this is such a popular walk.

A shorter version of this trail is possible by alighting at Brentford and starting at the Magpie & Crown, but this means you'll miss Syon Park and some excellent pubs!

The Great Conservatory in Syon Park

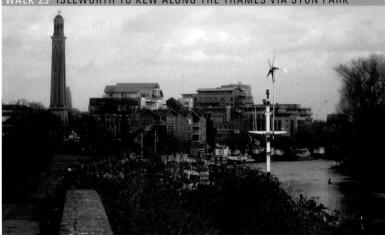

Thames Path in Brentford, looking towards Kew Steam Museum

This is a train trip, so start at Waterloo or Clapham Junction and take the frequent South West Trains service to Isleworth (35 minutes from Waterloo). For a shorter version of this trail, omitting the first two pubs and the walk through Syon Park, alight at Brentford station, two stops before Isleworth, and walk down the main road southwards to the main Brentford High Street by the *Beehive*, a Fuller's house. Then turn right and walk along the High Street for five minutes to reach the Magpie & Crown (below).

For those on the full circuit, come out of the main entrance of the station at Isleworth, turn right, and right again under the rail bridge. This is Linkfield Road, and it's only a short walk down here to the first pub. The **Red Lion** 1 is a large and distinctive building in a fairly nondescript suburban street, but it's also out of the ordinary in terms of its status both as a hub of the local community and as a beacon of beer excellence. The large and homely public bar offers plenty of drinking areas, and there's a separate, comfortable lounge. With nine constantly changing and well-kept beers (not to mention five ciders and perries) the choice is one of the best for miles around; no wonder then that the Red Lion has scooped the local CAMRA branch's top pub gong on no fewer than four occasions in the last decade! There always seem to be something happening here, including live music and a biannual beer festival showcasing champion beers. If you're after a lunchtime bite avoid Mondays but otherwise you'll be in luck. It's a good pub to kick off any trail, and a hard one to leave, but there's a task ahead!

TIMING TIP

A good route for the daytime, when you'll get the most from the views of the river and the parkland between Isleworth and Brentford. Most of the pubs are open all day, but watch out for limited hours at the Express, and see the note under the entry for the Watermans Arms, below.

Key

- - - - Walk route

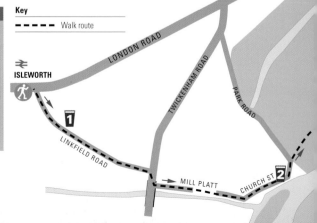

A good beer range at the London Apprentice

Leaving the Red Lion continue down to the far end of Linkfield Road, where turn right onto the main road, and almost immediately bear left by the river bridge into Mill Platt, an ancient route, now a pedestrian alleyway. Just south of the Platt is the bridge over the Duke of Northumberland's River – an artificial river, a branch of the River Colne, constructed sometime in the 15th or 16th century to provide power to the manorial water mill at Isleworth just downstream from

here. Pass the Ingram Almshouses, a terrace of six built by Sir Thomas Ingram, erstwhile Chancellor of the Duchy of Lancaster, and emerge by the site of the old mill by the Thames in Old Isleworth village. Saunter left here through the old village street down to the **London Apprentice 2**. This large and attractive pub has early 18th century origins and takes its name from the City livery company (trade association) apprentices, who stopped here for refreshments after their long row upstream. The interior sub-divisions have gone, only the multiple doorways remain, but there's enough of historic interest for it to merit a Grade II* listing. Look out for the fine 'Isleworth Ales' etched glass (the Isleworth Brewery was bought out by Watneys in

Isleworth Ales window at the London Apprentice

LEFT: **The Express Tavern** RIGHT: **Waterman's Arms**

1923). The beer menu has improved significantly in the past few years and you can now choose from up to four guests in addition to the regulars, Fuller's London Pride and Sharp's Doom Bar. If you didn't eat at the Red Lion you'll be pleased to learn that food is on offer here throughout the day and evening. The upstairs Riverside Room offers great views over the Thames if it's not being otherwise used, and there's also a riverside terrace.

Moving on, continue along the street passing some handsome old buildings and then the pretty tower of Isleworth church; it's now flanked with incongruous modern buildings, after schoolboys burnt the rest of it down in the 1940s! Just along the riverside past the church, pick up the well-signed Thames Path leading to the right into Syon Park. Originally the site of a medieval abbey, and described by John Betjeman as 'The Grand Architectural Walk', Syon House and its 200 acre park is the London home of the Duke of Northumberland (he of the river), whose family has owned it for 400 years. Walk up the roadway through the park (the house and gardens are open summer Wednesdays, Thursdays and Sundays, £10.50 see www.syonpark.co.uk). Beyond, keep to the cycle

route through the car park and house precincts if you feel you are about to lose your way, but the Thames Path then emerges on the busy A315 road just west of Brentford High Street. Turn right, pass two or three pubs and the Grand Union canal bridge before, tucked a little bit back off the street frontage, you'll come upon the next official stop, the **Magpie & Crown** 3 . A *Good Beer Guide* regular, this is a very good pub which has long been a great supporter of microbreweries and interesting beers. Since licensee Tam took over a couple of years ago she has re-established the place as Brentford's premier ale house, and offers the customer a wider-than-ever choice with, usually, six ales (including one from well-regarded local micro Twickenham) a cider and a perry, at reasonable prices. There's also a decent range of draught and bottled continental (mainly Belgian) beers. All in all it's another pub that can easily kill off a pub walk and turn it into a long sedentary session! Did you spot the old Watneys badge above the pub sign?

Continue east along the High Street for a short while, and before the traffic lights and the *Beehive* opposite turn right down Catherine Wheel Road. This is an area of mixed land use, industry giving way in places to new river and canalside apartments. Right by the junction of the canal and the river, and accessed via steps which is a reminder of the flood risk here, stands the **Brewery Tap** . This Fuller's local, whose name recalls a long-defunct takeover victim, still has a community feel and some vestiges of its former multi-roomed layout. Expect four Fuller's beers plus a rotating guest. Upon exit a narrow path opposite leads across a creek to the Grand Union Canal. Follow along to the lock and cross the bridge, but don't turn right (upstream) here on the Thames Path; rather, head downstream and follow the path along the wharfage with new developments and a marina as company. At Ferry Road, after circumnavigating a small inlet, and by a section of old wharf-side rail line, head up between the new apartments with an older brick house ('Peerless Pumps') on the corner, to the attractive **Watermans Arms** on the corner of the main road. With a fine period frontage featuring half-timbering, tiles and leaded windows, this Greene King house has a welcoming appearance. Inside despite a recent makeover it's still quite traditional in layout. Then three beers always feature Greene King IPA and Abbot Ale with a changing guest, sometimes from another brewer. The interesting menu features Japanese as well as more traditional

dishes. The pub usually closes in the afternoons during the midweek, especially in winter, but if you phone ahead in good time they may stay open for a group.

Leaving the pub and walking the few steps up to main road, the continuation to Kew Bridge is a walk of a shade over half a mile to the east (right). You could take the bus – the frequent 65 will drop you at the Express Tavern in no time – but to walk along the river, follow the road to the traffic lights and return to the riverside by the 'Thames Path via Watermans Park' sign. Current redevelopment hereabouts may open up more of the riverfront, so you could take local advice or check. It's a pleasant stroll past an array of house boats, emerging at Kew Bridge. Now, assuming you have done your homework with the opening times, the **Express Tavern** is a short walk back to the left, right on the busy road junction. You'll find well-kept beers in this tastefully decorated old house; although greatly remodelled the old character persists, and there are three interlinked rooms. The rear room, not originally part of the public drinking area, is particularly handsome, with thirties features, and leads to a pleasant garden. A framed award commemorates the founding of the local branches of CAMRA in this pub in 1974; and it has seen very frequent appearances in the *Good Beer Guide* since. As to

The bar at the Botanist

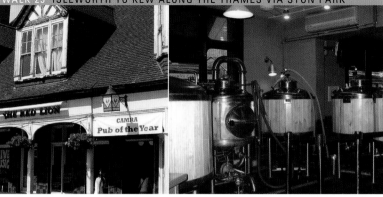

LEFT: **The Red Lion** RIGHT: **Visitors to the Botanist can view the brewhouse alongside the bar**

the beers: Draught Bass is the pub's trademark beer, and Young's Bitter is a regular too – in addition there may be up to four guests.

Cross the bridge and walk down on the main road to the south side of Kew Green, the centre of the old village, now riven in two by the nasty and busy South Circular road. Just beyond the Green on the right lies the **Botanist 7** brewpub. This newish venture by the Convivial Pub Company is aimed squarely at Kew's well-heeled young professionals and their free-range kids so you might want to aim for a time when the latter are at school or in bed; if you do, you'll be rewarded with an interesting range of home-brewed beers from the in-house microbrewery,

supported by the odd guest and a very decent list of bottled beers in support. The bright and cheery interior is quite tastefully done, and makes for an invigorating contrast to the largely traditional pubs earlier on this walk. Needless to say you can eat here, the menu is on the pricey side for pub food but with a wide range.

From here, Kew Bridge station is back across the river and just beyond the Express Tavern; and Kew Gardens on the Undergeround and Overground is a similar distance in the oppsite direction – consult your A to Z or ask. Alternatively, buses 65 and 391 from the oppsite side of the Green will take you down to Richmond station and town in about 20 minutes.

PUB INFORMATION

1 Red Lion
92-94 Linkfield Road, Isleworth,
TW7 6QJ
020 8560 1457
www.red-lion.info
Opening Hours: 12-11.30 (11
Tue; midnight Fri & Sat); 12-11 Sun

2 London Apprentice
62 Church Street, Old Isleworth,
TW7 6BG
020 8560 1915
www.thelondonapprentice.co.uk
Opening Hours: 11-11 (midnight
Fri & Sat)

3 Magpie & Crown
128 High Street, Brentford,
TW8 8EW
020 8560 4570
www.magpieandcrown.co.uk
Opening Hours: 12-midnight
(1am Thu-Sat)

4 Brewery Tap
47 Catherine Wheel Road,
Brentford, TW8 4BD
020 8568 6006
www.brewery-tap-brentford.co.uk
Opening Hours: 12-midnight

5 Watermans Arms
1 Ferry Lane, Brentford, TW8 0AW
020 8560 5665
www.watermans-arms.com
Opening Hours: 12-2.30, 5-11.30
Mon-Thu; 12-11.30 Fri-Sun

6 Express Tavern
56 Kew Bridge Road, Brentford,
TW8 0EW
020 8560 8484
Opening Hours: 11.30-3, 5.30
(6.30 Sat)-11 (midnight Thu-Sat);
12-11 Sun

7 Botanist
3-5 Kew Green, Kew, TW9 3AA
020 8948 4838
www.thebotanistkew.com
Opening Hours: 12-11 (midnight
Fri & Sat); 12-10.30 Sun

Chiswick – London's brewing heartland

WALK INFORMATION

Start: Chiswick Park, or Gunnersbury then bus

Finish: Fuller's brewery

Distance: 2 miles (3km)

Access: District Line from Central London, or Overground

Key attractions: Hogarth's House; Chiswick House and gardens; Fuller's Brewery

The pubs: Old Pack Horse; Lamb Brewery; Tabard; Duke of York; Fox & Hounds/ Mawson Arms

Chiswick Park Underground station, designed by Charles Holden in the early 1930s

The home territory of London's only remaining large brewery merits inclusion in this volume not just on that account but also on the strength of its historical architectural and cultural interest. The brewery is close to the original riverside settlement of Chiswick; the modern Chiswick, along the High Road, is more properly Turnham Green. Culture vultures may also enjoy the house of William Hogarth, painter, engraver and satirist, perhaps too close for comfort nowadays to the modern roundabout named after him; and the Palladian Chiswick House nearby with its noted gardens. The new Lamb Brewery, cheekily borrowing the name from the defunct Young's brewery, and the handsome Tabard add some welcome variety to the beer range on this interesting walk.

Tours of Fuller's brewery are available on weekdays and conclude with a beer tasting, but need to be booked in advance – see the brewery website www.fullers.co.uk or phone 020 8996 2063 for details.

CHISWICK PARK STATION

Start by taking the Underground (District Line) to Chiswick Park station (failing this, Gunnersbury station on the Overground is just two stops away by bus, just walk up to the A315 and cross over). Another Underground station designed by prolific architect Charles Holden in the early 1930s and now listed, its distinctive circular shape was ahead of its time and sets a nice tone for the walk to come. From the station, walk south away from the station down Acton Lane to join the Chiswick High Road right by the

> **TIMING TIP**
>
> Fuller's 'brewery tap', the Fox & Hounds/Mawson Arms, is as a rule closed at weekends; but the nearby George & Devonshire, passed *en route*, makes a perfectly adequate substitute.

first pub of the day, the impressive **Old Pack Horse 1** . Occupying a bold corner site which you shouldn't miss if you're coming by bus either, this is one of several pubs in the area designed by architect Thomas Henry Nowell Parr, this one in 1910 for Fuller's brewery to replace an earlier building acquired in 1849. Its attractive frontage has a deep brown faience at ground floor level where three original rooms are still clearly discernible via their names in the etched window glass, some of it gently curved. Don't miss the fine entrance porch to the former saloon on the Acton Lane. Inside, following a recent and fairly heavy internal makeover, a good deal of Nowell Parr's character has, I fear, been lost, not least in the old saloon: Parr's 'trademark' was his use of distinctive Tudor-style pointed archways. Here,

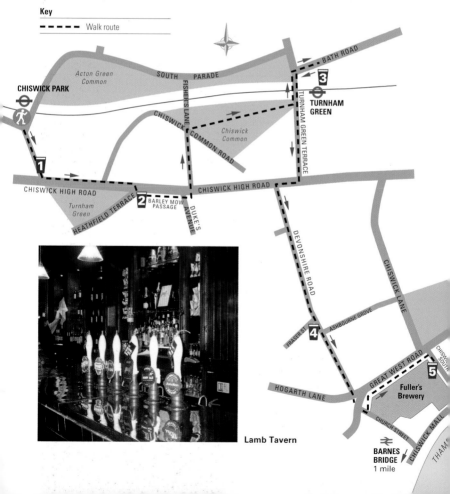

Lamb Tavern

BARNES
BRIDGE
1 mile

The Old Pack Horse, the work of noted pub architect Nowell Parr

a Tudor arch leading into a shallow alcove with original fireplace is now rebranded 'the snug' and guarded by a couple of buddhas. I had imagined that the scramble to 'turn Thai' on the food front was on the wane, but here it's still on the march. Even the old clock above the bar counter has at the time of writing been removed, only temporarily I hope; and the lovely old tiled floor has gone, or is at least buried, under modern stripped pine. An excess of cash accompanied by a deficiency of good taste once again, in the author's humble opinion. Nonetheless, despite an interior which feels increasingly like a modern restaurant rather than a pub, it's still worth a visit on account of a very good range of beers on seven handpumps, including up to three changing guests.

Upon exit, walk eastwards along Chiswick High Road, with Turnham Green opposite. Pass the listed *Crown & Anchor*, another victim of heavy modernisation but retaining an attractive exterior with distinctive inter-war tile work advertising Young's, the then owners. At the far end of Turnham Green by the lights, cross to the south side of the road for here on the corner is the newest of the beery attractions of this area, the **Lamb Brewery 2**. Fronted by a pleasant terrace, this is a good renovation of a former 'sports bar', and owners Convivial have shamelessly exploited the

name of the old Lamb Brewery to suggest a chain of history. In fact there's no connection apart from piggybacking on the name, for the old brewery was nearly a mile away (see box).

THE OLD LAMB BREWERY

The Lamb brewery in Old Chiswick occupied a site almost adjacent to that of Fuller's, and in fact the tower of the old brewery still survives in Church Street. For a good period of the nineteenth century it was considered to be comparable in size and significance to Fuller's. It was very closely associated with the Sich family and it had an estate of tied pubs, including the 'Lamb' itself, the brewery tap, which also survives although no longer a pub. It was sold to the Isleworth Brewery in 1920 and closed soon afterwards; and in turn, Isleworth was gobbled up by Watneys, and the rest, as they say, is history…

The Tabard, with the intimate Tabard Theatre upstairs

By the time you read this the brew kit in the building will have been replaced by another set geared to carbonated craft beers, but there are no plans to change the format as regards the cask ales – currently there are six handpulls dispensing a mixture of beers from the Botanist Brewery at nearby Kew (see page 156) and changing guests, with Shepherd Neame a favourite alongside locals such as Sambrook's. There's a small but interesting range of bottled beers too. The long narrow chalet-style interior (with rear dining room) won't appeal to all, but it's a welcome addition to the portfolio of drinking options in Chiswick, and the wide-ranging and varied food menu is currently reasonably priced.

Now cross back to the north side of the road and continue eastwards, looking out for Fisher's Lane very shortly on the left. Bear left up here, crossing just before the railway bridge to take the footpath striking across what's left of Chiswick Common, the railway embankment and tennis courts on your left. Reaching the road at the far end, bear left

Tiles by Walter Crane inside the Tabard, Turnham Green

under the rail bridge at Turnham Green station, then across on the right, just beyond the corner, you'll spot the architectural highlight of this walk, the **Tabard 3**. This is no ordinary pub, having been designed by architect Norman Shaw to serve the adjacent model village of Bedford Park in 1880. Inspired by the industrial model villages like Saltaire and Bournville, Bedford Park was always much more well-to-do but very much part of the coming garden city movement. It soon became a community of writers, artists and other bohemians. (If you want a flavour of the residential estate, walk just beyond the Tabard and take first left into Priory Gardens.) The rest of this considerable building was formerly stores to serve this estate. The Tabard was restored in 1971 and, in keeping with Bedford Park's artistic origins, now includes a theatre. The interior of this Grade II*-listed building is still a delight even though there has been some opening out. Undoubtedly a highlight is the fine original tilework by William De Morgan both in the entrance lobby and, more extensively, in the right hand bar room. Don't miss further tiles, by the artist Walter Crane, in a style that was a precursor of Art Nouveau, around the fireplace to the left of the bar. The beer range is much improved these days: expect up to eight well-kept and constantly changing beers from the SIBA list, with a local emphasis as regards sourcing. CAMRA members can obtain a 10% discount on beer on production of a valid membership card. Food is available all day.

Now retrace your steps back around the corner but continue down past the shops to the traffic lights on the Chiswick High Road, turn right, cross the road again and take Devonshire Road, the next turning left. This pleasant residential street which runs down towards the notorious Hogarth roundabout is home to two more pubs almost opposite each other which show the work of Nowell Parr. Sadly that on the left, the *Devonshire*, is currently closed and boarded up with an uncertain future; but opposite, on

Original screen panel in the Duke of York

a corner site, the attractive little **Duke of York** 4 is very much in business. It's a handsome inter-war brick building, very much a traditional local in contrast to the changing bars on the High Road; and inside, much of the original work survives, including the bar-back, bar counters and one original stained glass screen between two seating alcoves. Two hand pumps dispense London Pride and a changing second ale (often ESB) from Fuller's brewery just down the road, of whose estate the pub has been a part since 1834.

Upon exit, continue south down the road until you reach the tangled mass of roads which is the Hogarth Roundabout and Chiswick Flyover. With Fuller's brewery beckoning you from across the road, do not even consider not taking the subway, otherwise you may not even survive to reach the final refreshment stop on the route. The underpass leads you safely to the southern side, right adjacent the *George & Devonshire* and the northern end of Church Road in the centre

Duke of York

Fuller's brewery tap is the only pub in the UK with two names

of the old village. As suggested in the preamble this Fuller's house makes a perfectly acceptable alternative to our last stop, and at weekends, a substitute for it, but for now, cross Church Road and walk along the perimeter wall of Fuller's brewery to arrive at the oddly-named brewery tap, the **Fox & Hounds/ Mawson Arms** 5. There's more than one story in circulation as to how the place came by its name: the most colourful is of a dispute between two brothers who owned the place and

as a result had it divided with a wall! Wherever the truth lies, it's a pleasant place to hole up and relax with, as you'd expect, a wide choice of up to eight beers from the adjacent brewery. The quality of the ale here is as you'd expect it to be for Fuller's showpiece outlet, although food is only available at lunchtimes. If you want to round off with a meal, try the George & Devonshire which serves food until 9pm (6pm Sunday).

Old Chiswick is not well served by public transport. If you fancy working off some of the excesses of the day, by far the nicest finish is the mile or so walk to Barnes Bridge rail station, via the charming old Church Road (left just before the George & Devonshire). Upon reaching the river, take the Thames Path (signed) by some modern flats heading upstream. The first couple of hundred yards take us along a semi-privatised riverside past a modern housing development but then the path skirts some open space before Barnes Bridge comes into view with the old village visible on the other side of the river. Cross the bridge alongside the railway line to the station. Locally your best bet is the useful 190 bus, south (same side as the pub, bus stop beyond the George & Devonshire) towards Richmond for good rail links to London Waterloo and Clapham Junction and northwards back to Chiswick for the Underground.

PUB INFORMATION

1 Old Pack Horse
434 Chiswick High Road,
Chiswick, W4 5TF
020 8994 2872
www.oldpackhorsechiswick.co.uk
Opening Hours: 11-11 (midnight
Thu-Sat); 12-10.30 Sun

2 Lamb Brewery
9 Barley Mow Passage, W4 4PH
020 8994 1880
lambbrewery.co.uk
Opening Hours: 8am (7am
Sat)-11 (1am Fri & Sat); 7am-
10.30 Sun

3 Tabard
2 Bath Road, Turnham Green,
W4 1LW
020 8994 3492
Opening Hours: 12-11 (midnight
Thu-Sat)

4 Duke of York
107 Devonshire Road, W4 2HU
020 8747 0904
www.duke-of-york-chiswick.co.uk
Opening Hours: 12-11 (11.30
Fri & Sat)

5 Fox & Hounds/ Mawson Arms
110 Chiswick Lane South,
Chiswick, W4 2QA
020 8994 2936
www.mawsonarmschiswick.co.uk
Opening Hours: 11-8; closed
Sat & Sun

1960s price list in the Mawson Arms

South down the Northern Line

WALK INFORMATION

Start: Clapham South

Finish: South Wimbledon (Merton)

Distance: 4.7 miles (7.5km)

Access: Northern Line from Central London, or via Clapham Junction or Victoria to Balham then walk

Key attractions: Clapham and Tooting Bec Commons; Wandle Trail; Merton Abbey Mills market; Underground architecture; Tooting curry houses

The pubs: Nightingale; Balham Bowls Club; Wheatsheaf; King's Head; Tooting Tram & Social; Antelope; Sultan

The southern extension to the City & South London Railway as far as Morden was opened in 1926, with several new stations designed by now-iconic architect Charles Holden. The line itself didn't become the 'Northern Line' until 1937, but all the stations on this pub tour are now listed buildings, having suffered relatively little damage from subsequent development (unlike Morden itself). The pubs won't let you down either: no fewer than four were in the portfolio of pubco Antic, who have gained a reputation for imaginative refurbishments, although they have recently hived off two of these. Thrown in for good measure is a favourite from Young's, and the Hop Back brewery's only London tied house. The route itself could also be quite conveniently accomplished on a bicycle, but I recommend you take to the train. Or, if you are averse to the Underground, the route can be accomplished by bus: the 155 down the A24 as far as Tooting Broadway, then the 219 or 57.

The Nightingale, Clapham

TIMING TIP

Don't be caught out by the limited hours at several of these pubs, particularly those in the Antic/Gregarious stable. Avoid Mondays, and don't start before late afternoons during the other weekdays, if you want to visit the whole set. That said, weekend evenings can see the pubs rammed and noisy with slow service. Aim for a summer midweek evening if you can.

Balham Bowls Club

Clapham South station lies at the southern extremity of Clapham Common, surely the most well-known (but not the prettiest) of South London's numerous Commons. Nightingale Lane is the road running off to the left (west) from the station, and our first pub is about half a mile down this road. Alternatively, catch the G1 or 690 bus from around the corner for two stops to Ramsden Road and continue walking for a short way to get to the **Nightingale 1**. A pretty mid-Victorian listed building, it has some handsome brickwork and windows giving it a cottage-style appearance. More importantly, it has so far escaped Young's obsession with turning their pubs into gastro eateries (and turning their backs on the humble drinker), although you can certainly eat here. The front bar in particular is much as my generation of former Young's fans remember many of their old South London pubs: a simple but solidly attractive bar counter with a well-worn boarded floor, all in good old-fashioned brown. The very well-kept beers include not only Wells & Young's staples and a seasonal, but Sambrook's Wandle and often another guest. In addition, Meantime beers are available on keg, and you can sample a range, since there are third-pint glasses available. All in all, a pub which has got the balance right and which remains a firm community favourite.

Now, to get to the next pub, you can walk: it's only a few minutes. Follow Western Lane at the side of the pub and swing round left to join Endlesham Road. Turn right, and head south until the junction with Norgrove Street, and turn up here to join Ramsden Road, when a short distance to the right you'll find the distinctive **Balham Bowls Club 2**. [If you want to be a Northern Line purist (and why not?) return to Clapham South, head one stop south to Balham and, upon exit, cross the High Road diagonally and take

the second turn left along the road]. The building greets you with a frontage which suggests a more rural location and a previous era, an impression reinforced once you're inside. It still feels like the club house it once was, and much of the old décor remains, in a deliberately retro refurb by Antic in 2006. The rambling interior has several rooms, many with lovely parquet flooring complemented by panelled walls. Seating is eclectic like the rest of the furniture – sofas, old chairs and tables, although there's also quite a bit of vertical drinking at the bar. One of the rooms is mainly used as a restaurant, and there's a pleasant walled patio garden, though the old bowling green itself isn't part of the property any more. On the four handpumps you'll find regular Purity Ubu, one from Adnams and a couple of rotating guests. It's a likeable place but be warned, it can get very, very busy, especially on Friday and Saturday nights.

Key

- - - - - Walk route

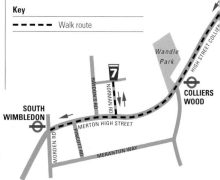

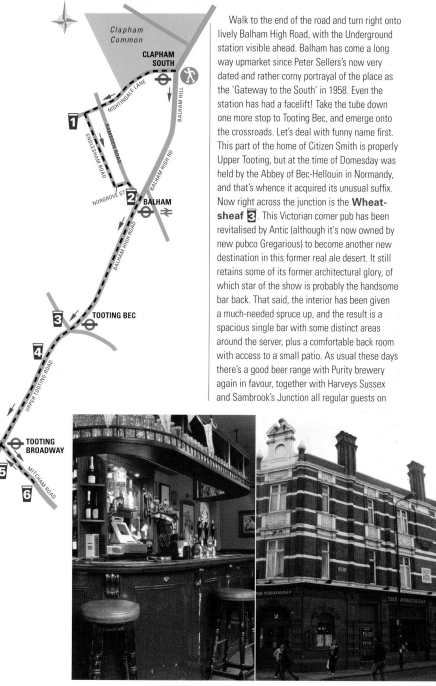

Walk to the end of the road and turn right onto lively Balham High Road, with the Underground station visible ahead. Balham has come a long way upmarket since Peter Sellers's now very dated and rather corny portrayal of the place as the 'Gateway to the South' in 1958. Even the station has had a facelift! Take the tube down one more stop to Tooting Bec, and emerge onto the crossroads. Let's deal with funny name first. This part of the home of Citizen Smith is properly Upper Tooting, but at the time of Domesday was held by the Abbey of Bec-Hellouin in Normandy, and that's whence it acquired its unusual suffix. Now right across the junction is the **Wheatsheaf 3**. This Victorian corner pub has been revitalised by Antic (although it's now owned by new pubco Gregarious) to become another new destination in this former real ale desert. It still retains some of its former architectural glory, of which star of the show is probably the handsome bar back. That said, the interior has been given a much-needed spruce up, and the result is a spacious single bar with some distinct areas around the server, plus a comfortable back room with access to a small patio. As usual these days there's a good beer range with Purity brewery again in favour, together with Harveys Sussex and Sambrook's Junction all regular guests on

LEFT: **Solidly attractive bar counter at the Nightingale** RIGHT: **The Wheatsheaf**

Splendid screenwork inside the King's Head

the five ale pumps. During the week, food service starts at 6pm. Once again, I'd issue my warning about Friday and Saturday evenings.

Take to your feet for the next pub on this trip, for it's only a few minutes walk south down the main road. Upper Tooting Road is lively but rather tatty, with nondescript shops in abundance – an unlikely place to run into our next pub, which has been described as one of the most important historic pub interiors south of the river, a view with which it's almost impossible to disagree. The **King's Head** 4 designed in 1896 by the prolific pub architect W. M. Brutton and regarded as possibly his best work, is a remarkable building on the outside too, best viewed from the other side of the street. Although there has been a degree of opening out inside, there is enough remaining to recall the sheer quality and extravagance of the late Victorian interior. Several splendid screens with fine glass have survived, along with some quality bar fittings. The snug on the left has some good floor tilework, whilst to the right-hand side, various doors show how there were formerly several separate areas. It's remarkable enough that the Taylor Walker (part of Spirit Group) website doesn't even categorise this place as an historic pub, the more so when one sees what mediocre places *are* given the accolade! There's a small range of ale from the Spirit list which occasionally features something

interesting, but this is firmly one to savour for the building, and not to be missed.

Now, if you're planning to take in a Tooting curry house on this tour, and anyone in the know will tell you that there's no better place in London for one just now, the main drag down to Tooting Broadway has some of the finest. Whether you'll feel able to resume the pub tour afterwards is your call, so an alternative option is to finish the latter first and return to the Broadway for your curry meal, in which case, if you're doing things by the book, the only way is back, to Tooting Bec, for the tube to Tooting Broadway.

From the crossroads at the Broadway, the next pub is pretty well hidden, though only a few yards away. Turn right out of the station and head along the Mitcham Road (signed to Croydon on the ornate metal fingerboard on the traffic island). Just past the *Graveney & Meadow*, another recent Antic-inspired refurbishment, and before the old cinema, now a bingo hall, look for an entry to the right, and through the gates is the **Tooting Tram & Social** 5. The understated entrance, without even a sign, is in stark contrast to the interior which, being a former tram shed, is overwhelming by its sheer size. Judge for yourself the interior with the eclectic furniture and fittings, but during the week the atmosphere is relaxed and there are plenty of tables, chairs and sofas to choose from. Now acquired by Gregarious pubco, there's a more limited cask beer range than nearby Antic venues, with Purity beers (Mad Goose, Pure Gold etc) the main offering. Be aware, the place functions more like a club at the end of the week, Thursday to Sunday, with live acts and large crowds, some no doubt loyalists from its former days as a yoof-oriented 'Scream' chain venue; it's also closed on Mondays!

The next port of call is a short distance further down the Mitcham Road, on the same side of the street. Another Antic acquisition, but this time in a far more conventional building. Nonetheless, like the Wheatsheaf, the **Antelope** 6 is a conversion of a substantial late Victorian building with some character. The spacious interior is dominated by the central servery, with the usual mixture of sofas, chairs and tables making the place feel cosier and more intimate than one might expect for its size. This place takes its food seriously and the dining area at the rear is a good choice if you plan to eat somewhere on this tour. There's also an outdoor drinking area at the rear of the pub. The beer range is wider here, and there are usually four rotating and often interesting guests alongside the Adnams and Purity regulars.

It's a short walk back to Tooting Broadway for the tube to Colliers Wood. Once known as Merton Singlegate after the toll house on the

Tooting Tram & Social

turnpike road here, it's now more notorious as the home of the grim tower block which was voted London's ugliest in a 2006 poll. But if you can turn a blind eye to it as you cross the road by the station, there are more pleasant sights, and much history, in this locality. One such is Wandle Park on your right. Under the influence of early open spaces campaigners like Octavia Hill, co-founder of not just the National Trust but also the Wandle Open Spaces Committee, Wimbledon Corporation bought the ten acre estate of Wandle Bank House when it came onto the market in 1907.

The King's Head, Tooting, architecturally one of South London's most remarkable pubs

The Sultan – a great place to sample Hop Back beers

The house, once home to James Perry, a friend of Admiral Lord Nelson (who lived briefly across the road in Merton) has now gone, but the public park remains. Across the road, on the very site now occupied by the hideous boxy supermarket, once stood William Morris's Merton Abbey Mills workshops and, earlier, Nelson's Merton Place. The much tormented River Wandle still flows alongside the street, opposite the bus garage, although there are plans to restore its course through Wandle Park. Walk past all this, and look for Norman Road on your right, a few turnings along. Head down this street of humble Victorian terraces, until on a corner site to your right stands to you see the **Sultan** 7. A pretty intact postwar pub which retains its two room layout, the Sultan (named after a champion stallion)

is far better known as the only London pub in the small estate of the Wiltshire-based Hop Back brewery. It was their flagship beer Summer Lightning which many credit as being the first of the new breed of light hoppy beers that we now take for granted, and the pub has won hatfuls of accolades for its well kept beers ever since it opened under Hop Back's colours in 1993. Expect a wide range of Hop Back beers including the tasty session ale GFB, and the full-bodied Entire Stout. There's an occasional guest from the Downton brewery. It's not a food pub, so if you're peckish try a packet of crisps!

Leaving the pub, head back the way you came. When you get back to the main road, Merton High Street, you're as near to South Wimbledon tube station as Colliers Wood, so turn right and it's about 7-8 minutes. Note the impressive tiled exterior to the *Nelson Arms* across the street, and Nelson Wines beer shop on the right halfway down, one of the best bottle shops for miles around. Although not officially included here, the excellent *Trafalgar Freehouse* (see the Tramlink Beer Tour, Walk 29) a frequent local CAMRA branch accolade winner and 2008 CAMRA London Pub of the Year, is just five minutes away: turn left down Pincott Road, just beyond Nelson Wines.

PUB INFORMATION

1 Nightingale
97 Nightingale Lane, SW12 8NX
020 8673 1637
Opening Hours: 11 (12 Sun)-midnight

2 Balham Bowls Club
7-9 Ramsden Road, SW12 8QX
020 8673 4700
www.balhambowlsclub.com
Opening Hours: 4-11 (midnight Thu); 2-1am Fri; 12-1am Sat; 12-11 Sun

3 Wheatsheaf
2 Upper Tooting Road, SW17 7PG
020 8672 2805
wheatsheaftootingbec.com
Opening Hours: 4-midnight (1am Fri); 12-1am Sat; 12-11 Sun

4 King's Head
84 Upper Tooting Road, SW17 7PB
020 8767 6708
Opening Hours: 12-midnight

5 Tooting Tram & Social
46-48 Mitcham Road, SW17 9NA
020 8767 0278
www.antic-ltd.com/tooting
Opening Hours: 5-midnight; 4-2am Fri; 1-2am Sat; 1-midnight Sun; closed Mon

6 Antelope
76 Mitcham Road, SW17 9NG
020 8672 3888
www.theantelopepub.com
Opening Hours: 4 (12 Sat)-11 (midnight Fri; 1am Sat); 12-11 Sun

7 Sultan
78 Norman Road, SW19 1BT
020 8544 9323
Opening Hours: 12-11 (midnight Fri & Sat)

The Nightingale

Riverbus pub hopscotch

WALK INFORMATION

Start: Embankment Pier

Finish: Charing Cross

Access: Via Charing Cross

Key attractions: River views; Tower of London; Greenwich museums, Observatory and Park

The pubs: Greenwich Pier: Old Brewery; Plume of Feathers. Canary Wharf Pier: North Pole; Ledger Building. Tower Bridge Millennium Pier: Draft House Tower Bridge. Blackfriars Pier: Black Friar; Cockpit. Embankment Pier: Ship & Shovell. Try also: Tower Bridge Millennium Pier: Liberty Bounds

Riverside warehouses, and the distinctive Shard

As a lifelong Londoner I have to confess I had never been on a river trip until I did the punishing research putting this circuit together. I can only hope you enjoy the route as much as I did: once the commuters have melted away there's enough space on board the fast and frequent Thames Clipper services to relax and enjoy the views which are first class throughout. The River Roamer ticket (currently almost £13 but discounted by a third if you have a valid Travelcard) allows you to jump on and off the services at will, which is what we need to visit the pubs on this trail. Check the maps and timetables in advance at www.thamesclippers.com but you can just turn up at the pier and buy your ticket at the booth at no extra cost. Starting at the Embankment Pier by Charing Cross rail bridge, I recommend heading non-stop down to Greenwich and thence making your way back in several stages, but as usual there's nothing to stop you composing your own variations. The clippers run very frequently so you can pretty much turn up and go; there are pocket timetables on board — be aware that some services omit some stops, notably Blackfriars.

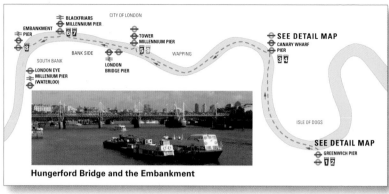

Hungerford Bridge and the Embankment

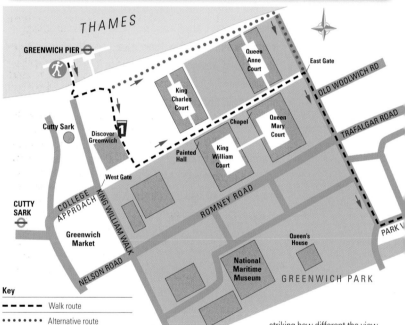

Key

- - - - Walk route

••••••• Alternative route

Catch your Thames Clipper from Embankment Pier. The pubs in Greenwich are open early, and the Roamer tickets are valid from 9am, so you can happily make an early start for what can be a full day if you take in the sights as well as the pubs. Describing the variety of sights and attractions on view all the way down to Greenwich is beyond the scope of this book, and unless you prefer to relax inside and enjoy a coffee and pastry on board, I recommend you take a map and guide to make the most of them. Having said that, it's quite striking how different the view of a familiar city is from the water.

The first stop for the boat (not for us) is the London Eye, and thereafter it's downstream all the way to Greenwich. Obvious highlights are the bridges, the Tower of London, the riverside warehouses, and some fine churches, a few of which are still able to show a face to the river despite the proliferation of brash modern blocks. Look out in particular for St Paul's Church, Shadwell, close by the *Prospect of Whitby* at Wapping; the tower is very graceful. The Clippers don't hang about, particularly beyond Tower Bridge when they're allowed to get moving.

The views of the Docklands towers are very striking, with the original 'Canary Wharf' block, 1 Canada Square, to give it its proper title (the one with the slopy roof!) now joined by many others of differing heights. Unless you fancy going down to the O2 and back for the ride (and the view of the new cable car crossing), then alight with most of the other trippers at Greenwich.

There's enough to see in Greenwich that even if you arrive before opening time, you should be fully entertained. The *Cutty Sark* is of course one of the stars, right in front of you as you exit from the pier. She was the fastest sailing ship of her day and after being launched at Dumbarton in 1869 she initially sailed the tea route to China, once doing the trip from Shanghai in just 107 days. Later on, she brought back wool from Australia, but has been in dry dock in Greenwich since 1954. Bear downstream on the signed route 'cycle path' in front of the Old Naval College buildings, which was originally the Greenwich Royal Naval Hospital. The hospital was built by Christopher Wren between 1696 and 1712 and closed in 1869. Between 1873 and 1998 it functioned as the Royal Naval College. A charitable trust, the Greenwich Foundation for the Royal Naval College, assumed responsibility for the site when the Royal Navy moved out in December 1998. Go to www.ornc.org/visit to see what's on offer here. One important attraction for us is just yards away, across the lawn in the near side of the cluster of the old College buildings: the **Old Brewery** ■1 is the microbrewery, bar and café venture by Greenwich-based Meantime Brewery. The name celebrates a surprisingly long association with brewing on this site, set out in the timeline running around the wall of the café building housing the microbrewery. A brewery opened on the site in 1717 to supply the hospital, and operated until 1868. This recent venture gives the buildings an agreeable, but very modern makeover. The airy café bar opens at 10am, and the bar next door, with its scrubbed up brick walks and roof, at 11am. On tap are around eight different Meantime beers, but these, although highly regarded by many, are not cask ales, and I find them too cold for my palate. There are a couple of cask beers, typically Dark Star Hophead and Adnams Bitter. There's also a garden leading off the bar.

The very modern Old Brewery

The prices are not great value, far too expensive for beers brewed mostly on site. At over £6 a pint for one beer under 5% on my research visit, one wonder how far prices can climb before customers call time? I'll break my price rule for this one though for as a drinking experience, it's still worthwhile: save up.

There are a number of other pubs in town which serve a passable pint. My second choice is a far more traditional affair a few minutes' walk away. Either exit the Old Brewery on the town side, onto the main vista running west-east through the Old Naval College site, and walk left to the East Gate onto Park Row; or return to the riverside path and follow it down to the Trafalgar Gate by the big old riverside pub of the same name, turning 'inland' up Park Row. Head away from the river, up Park Row and cross the main road towards the park entrance ahead, following the road left by the park gates into Park Vista, when you'll catch sight of the **Plume of Feathers** ■2 . This attractive street was at one time the main east-west route through Greenwich, dividing the park from the Tudor palace that stood by the river. Just before you reach the pub, look out for the meridian line, set as series of studs in the road leading to a metal groove in the footpath and a wall plaque on the right. So once you are safely inside the Plume, the easternmost entry in this guide, you will have drunk in both hemispheres in one day! This comfortable pub dates from 1691 and not surprisingly, given its location, contains many naval artefacts. The carpeted bar assumes a horseshoe shape around the servery, where a choice of four beers (London Pride, Harveys Sussex, Sharp's Doom Bar and a guest)

LEFT: **Tower Bridge Draft House** RIGHT: **Ship & Shovel**

are what you can expect. There's a dining area to the rear with a lunch and evening menu.

Unless you're heading up the Observatory, the Park and/or Greenwich's other attractions (all worthwhile but we've a long day ahead) return back to the Pier for a westbound clipper.

Next stop for us is Canary Wharf. As one would expect, the majority of the watering holes in and around the towers of international banking are pretty soulless modern joints designed primarily to unload large sums of cash from the overpaid occupants whilst they talk loudly to each other on their mobiles. Right, now we have the stereotypes dealt with let's try a couple of the better places! Ascend the steps from the piazza in front of the pier, and cross the large traffic circus with the original tower, 1 Canada Square, directly in your sights. Once across the two roads, head slightly left through the arch advertising 'Columbus Place' to emerge in a pedestrian courtyard. Over to the left is a piece of artwork in light and dark blue glass, the 'Columbus Screen'. To the right of this is a well-hidden staircase down to the street below. Now follow the sign for the Docklands Museum for about 100 yards and you'll come across the **Ledger Building** 3. It's refreshing to find a few surviving old buildings here in the midst of the largely mediocre modern stuff, and this one with its classical portico, has been restored with the care that characterises the work done by the J D Wetherspoon chain. Its neighbour, is the very different but equally attractive Museum of Docklands. The name of the

Ledger Building stems, as one might expect, from the building's original use: to house the ledgers of the West India Docks. The light and spacious bar room, according to reviewers, attracts a slightly lower quotient of suits than neighbouring establishments so you should have a fighting chance of getting a seat if you want one. There's a good range of up to five interesting guest ales as well as the four 'regulars' further along the bar, and of course the usual JDW fare on the menu.

An alternative venue well worth a trip is the **North Pole** 4. This is probably the last remaining traditional East End boozer in the area, and a surprising survivor given its proximity to the tower blocks nearby. To get there, either walk back to the piazza in front of the riverbus station and head down the waterside path downstream until you reach Cuba Street (consult the map) then inland; or perhaps call a cab. Manilla Street seems to be rife for redevelopment: comprising a few down at heel industrial buildings plus the North Pole itself, in a 1970s time warp inside and out. Timber panelling adorns all the walls, seating consists of red mock leather seats around the perimeter with an eclectic mix of stools and chairs around nostalgia-ridden Formica tables. The Artex ceiling, still yellow from smoking days, even has genuine fake beams, whilst the red carpet and background piped music adds to the social club ambience. Happily the beers are far more drinkable than they would have been in the seventies. Expect a safe choice: London Pride, Taylor Landlord and Sharp's Doom Bar, but don't expect more than a few nibbles on the food front.

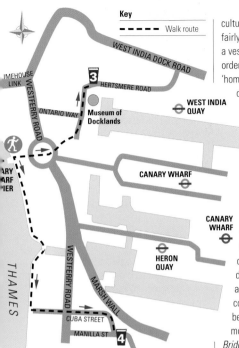

Key
- - - - Walk route

WEST INDIA DOCK ROAD

LIMEHOUSE LINK

HERTSMERE ROAD

3

ONTARIO WAY

Museum of Docklands

WEST INDIA QUAY

WESTFERRY ROAD

CANARY WHARF

CANARY WHARF

ARY ARF IER

HERON QUAY

THAMES

WESTFERRY ROAD

MARSH WALL

CUBA STREET

MANILLA ST

4

culture, the place has a layout and atmosphere fairly typical of the new breed of bars, but retains a vestige of 'pubbyness' within too. Drinkers can order third of a pint 'samples' at this self-styled 'home of the third', complemented by a range of beer-friendly food. At the time of writing there are plans to expand the range of cask ales beyond the current three, but there's a good range of both bottled and draught craft keg beers, the latter including popular North London micro Camden Town. The enthusiastic and knowledgeable staff seem to know what they're doing, making the visit a positive experience.

If you're game for another beer my advice would probably be to stay here, but if it's another nearby pub or bar you're after, you could try the *Pommeller's Rest* a few doors down. The former Tower Bridge Hotel has had a rather bland (by Wetherspoon standards) conversion but there's a good selection of beers, well kept when I have been in, and most punters seem to be fairly impressed. The *Bridge House* further back on Tower Bridge Road which you passed earlier is Adnams' only London tied house but frankly the place is rather lacking in atmosphere and the schoolboy errors on their website seemed to be matched by the rather uninformed and unenthusiastic staff on my last visit, so I can't really recommend it.

If you're pushed for time at the pier, then I would try the **Liberty Bounds 9** a couple of minutes' walk from the boat (just keep directly away from the river on the path, weave through the tourists and it's pretty well directly ahead at the road crossing). Another J D Wetherspoon house, in a handsome Edwardian block, there's decent range of beers which, although pricier than normal JDW offerings, are still very good value for the area.

Return to the pier (if you fancy stretching your legs, another option is to head down Queen Elizabeth Street opposite and then make your way down to City Hall and walk along the Thames Path to pick up your boat at the London Bridge City Pier in a few minutes).

Check that your departure is scheduled to stop at Blackfriars, or be prepared to miss out on one of the definite highlights of the tour. Disembarking from the riverbus at Blackfriars Millennium Pier,

Despite the advertised hours you might be advised to phone ahead before setting out for the North Pole, if you plan to be there for some time.

Return to the Pier and head further back upstream to our next port of call, the Tower Bridge Millennium Pier. Here you'll be sharing the stage with a very different clientele, the hordes of tourists who make this the most popular of the Royal Palaces. Unless you've scheduled a visit yourself, work your way along the riverside back towards Tower Bridge, and climbing up onto the roadway, cross the bridge to the south shore. The area around Butlers Wharf and Shad Thames on the South Bank here, close to City Hall (the elliptical building which you can't miss on the riverside) has been transformed into a bit of a destination, with numerous upmarket bars and eateries where once there were riverside wharves and warehouses. In that sense it's a symbol of the changes you will have seen from the riverbus. My recommendation for some interesting beers on this strip is the **Draft House Tower Bridge 5** on the left, 200 yards beyond the bridge, past the Bridge House (see below). One of a small (currently five) but growing chain of alehouses aiming at the new aficionados of beer climb up to the Victoria Embankment and walk back up to Blackfriars Bridge. Crossing the roads here is one of the day's more taxing undertakings, but heading up away from the river you'll spot the distinctive prominent shape of the **Black Friar** 6 on the prominent apex, surrounded by modern buildings jammed against the railway line. For a full description, see its entry on Walk 9, the Central London Heritage Pub tour.

If you'd like a second pub before you return to the boat, turn left out of the Black Friar under the rail bridge and left again up Black Friars Lane, turning right into Playhouse Yard which becomes Ireland Yard ahead. At the end of this passageway you'll find the **Cockpit** 7. The dark exterior looks the part, notably the fine entrance on the apex of the two streets. The interior is comfortable, although quite confined, and perpendicular drinking is common here. The story goes that at one time there was cockfighting here until it was outlawed early in Victoria's reign, but the current interior in a curious quasi-medieval style complete with mini minstrel's gallery dates back to an 1890s remodelling. This increasingly popular little pub offers five beers, four regulars from national brewers headed by Adnams Bitter, and a guest from the Enterprise list.

Return to the pier and catch the next clipper down to Embankment, where we started this mini marathon. The last stop is reassuringly close by. Cross the road by the pier and walk through the concourse to the Underground station, and continue straight up busy Villiers Street. The street is named after George Villiers, first Duke of Buckingham, who was a fashionable courtier and friend of James I. He had a substantial mansion nearby, the only remnant of which is the York Water Gate in the Embankment Gardens alongside the street. This marked the old line of the Thames before the Embankment reduced its width. Look for the tunnel running under the railway station on the left (and note, for later, the new access to the station immediately on your left as you walk down it). At the far end of this arch lies the curious **Ship & Shovell** 8. Curious, since it's the only pub in the land which is divided into two parts, on opposite sides of the passage. The spelling of the name refers to Admiral Sir Cloudesley Shovell whose fleet was grounded on the Scilly Isles in 1707 with the total loss of several of his ships and over two thousand of his crew. His portrait hangs in the main bar. The smaller bar (on the left) is probably the more atmospheric, with some cosy corners and plenty of dark wood panelling. Of more importance is the beer range, which comes from Hall & Woodhouse and includes favourites such as Tanglefoot and their take on the old King & Barnes Sussex Best Bitter. You have just passed the nearest British Rail and Underground station – if it's buses you're after walk up to the top of Villiers Street to the Strand.

PUB INFORMATION

1 Old Brewery
Pepys Building, The Old Naval College, SE10 9LW
020 3327 1280
www.oldbrewerygreenwich.com
Opening Hours: 11-11; 12-10.30 Sun

2 Plume of Feathers
19 Park Vista, SE10 9LZ
020 8858 1661
www.plumeoffeathers-greenwich.co.uk
Opening Hours: 11-11 (midnight Fri & Sat); 12-11

3 Ledger Building
4 Hertsmere Road, E14 4AL
020 7536 7770
Opening Hours: 8am-midnight (1am Fri & Sat); 8am-11pm Sun

4 North Pole
74 Manilla Street, E14 8LG
020 7987 5443
Opening Hours: 11-3, 5-11; closed Sat & Sun

5 Draft House Tower Bridge
206-208 Tower Bridge Road, SE1 2UP
020 7378 9995
www.drafthouse.co.uk
Opening Hours: 12-11 (10.30 Sun)

6 Black Friar
174 Queen Victoria Street, EC4V 4EG
020 7236 5474
www.nicholsonspubs.co.uk/theblackfriarblackfriarslondon
Opening Hours: 10-11 (11.30 Fri & Sat); 12-10 Sun

7 Cockpit
7 St Andrews Hill, EC4V 5BY
020 7248 7315
Opening Hours: 11-11; closed Sat & Sun

8 Ship & Shovell
2-3 Craven Passage, WC2N 5PH
020 7839 1311
Opening Hours: 11-11; closed Sat & Sun

TRY ALSO:

9 Liberty Bounds
15 Trinity Square, EC3N 4AA
020 7481 0513
Opening Hours: 8am-midnight (1am Wed & Thu; 2am Fri & Sat)

A Tramlink beer tour

WALK INFORMATION

Start: Beckenham Junction

Finish: Morden Road, or South Wimbledon

Access: Frequent services by train from London Victoria (20 mins). From London Bridge, alight at East Croydon and take the Beckenham Junction tram

Key attractions: Mitcham Common; Morden Hall Park; Wandle Trail

The pubs: Jolly Woodman; Cricketers; Claret Free house; George; Ravensbury; Prince of Wales; Trafalgar Freehouse. Try also: Builders Arms

Ravensbury in Mitcham

Tramlink was opened in May 2000, after over 12 years of development and construction. Around 30 million journeys annually are now made on the system: it's a remarkable success story. London's only tram network is most closely associated with Croydon where the trams run on-street, but making use of old and new tracks the eighteen mile tram system extends from Wimbledon to Beckenham. When the Tramlink opened the local CAMRA branches produced a beer guide to the tram network, but pubs have come and gone since then. I humbly present this as the discerning drinker's best choices as they stand today. If you do this walk during the daylight hours you'll enjoy the open spaces to their maximum, and there are some potentially pleasant detours. Taking the route in the recommended east to west direction will enable you to hole up in the CAMRA award-winning Trafalgar in Merton, with Tooting's famous curry houses not far away if you wish to end the day with a meal.

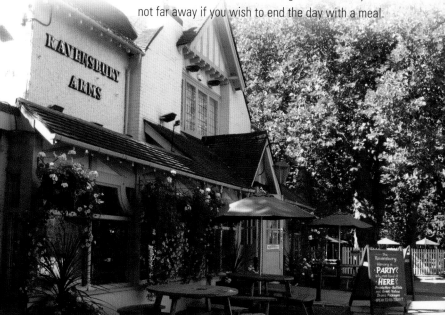

TRAM ROUTE HEADING

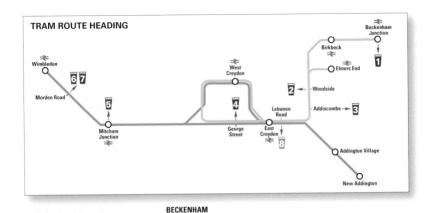

TIMING TIP

Trams are frequent so research-
ing timetables ahead should not
be necessary. Do this route in
daylight if possible to get the
most from the walks to the pubs;
but note that during the week the
Trafalgar opens at 3pm, which
shouldn't be a problem by the
time you get there!

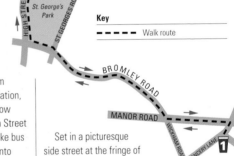

BECKENHAM JUNCTION

Key

- - - - Walk route

Take the train or tram to Beckenham
Junction and, emerging from the station,
walk across to the road junction and it's now
either a 10-12 minute walk down the High Street
and left along Bromley Road or you can take bus
162 or 227 to Wickham Road. You'll turn into
Chancery Lane by the *Oakhill Tavern* (or enter
from the southern end if alighting from the 162).

Set in a picturesque
side street at the fringe of
the town centre, the **Jolly
Woodman** 1 feels a bit
like a rural pub that has been
absorbed by suburbia. It still exhibits some brew-
eriana from its Charrington days. There are even
a couple of rustic old oak tables inside the bar.
Highly rated by the cask ale fraternity for its good
range of well-kept ales, expect to find Harveys
Sussex, Timothy Taylor Landlord plus three changing guests. There's a limited but tasty food menu
if you're already feeling peckish.

Make your way back to the town centre
retracing your steps or your bus journey (if walking
remember to fork right at the junction in about 200
yards), and board the next tram. The tram stop, in
case you missed it before, is right adjacent Beckenham Junction rail station. The route utilises one
of the former British Rail tracks as far as Birkbeck,

Inside the Jolly Woodman, Beckenham

Mitcham is home to one of South London's largest commons

before swinging off south on new track. Pass the Croydon Arena and alight at Woodside, which was another former BR station, walking up to join the road by the old station building. Turn to your right and, if it's daylight, you can cut into Ashburton Park. Head for the diametrically opposite corner, using the cedar trees as a guide. This will bring you out on the A222 Long Lane close to the junction with Shirley Road. If the park gates are locked simply walk around the road bearing right at the junction.

At the traffic lights head up Shirley Road for a few minutes to the **Cricketers 2**. You'll probably see the impressive pub sign before the pub itself. Enthusiastic guv'nor Ray Snadden has clocked up ten years at the pub now, turning it around from a nondescript local into a top beer destination in the Croydon area, and has twice won the local CAMRA Pub of the Year award, most recently in 2010. The spacious interior with no fewer than three real fires is a pleasant spot to enjoy Harveys Sussex Bitter plus up to four changing guests. If you're lucky you may stumble upon one of Ray's regular beer festivals. There's a rear patio and garden if the weather merits it.

You can either retrace your steps to Woodside, in which case take the tram two stops further to Addiscombe, or as an alternative, it's hardly any further to walk directly to the next pub which is a

On the bar at the Claret Free House

stone's throw from Addiscombe tram stop: simply take Bingham Road, directly opposite the Cricketers, and walk to the very far end of it! Either way, make your way onto the A222 Addiscombe Road and you'll find the **Claret Free House 3** in the parade of shops backing onto the tram platform. It looks a bit like a shop itself, having been converted from one, so it won't win any heritage awards, but there's no pub in the Borough of Croydon which has picked up more CAMRA awards than the Claret. Quirkily, it's a loyal and very rare outpost for Palmers of Bridport, whose IPA sells faster here than in any other UK outlet! There are five other regularly changing guests to tempt you in this cosy drinkers' den.

Back at the tram stop, continue on towards Croydon. Just before the Sandilands stop rail enthusiasts should look out for the 90 degree curve and junction with the New Addington branch curving away into a tunnel, part of an old British Rail line which has been re-used for the tramway.

An optional addition at Lebanon Road is to alight and visit the **Builders Arms 8** , which is a 5-minute walk down to the end of Lebanon Road itself, opposite the tram stop. This Fuller's house is still an attractive building externally, although I think that much of the interior character it once had has been lost. It still retains two

The Ravensbury in Mitcham is bright and spacious

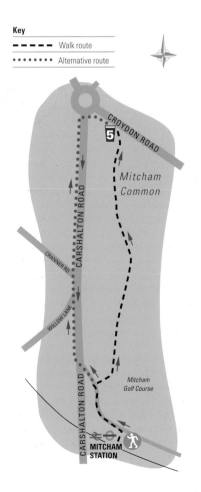

Key

▬ ▬ ▬ Walk route

• • • • • • • Alternative route

CROYDON ROAD

Mitcham Common

CARSHALTON ROAD

CRANMER RD

WILLOW LANE

CARSHALTON ROAD

Mitcham Golf Course

CARSHALTON ROAD

MITCHAM STATION

interconnected rooms, that on the right being the more upmarket with comfortable seating extending to a pleasant secluded garden at the rear. Expect regulars and seasonals from the Fuller's stable including their take on Gales HSB.

The next stop on the tram beyond Lebanon Road is East Croydon, but stay put until the following stop, George Street, right in the centre of town. Walk back a few yards after alighting from the tram, and you'll see the **George 4**. Under the stewardship of Steve Meeke who before he came here worked wonders at another Croydon Wetherspoon, the *Skylark* (see page 134) this town centre shop conversion has shot into the top ten in the whole of the Wetherspoon estate for beer sales. What's more not only is the selection extensive, the quality is exceptional, enough to see this pub voted as local CAMRA Pub of the Year in 2011. Expect, apart from 'Spoons 'usual suspects', Dark Star Hophead and Oakham JHB, along with a great range of changing guests, with local micros much in evidence. Don't miss the second array of handpumps at the rear of the pub as well.

This is the obvious place to 'jump tram' if you want to stay in Croydon – see Walk 21 for other pub recommendations; otherwise, wait for a Wimbledon tram and settle down for a longer journey of several stops, passing Wandle Park and the retail warehouses of the Purley Way before alighting at Mitcham Junction. Here, the tram shares the station with a British Rail line, and the easiest way to find the route to the next pub

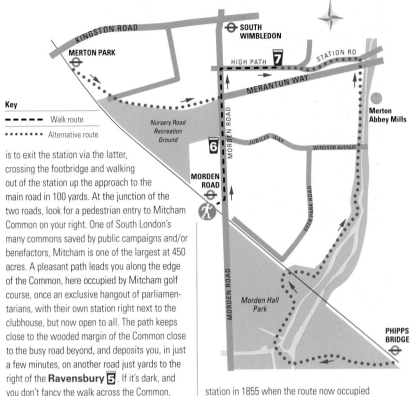

Key

━ ━ ━ ━ Walk route

• • • • • • • Alternative route

is to exit the station via the latter, crossing the footbridge and walking out of the station up the approach to the main road in 100 yards. At the junction of the two roads, look for a pedestrian entry to Mitcham Common on your right. One of South London's many commons saved by public campaigns and/or benefactors, Mitcham is one of the largest at 450 acres. A pleasant path leads you along the edge of the Common, here occupied by Mitcham golf course, once an exclusive hangout of parliamentarians, with their own station right next to the clubhouse, but now open to all. The path keeps close to the wooded margin of the Common close to the busy road beyond, and deposits you, in just a few minutes, on another road just yards to the right of the **Ravensbury 5**. If it's dark, and you don't fancy the walk across the Common, simply cross the main road (there's no continuous footway on the nearside) and turning right, walk up the Carshalton Road, keeping directly ahead at the first junction, to the roundabout where the pub is round the corner on the right. New management after a period of closure have turned the fortunes of this prominent roadhouse upwards: the interior is spacious, cheery and modern, with a smart wooden floor, and there's a welcome array of handpumps to greet one upon entry. Expect Fuller's London Pride and Doom Bar as regulars, with three additional and changing guests. Food is available throughout the day and into the evening.

Retrace your steps back to the tram stop, and continue on the route towards Wimbledon. Rail enthusiasts should note that although not visible from the tram stop the former station building at Mitcham, the next stop, is one of the oldest station buildings in Britain, and therefore the world. The handsome Georgian building with its archway was built around 1800 and became a railway

station in 1855 when the route now occupied by the Tramlink became part of the rail network but it had possibly been used by the Surrey Iron Railway, the world's oldest public railway, which once ran along this course.

Another opportunity for diversion arises at Phipps Bridge two stops further on. Here the path across the tram tracks leads into Morden Hall Park, a former deer park astride the River Wandle now in the hands of the National Trust. Unusually for the National Trust and thanks to the will of the last owner Gilliat Hatfeild the park is always open and with no admission charge. There's a cafe, visitor centre (in converted stables) and other attractions close to the river. It's also possible to take a very pleasant walk along the Wandle Trail from here to Merton Abbey Mills and on to the Trafalgar Freehouse – see the map. The tram itself continues to Morden Road which is the best point at which to alight for the next pub stop. Climb up to the busy Morden Road and bear left for a five minute walk down to the **Prince of Wales 6**.

The handsome Victorian building reverted to its original name in 2010 (it was renamed the Princess of Wales in 1997) after a sympathetic refurbishment aiming to capture some of the atmosphere of the past. Today it's a one-bar pub with three fairly distinct areas, and with a variety of seating. There's a small garden at the rear. It's now a free house (Young's having sold it in March 2013) and offers well-kept Young's Bitter, Fuller's London Pride and a guest.

From here it's a short walk northwards (but purists could return to the tram stop and head down to Merton Park from whence there's a more pleasant walk along a signed footpath back to the Morden Road). In both cases continue as far as the pedestrian crossing within sight of the traffic lights at Merton High Street; and cross into High Path, with a small church on your right and post-war flats on the left. This quiet little back street is a fitting location for the last pub on this tour, and it's no ordinary pub, since the **Trafalgar Freehouse 7** is a regular recipient of accolades from the local CAMRA branch and in 2008 won the Greater London Pub of the Year Award. This is no mean feat in a part of London not short of good quality pubs.

It's very much your back-street corner local, a modest enough building from the outside and quite dinky inside too. The man behind the success of this former Charrington's house is Dave Norman who sources his beers from far and wide but with an emphasis on the more local. The house beer, Market Ale, is brewed exclusively for the 'Traf' by Ascot, and is a traditional 'brown' session ale. There are five more handpumps dispensing a changing variety of interesting beers. Nelson-related prints decorate the walls for, unlikely as it may seem, the great man's last home before he died at Trafalgar was at Merton Place which stood on a site pretty much opposite the pub. If I were to criticise anything in this otherwise excellent little pub it would be the presence of a TV at both ends of the narrow interior; there's no escape if both are switched on.

Consult your map for the best option for your homeward journey but if you prefer the Northern Line to Tramlink swing left out of the pub and up Pincott Road to Merton High Street where the very good bottle shop, Nelson Wines, is opposite, and South Wimbledon Underground station, with trains to Tooting Broadway and its excellent curry houses, is less than a five minute walk to your left.

PUB INFORMATION

1 Jolly Woodman
9 Chancery Lane, Beckenham,
BR3 6NR
020 8663 1031
Opening Hours: 11 (4 Mon)-11
(midnight Fri & Sat)

2 Cricketers
47 Shirley Road, Addiscombe,
CR0 7ER
020 8655 3507
Opening Hours: 12-midnight
(11 Sun)

3 Claret Free House
5A Bingham Corner, Lower
Addiscombe Road, Addiscombe,
CR0 7AA
020 8656 7452
Opening Hours: 11.30-11
(11.30 Thu; midnight Fri & Sat);
12-11 Sun

4 George
17-21 George Street, Croydon,
CR0 1LA
020 8649 9077
Opening Hours: 8am-midnight
(1am Fri & Sat)

5 Ravensbury
260 Croydon Road, Mitcham,
CR4 4JA
020 8648 9964
www.theravensbury.co.uk
Opening Hours: 8am-11 (midnight
Fri; 10.30 Sun)

6 Prince of Wales
98 Morden Road, Merton,
SW19 3BP
020 8545 0509
Opening Hours: 12-11; 11-mid-
night Fri; 11-11 Sat; 12-10.30 Sun

7 Trafalgar Freehouse
23 High Path, SW19 1JY
020 8542 5342
www.thetraf.com
Opening Hours: 3 (12 Fri-
Sun)-11

TRY ALSO:

8 Builders Arms
65 Leslie Park Road, Croydon,
CR0 6TP
020 8654 1803
buildersarmscroydon.co.uk
Opening Hours: 12-11 (midnight
Fri & Sat; 10.30 Sun)

Central excursion by 'beer bus'

WALK INFORMATION

Start: Paddington

Finish: Old Street

Distance: Less than a mile on foot

Key attractions:
Madame Tussauds, London Planetarium; London Zoo & Regents Park

The pubs: Victoria; Barley Mow; Albany; Euston Tap; Parcel Yard; Old Fountain

When the railway companies were building their lines into London in the nineteenth century, they were forbidden to drive their lines into the heart of the city, which is why many of the termini today lie in a line along the axis of the Euston & Marylebone Roads. Happily this axis is the route followed today by bus 205, which not only links the stations, it connects a ribbon of good quality, interesting drinking holes that don't feature elsewhere in this compendium. More than one of the pubs has noteworthy architectural and/or heritage features, whilst the beer range is, as usual in London these days, surely wide enough for even the most discriminating imbiber.

The Barley Mow

Unless you're starting at the *Cleveland* (see 'timing tip') exit Paddington station onto Praed Street, and look for the road leading off at the left-hand (south-east) corner of the station – London Street. (If you're getting off the bus walk back to the first road junction.) Head down past the parade of shops, by which time you may see a stern picture of our longest serving monarch staring lugubriously at you in the distance. She might have been cheered by the pub which takes her name, however, for the **Victoria** 1 , at the corner of Strathearn

Place, is a high-quality rarity in the context of London pub interiors. The rounded, stuccoed exterior is appropriately tasteful for the locality, but what sets the place apart architecturally are the interior fittings which seem to have survived the late Victorian frenzy of redecoration and replacement and, if we believe the date on the clock, go back to 1864. Pride of place probably goes to the glass and mirror work, especially the gilded glass set in the wonderful bar back and screen on the back wall. The interior décor gets it right with smart floorboards and a variety of comfortable seating areas. Do not miss a trip upstairs to both the theatre bar (which although more modern has an agreeable ambience), and the very impressive library room with its leather seats and an atmosphere redolent of a gentlemen's club. The beers are from Fuller's, and a varied food menu is served throughout the day. All in all just the sort of place to set you up for an enjoyable day's drinking!

Walk back to the bus stop, on the northern side of Praed Street, and take the next 205 for five stops alighting right outside Baker Street station. If you value your life you are advised to take the subway to reach the southern side of the Marylebone Road in safety: it's inside the station entrance. Then walk down Chiltern Street for a few minutes, and Dorset Street is the third on the right. The **Barley Mow** 2 is a few yards along. It was built in 1791 and as such claims to be the oldest pub in Marylebone. It's certainly remains a very traditional

The Victoria at Paddington

TIMING TIP

The Old Fountain is closed at the weekend, but as an alternative weekend finish try the *Wenlock Arms*, (see page 115) 5 minutes from the bus. If in a group, you might want to convene at the *Cleveland Arms* (see page 71) after 11am before strolling round to Chilworth Terrace, the western terminus of the 205.

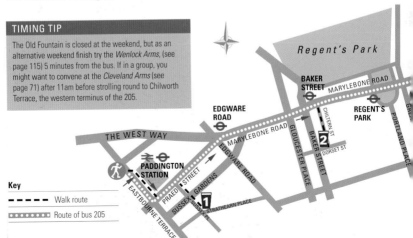

Regent's Park

BAKER STREET

MARYLEBONE ROAD

EDGWARE ROAD

REGENT'S PARK

CHILTERN ST

GLOUCESTER PLACE

BAKER STREET

DORSET ST

PORTLAND PLACE

THE WEST WAY

MARYLEBONE ROAD

EDGWARE ROAD

PADDINGTON STATION

PRAED STREET

EASTBOURNE TERRACE

SUSSEX GARDENS

SUSSEX PL

STRATHEARN PLACE

Key

– – – – Walk route

••••••••• Route of bus 205

The Albany on Great Portland Street

pub which has a comfortable, well-worn feel throughout. The pub is rightly renowned for a pair of small all-wooden drinking cubicles, now unique in London. Some claim they were used for pawnbroking transactions but in reality they're very probably simply another example of the Victorian passion for privacy! Look out also for the little rear room with some very old panelling. In keeping with the trend throughout London the beer range is much improved since the first edition of this book was published: Fuller's London Pride has a constant presence, with changing beers on the other five hand-pumps, Mighty Oak and Sharp's being among the more favoured breweries along with Fuller's seasonals. Food-wise it's toasted sandwiches until 4pm, with a daily special – a hot meal – available all day.

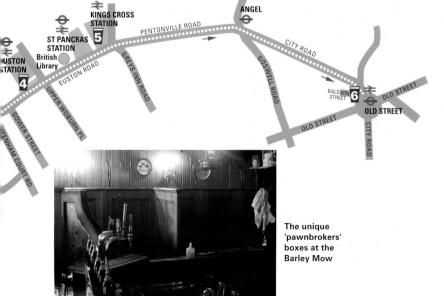

The unique 'pawnbrokers' boxes at the Barley Mow

The stunning new roof in King's Cross station

Retrace your steps to the bus stop, and continue by the next 205 the short distance, three stops, to Euston Road/Great Portland Street. Again it's the south side of the road we want and this time using the crossing is mandatory. Once across the street bear to the left of the Underground station island and you'll see the **Albany** 🔳 on the left, at the northern end of Great Portland Street itself. In a handsome

Euston Tap

Victorian building built of London's famous yellow stock bricks, the single split level bar room with its textured ceiling is well-endowed by natural light via wide arched windows. It's yet another pub which has recently been given the modern makeover and is now run by enthusiastic young management who are serious about their beer. Five real ales rotate regularly, and you'll find national favourites like Taylor Landlord and Doom Bar alongside more interesting offerings from say Thornbridge or Sambrook's. In support is a lengthy list of draught keg offerings including beers from Sierra Nevada, Camden and BrewDog; as well as some Belgian and other interesting bottles in the fridge. A generally lively and youthful crowd occupies the eclectic furniture, and it can be noisy, but it's a far better port of call for the imbiber than it was in its Firkin days. As you might expect, it takes its food seriously and this is probably the best eating option on this particular route. Check the website for menus.

Return to the same bus stop, and it's only three more stops on the 205 until you alight at Euston station. Just at the entrance to the bus stances is the next bar on the route (they get very touchy if you call it a pub), the **Euston Tap** 🔳. With almost 30 changing cask and keg options, this is the ultimate beerhound's Tardis, and my favourite of several decent drinking options a stone's throw from Euston station. It occupies one of the small pavilions which once flanked the station's late lamented Doric Arch, demolished in 1962 in surely one of the worst acts of British railway vandalism. At least these two little survivors (the other, under the same ownership, is now a cider bar) are now being put to imaginative and productive use after years of neglect! Be warned, it's tiny inside, and not given to comfort: there are at least some seats 'upstairs' but these, along with the diminutive toilets, are only accessed via some rather perilous spiral stairs which, given the strength of some of the beers, must be a health and safety hazard! The Tap's web and social network sites provide updates on the latest beers, but frankly whenever you turn up there'll be more than enough choice to satisfy.

It's back on the bus for the short hop down to King's Cross, and, at the time of writing, the newest of the rash of railway station bars which are springing up all over the country. The nearby *Betjeman Arms* has been open at the revamped St Pancras for a while now, but I am plumping for the **Parcel Yard 5** in adjacent King's Cross. To access it, you need to traverse the splendid new concourse with its magnificent metal lattice roof,

spreading in a half-cylinder span of 52 metres. For once Network Rail has spent some money to come up with something which stands comparison with the Victorian railway era. The pub is up a flight of steps at the far end of the concourse: it's a clever renewal of Thomas Cubitt's original GNER parcel office of 1852, a bright, spacious, and functional bar with several separate spaces retaining a good deal of the original materials; you can even look out onto the platforms from the further rooms. The pub is one of the few Grade I listed pubs in London, and Fuller's deserve credit for producing something which is a worthy complement to the wider setting. In this context one is more forgiving about the stratospheric prices than might otherwise be the case! You can expect the entire Fuller's range of beers (including seasonals) on the bar as well as one or two guests; and there's a fairly extensive food menu, viewable on the website.

Once back on the next 205 eastwards, you can relax for a while as the final pub of the sextet is some nine stops away: the bus passes Angel and heads down the City Road before you need to alight at Old Street Station. Baldwin Street is directly across the busy artery but you'll need to walk the few yards down to the junction to cross safely. Head into the short side road and you'll spot the **Old Fountain 6** a few yards along

The Old Parcel Yard is a clever renewal of the old parcel office at King's Cross

The Theatre Bar in the Victoria

on the right. Sporting a distinctive external paint job and some handsome leaded windows this otherwise unassuming-looking local has become a real destination for beer aficionados, winning the local CAMRA Pub of the Year award in 2011. The pub sign is interesting: the pub apparently took its name from one of the local medicinal springs, and at one time the emblem, a portcullis surmounted by a ripple design was widespread. This free house has been in the same family for a long time, and has two bar rooms, with a new roof garden for those warmer days. The comprehensive beer range comes mainly from local and microbreweries; the pub is noted for new brews and an extensive range of local bottled beers. Food is

available at lunchtimes, and in the evenings until 10. Check the website for beer festivals.

Getting home, Old Street on the Underground is just a step away, or you can stay with the 205 for Liverpool Street station; the 135 bus from East Road will take you to Shoreditch for the London Overground.

LINK If you alight two stops before the Old Fountain, at Windsor Terrace, it's a five minute walk to the excellent *Wenlock Arms* (see Walk 18), which you can do as a stand-alone extra pub or continue and visit the other pubs along the Regent's Canal.

PUB INFORMATION

1 Victoria
10A Strathearn Place, W2 2NH
020 7724 1191
www.victoriapaddington.co.uk
Opening Hours: 11-11;
12-10.30 Sun

2 Barley Mow
8 Dorset Street, W1U 6QW
07967 484596
www.thebarleymowpub.com
Opening Hours: 11-11;
closed Sun

3 Albany
240 Great Portland Street,
W1W 5QU
020 7385 0221
www.thealbanyw1w.co.uk
Opening Hours: 12-midnight
(10.30 Sun)

4 Euston Tap
West Lodge, 190 Euston Road,
NW1 2EF
020 3137 8837
www.eustontap.com
Opening Hours: 12-11.30
(10.30 Sun)

5 Parcel Yard
King's Cross Station, N1 9AL
020 7713 7258
www.parcelyard.co.uk
Opening Hours: 8am-11; 9am-
10.30 Sun

6 Old Fountain
3 Baldwin Street, EC1V 9NU
020 7253 2970
www.oldfountain.co.uk
Opening Hours: 11-11; closed
Sat & Sun

Old Fountain

Pub index

LocAle

A number of entries in the book refer to pubs offering a LocAle. This scheme was devised by CAMRA members in Nottingham and is now in widespread use throughout the UK.

The aim is to encourage publicans to stock at least one cask beer that comes from a local brewery – the distance between pub and brewery varies but is now generally accepted to be not more than 30 miles. The scheme also encourages publicans to use the Direct Delivery Scheme run by SIBA, the Society of Independent Brewers. SIBA members deliver direct to pubs in their localities rather than going through central warehouses.

The overall aim of LocAle is to cut down on 'beer miles'. Research by CAMRA shows that food and drink transport accounts for 25 per cent of all HGV vehicle miles in Britain. Taking into account the miles that ingredients have travelled on top of distribution journeys, an imported lager produced by a multi-national brewery could have notched up more than 24,000 'beer miles' by the time it reaches a pub.

£10 spent on locally-supplied goods generates £25 for local economies. Keeping trade local helps enterprises, creates more economic activity and jobs, and makes other services more viable. The scheme also generates consumer support for local breweries.

Pubs that support the LocAle scheme receive a special window sticker. For more information, see the CAMRA website: www.camra.org.uk

Beer index

Books for beer lovers

CAMRA Books, the publishing arm of the Campaign for Real Ale, is the leading publisher of books on beer and pubs. Key titles include:

Good Beer Guide 2013

Editor: Roger Protz

The *Good Beer Guide* is the only guide you will need to find the right pint, in the right place, every time. It's the original and best-selling independent guide to around 4,500 pubs throughout the UK. Now in its 40th year, this annual publication is a comprehensive and informative guide to the best real ale pubs in the UK, researched and written exclusively by CAMRA members and fully updated every year.

£15.99   **ISBN 978-1-85249-290-8**

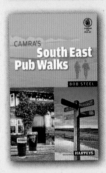

South East Pub Walks

Bob Steel

CAMRA's South East Pub Walks helps you to explore the beautiful countryside of the South Eastern corner of England, whilst never straying too far from a great pint. A practical, pocket-sized guide to some of the best pubs and best walking in the South East, this guide features 30 walks of varying lengths, all accessible by public transport and aimed at both the casual walker and more serious hiker. Each route has been selected for its unique and varied landscape, and its beer – with the walks taking you on a tour of the best real ale pubs the area has to offer.

£9.99 ISBN 978-1-85249-287-8

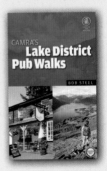

Lake District Pub Walks

Bob Steel

A pocket-sized, traveller's guide to some of the best walking and best pubs in the Lake District. The 30 walks are grouped geographically around tourist hubs with plenty of accommodation, making the book ideal for a visitor to the Lakes. The book is fully illustrated, with clear Ordnance Survey mapping and written directions to help readers navigate the routes. Lake District Pub Walks also explores some of the region's fascinating historical and literary heritage as well as its thriving brewing scene, and has useful information about local transport and accommodation.

£9.99   **ISBN 978-1-85249-271-7**

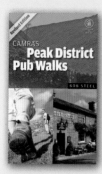

Peak District Pub Walks

Bob Steel

A practical, pocket-sized traveller's guide to some of the best pubs and best walking in the Peak District. This book features 25 walks, as well as cycle routes and local attractions, helping you see the best of Britain's oldest national park while never straying too far from a decent pint. Each route has been selected for its inspiring landscape, historical interest and welcoming pubs.

£9.99   ISBN 978-1-85249-246-5

Edinburgh Pub Walks

Bob Steel

A practical, pocket-sized traveller's guide to the pubs in and around Scotland's capital city. Featuring 25 town, park and coastal walks, Edinburgh Pub Walks enables you to explore the many faces of the city, while never straying too far from a decent pint. Featuring walks in the heart of Edinburgh, as well as routes through its historic suburbs and nearby towns.

£9.99   ISBN 978-1-85249-274-8

London's Best Beer, Pubs & Bars

Des de Moor

London's Best Beer, Pubs&Bars is the essential guide to beer drinking in London. This practical book is packed with detailed maps and easy-to-use listings to help you find the best places to enjoy perfect pints in the capital. Laid out by area, find the best pubs serving the best British and international beers wherever you are. Features tell you more about London's rich history of brewing and the city's vibrant modern brewing scene, where well-known brands rub shoulders with tiny micro-breweries.

£12.99   ISBN 978-1-85249-262-5

BOOKS

Order these and other CAMRA books online at
www.camra.org.uk/books,
ask at your local bookstore, or contact:
CAMRA, 230 Hatfield Road,
St Albans, AL1 4LW. Telephone 01727 867201

A Campaign of Two Halves

Campaigning for Pub Goers & Beer Drinkers

CAMRA, the Campaign for Real Ale, is an independent not-for-profit, volunteer-led consumer group. We campaign tirelessly for good-quality real ale and pubs, as well as lobbying government to champion drinkers' rights and promote local pubs as centres of community life. As a CAMRA member you will have the opportunity to campaign to save pubs under threat of closure, for pubs to be free to serve a range of real ales at affordable prices and for a fair rate of tax on beer.

Enjoying Real Ale & Pubs

CAMRA has over 150,000 members from all ages and backgrounds, brought together by a common belief in the issues that CAMRA deals with and their love of good quality British beer. From just £23 a year – that's less than a pint a month – you can join CAMRA and enjoy the following benefits:

Subscription to *What's Brewing*, our monthly colour newspaper, and Beer, our quarterly magazine, informing you about beer and pub news and detailing events and beer festivals around the country.

Free or reduced entry to over 160 national, regional and local beer festivals.

Money off many of our publications including the *Good Beer Guide*, the *Good Bottled Beer Guide* and *CAMRA's Great British Pubs*.

Access to a members-only section of our national website, **www.camra.org.uk**, which gives up-to-the-minute news stories and includes a special offer section with regular features.

Special discounts with numerous partner organisations and money off real ale in your participating local pubs as part of our Pubs Discount Scheme.

Visit **www.camra.org.uk/joinus** for
CAMRA membership information.